UNHEARD MELODIES

UNHEARD MELODIES

NARRATIVE FILM MUSIC

Claudia Gorbman

BFI Publishing, London

INDIANA UNIVERSITY PRESS
Bloomington & Indianapolis

To my mother and father

First published in the United States of America by
Indiana University Press
10th and Morton Streets
Bloomington, Indiana
and
Published in Great Britain by
The British Film Institute
127 Charing Cross Road
London WC2H OEA

Manufactured in the United States of America

Library of Congress Cataloging-in-Publication Data
Gorbman, Claudia.
   Unheard melodies.

   Bibliography: p.
   Includes index.
   1. Moving-picture music—History and criticism.
I. Title.
ML2075.G67   1987   782.8'5'09   86–45941
ISBN 0–253–33987–1
ISBN 0–253–20436–4 (pbk.)
1 2 3 4 5 91 90 89 88 87

British Library Cataloguing in Publication Data
Gorbman, Claudia
   Unheard melodies: narrative film music

   1. Moving-picture music
I. Title.   II. British Film Institute
782.8'5   ML2075
ISBN 0–85170–208–2
ISBN 0–85170–209–0 Pbk

Contents

Acknowledgments

My first thanks go to R. C. Dale and Alan Williams for two decades of consistently insightful criticism and guidance. I am indebted to Jim Naremore and Matei Calinescu for reading parts of the manuscript in draft form, and to my toughest untenured critics, Shari Zeck and Cynthia Erb. I warmly thank Tania Modleski for last-minute inspiration, as well as Nancy Wood, Simon Frith, and Kathryn Kalinak for sharing their knowledge and enthusiasm with me. Breon Mitchell provided generous support beyond the call of any chairman's duty; I also thank the Lilly Endowment for precious time released from teaching. Finally, I am deeply grateful to Barbara Klinger, Dr. Ernest Volinn, Beryl Gorbman, and Suzanne Jill Levine, who were no less essential to the realization of this book—as loving friends, critics, colleagues, and literal or figurative family.

For permission to include revised versions of previously published materials, I gratefully acknowledge the following: *The Velvet Light Trap*, for my essay "The Drama's Melos: Max Steiner and *Mildred Pierce*," which appeared in *VLT* #19 (1982), pp. 35–39; *Yale French Studies*, for my essay "Narrative Film Music," which appeared in *Yale French Studies* #60 (1980), pp. 183–203; the Purdue Research Foundation, for my essay "Clair's Sound Hierarchy and the Creation of Auditory Space," which appeared in the *1976 Film Studies Annual*, © Copyright by Purdue Research Foundation, West Lafayette, Indiana; and *Ciné-Tracts*, for my essay "Vigo/Jaubert," which appeared in *Ciné-Tracts* 1, 2 (Summer 1977), pp. 65–80. I also thank Warner Brothers for the film still from *The Jazz Singer*; Orbitron and R. C. Dale and Cinémathèque Française for the film stills from *Sous les toits de Paris*; and RKO Studios for the Max Steiner memo and the cue sheet and musical score from *So Well Remembered*.

Heard melodies are sweet, but those unheard
Are sweeter; therefore, ye soft pipes, play on . . .

Keats, "Ode on a Grecian Urn"

Introduction

Let us imagine for a moment that the commercial narrative cinema had developed a bit differently: let us imagine movies having no background music.[1] Raised in this hypothetical tradition, we are thoroughly accustomed to a cinematic world in which sounds (seem to) issue solely from the depicted narrative space. This cinematic world resembles the "real" world, more or less, in its conventions of depicting sonic space. Then one day, brought up in this relatively nonmusical tradition, we attend a screening of a film from another dimension—say, *Mildred Pierce*, with Max Steiner's lush and insistent score full of dramatic, illustrative orchestral coloration. What sheer artifice this would appear to the viewer! What a pseudo-operatic fantasy world! What *excess*: every mood and action rendered hyperexplicit by a Wagnerian rush of tonality and rhythm! What curious music, as well—robbed of its properly musical structure, it modulates and changes color, chameleonlike, in moment-to-moment deference to the narrative's images.

One hardly need emphasize that the acceptance of music in narrative cinema is purely a matter of convention. Such conventions have a long history, much of which predates the cinema itself. But does the notion of convention itself suffice to explain the operation of music in the movies?

Every moviegoer, every film scholar, tin ear notwithstanding, becomes aware from time to time of the ubiquity and psychological power of music in dramatic films. Such moments of lucidity tend to occur when we take note of how shamelessly emotional or copious a film score has been: what has been blaring in the background the entire time suddenly comes to the foreground of consciousness. Suddenly the story is perceived to inhabit a world strangely replete with musical sound, rhythm, signification . . . until, a few scenes or measures later, we drop off, become re-invested in the story again. Then the music is "working" once more, masking its own insistence and sawing away in the backfield of consciousness.

This book is for students and scholars of film who are curious about the ways of music in films. It should prove especially illuminating for those who most successfully block out film music—not only during viewing/immersion at the cinema, but also in the process of reading—conscious, analytical investigations of the cinema's workings. For if Marxist and Freudian theory have forever destroyed the romance of the autonomous perceiving subject, and if recent film theory has taken on among its primary missions to understand the historical, psychological, and textual positioning of the cinematic spectator, we need to start *listening* to the cinema's uses of music in order to read films in a literate way.

What is music doing in the movies, and how does it do it? These questions engender others in turn. What and how does music signify in conjunction with the images and events of a story film? What can we learn from dramatic forms of the past that employed music—nineteenth-century theater and opera—and in what ways does cinema's particular technological and historical situation give a specific thrust to this inquiry into the interrelations among media? Why do we tend not to hear music consciously in watching a story film? What business does music have in a movie in the first place? How have standard practices of composing, mixing, and editing evolved, and what alternative practices are possible/conceivable? How does music in film narration create a *point of experience* (note the visual chauvinism of saying "point of view") for the spectator?

The trajectory of this book follows, more or less, the history of my own inquiry into film music. I began in a structuralist-semiotic spirit to seek means of considering how music can signify in the narrative film.

It became clear that the semiological notion of codes is crucial to the study of how film music means. First of all, music has its own purely *musical* signification, creating tension and resolution through highly coded structure and syntax. Pure musical codes are operative in films, but only in a limited fashion, for in order to signify, they oblige the listener to *listen*—just as, in a restaurant, we may "hear" the din of human speech, but we cannot make sense of utterances until we listen to their vocabulary, syntax, and intonations. Some films, including Jean Mitry's *Pacific 231*, Walt Disney's *Fantasia*, and Jean-Marie Straub's *Chronicle of Anna Magdalena Bach*, subordinate cinematic/narrative logic to musical logic in this way.

But surely, the vast majority of films employ music in other ways. While they might contain sequences or "production numbers" devoted to musical performances, the organizing structure of such films—even musicals and "lives of composers" films—is, precisely, a classical narrative with its own demands for pacing, development, spatiotemporal structure, and so on. Music is subordinated to the narrative's demands.

Music signifies in films not only according to pure musical codes, but also according to *cultural* musical codes and *cinematic* musical codes. Any music bears cultural associations, and most of these associations have been further codified and exploited by the music industry. Properties of instrumentation, rhythm, melody, and harmony form a veritable language. We all know what "Indian music," battle music, and romance music sound like in the movies; we know that a standard forties film will choose to introduce its seductress on the screen by means of a sultry saxophone playing a Gershwinesque melody. As for cinematic codes: music is codified by the filmic context itself, and assumes meaning by virtue of its placement in the film. Beginning and end-title music, and musical themes, are major examples of this music-film interaction. Based on the Wagnerian principles of motifs and leitmotifs, a theme in a film becomes associated with a character, a place, a situation, or an emotion. It may have a fixed and static designation, or it can evolve and contribute to the dynamic flow of the narrative by carrying its meaning into a new realm of signification.

Maurice Jaubert stated in 1936:

> We do not go to the cinema to hear music. We require it to deepen and prolong in us the screen's visual impressions. . . . It ought, like the script, the cutting, the decor and the shooting, to play its own particular part in making clear, logical, truthfully realistic that telling of a good story which is above all the function of a film. So much the better if, discreetly, it adds the gift of a poetry all its own.[2]

What *is* the "own particular part" of film music?

Approaching this question, we must start by taking narrative, the "telling of a good story," into account. The conventional narrative film constructs a diegesis—a story world, a place of the action. Classical narratives emphasize the diegesis over the narration, efface narrational presence. Modernist forms, on the other hand, problematize the transparency of discourse, point out that it's the narration that constructs the diegesis. Music enjoys a special status in filmic narration. It can be diegetic (musicians can play in the story, a radio can be on)—in the trade this is called source music—or nondiegetic (an orchestra plays as cowboys chase Indians on the desert). The reader might object that the human voice is just as flexible in its freedom to be diegetic or nondiegetic. But the nondiegetic voiceover is perceived as a narrative intrusion, and music is not. Furthermore, music very often crosses the boundary, even in the most conventional films. We are all familiar with soundtrack music that suddenly ceases as a character leans over and turns off a radio; or, conversely, as in a scene in *North By Northwest*, what seems like piped-in music in a train's dining car becomes more and more clearly nondiegetic.[3]

This ease in crossing narrational borders puts music in a position to free the image from strict realism. As something not very consciously perceived, it inflects the narrative with emotive values via cultural musical codes. A music cue's signification—eerie, pastoral, jazzy-sophisticated, romantic— must be instantly recognized as such in order to work. The prevailing dialect of film-music language has therefore been composed of the nineteenth-century late Romantic style of Wagner and Strauss. Bernard Herrmann and others may have gone beyond this style by exploring dissonance, harmonic ambiguity, even atonality, and scores using jazz, electronic music, and music of other cultures have expanded those boundaries in other directions. But the core musical lexicon has tended to remain conservatively rooted in Romantic tonality, since its purpose is quick and efficient signification to a mass audience.

But enumerating the semiological functions of film music does not help to confront an issue that keeps returning to haunt us: why is film music there in the first place, even in the most "realist" film, in virtually all films abiding by rules of verisimilitude? Few would wish to claim that "classical realist cinema" is realist in the sense of approximating objective reality (if such a thing were representable)—film serves up fantasy in the guise of verisimilitude. Classical filmic discourse (mise-en-scène, camerawork, editing, sound recording, and mixing) contributes to the portrayal of a world, the representation of a diegesis. The nondiegetic shot or sound is the exception, not the rule—except in the case of music. Therefore: *why music*, in the tightly consolidated "realist" world of the sound film? It gives mood, pacing, emotion, yes—but why is it permitted into the narrative's regime at all?

For one thing, it has history on its side. Music has gone hand in hand with dramatic representation ever since the ancient Greek theater, and no doubt before, in ritual forms.

> When we read a play such as the *Suppliants* of Aeschylus, it is as if we were seeing only the libretto of an opera to which all music, dances, and stage directions are missing. It is so clearly a lyric drama that the music itself must have been the principal means by which the poet conveyed his meaning. Euripedes' *The Bacchae*, on the other hand, has far greater intrinsic substance, but even here the emotional intensity of the individual scenes often rises to such a pitch that music had to take over where the words left off; just as when a person is so overcome with feeling that words fail, and he resorts to inarticulate sounds and gestures.[4]

Tradition has it that the departure from the prosaic toward poetry, emotion, the irrational, is served by music. Merely to cite tradition, however, is necessary but not sufficient in the case of film music. Cinema's technological specificity obliges further analysis. Why did the resources of editing, framing, and cinematography not take over all the functions that music had in previous theatrical forms? In chapters 2 and 3, I explore some of the vicissitudes in the development from nineteenth-century melodramatic theater to the "fully diegetic sound film." This is by no means a history; for a history would entail a book in itself (Nicholas Vardac's 1949 *From Stage to Screen* is precisely such a study). But a sense of the historicity of some of the technological, generic, and contextual conditions that prevailed through the arrival of the feature sound film is, I think, necessary for assessing the strength of the "continuity of conventions" argument for explaining the persistence of background music into the classical narrative film.

What does music do in the sound film? The psychic payoff it brings to the realist regime of sound film must be considerable for it to have survived, and thrived, as an integral component of even the most "realistic" movies. What is there about music itself that affects an audience? To understand background music's functions better, and to shed momentarily any cultural snobbishness that might prevent us from considering its most basic functions—bodily functions before gastronomic arts, if you will—we might consider the social and psychological functions of music that is designed to be utilitarian: easy-listening music, Muzak. Both easy-listening and film music belong to larger contexts (dentist's office, film narrative); neither is designed to be closely listened to. Both employ familiar musical language, both bathe the listener in affect. Easy-listening music (at least in theory) helps the consumer buy, the patient relax, the worker work; its goal is to render the individual an untroublesome social subject. Film music, participating as it does in a narrative, is more varied in its content and roles; but primary among its goals, nevertheless, is to render the individual an untroublesome viewing subject: less critical, less "awake." This notion has several important consequences. Music may act as a "suturing" device, aiding the process of turning enunciation into fiction, lessening awareness of the technological nature of film discourse. Music gives a "for-me-ness" to the soundtrack and to the cine-narrative complex. I hear (not very consciously) this music which the characters don't hear; I exist in this bath or gel of affect; this is my story, my fantasy, unrolling before me and for me on the screen (and out of the loudspeakers).

Music lessens defenses against the fantasy structures to which narrative provides access. It increases the spectator's susceptibility to suggestion. The cinema has been compared to hypnosis, since both induce (at least in good subjects) a kind of trance. The trusting subject (trusting the hypnotist, the system of cinematic narrative) removes defenses to access to unconscious fantasies. The hypnotist has his/her induction methods: soothing voice, repetition, rhythm, suggestion of pleasantly enveloping imagery, and focusing the subject's attention on one thing to the exclusion of others. Narrative cinema has its own "induction methods"—including the harmonic, rhythmic, melodic suggestiveness and channeling effects of music. Film music lowers thresholds of belief. This begins to explain why it has continued to be indispensable even to "realist" narrative cinema.

The bath of affect in which music immerses the spectator is like easy-listening, or the hypnotist's voice, in that it rounds off the sharp edges, masks contradictions, and lessens spatial and temporal discontinuities with its own melodic and harmonic continuity. It lessens awareness of the frame; it relaxes the censor, drawing the spectator further into the fantasy-illusion suggested by filmic narration. When we shed a tear during a pregnant moment in a film melodrama (Mildred Pierce's little daughter quietly dying of pneumonia) instead of scoffing at its excess, music often is present, a catalyst in the suspension of judgment.

But what is it about music (especially tonal music) that has this power? What is the nature of musical pleasure? Why has it been regarded since Plato as having privileged access to the soul? Why are "depth" and "inner truth" evoked in accounting for the effect of music? Here, psychoanalytic investigations of sound and music hold particular appeal. Scholars have extended Freudian thought to theorize the auditory realm. According to the psychoanalytic scenario of psychic development, the infant is born into a sort of "sonorous envelope," and is as yet unaware of distinctions between self and other, inside-outside the body. Further, more than one writer claims that the "auditory imaginary" precedes the mirror phase: "the melodic bath (the mother's voice, her songs, the music she plays to the infant) provides [the infant] a first auditory mirror which it first uses with its cries."[5] The imaginary longing for bodily fusion with the mother is never erased; and, these writers argue, the terms of this original illusion are defined in large part by the voice.

Thus, primary experiences of sound may account for the characteristics of depth and inwardness, and of an ineffable, preverbal attachment to music (which is the conscious organization of sounds into harmony and melody). To insist on the auditory imaginary is to suggest a basis for understanding mechanisms of pleasure and identification in music. Of course, music is a highly structured *discourse* of sound: but its freedom from referentiality (from language and representation) ensures it as a more desirable, less unpleasurable discourse.

Music is pleasurable, signifying but nonrepresentational discourse. Not unlike the hypnotist's discourse, it guides the spectator-audience, and increases receptivity to the narrative in its excess. Music that is noticed, which calls attention to itself, swings away from the imaginary toward the symbolic. The goal of "classical" scoring is rather to place the auditor's ears in a subject position harmonious with the spectator's eyes: to create a unified phantasmatic body of identification, a heightened for-me-ness for the regressive ego.

This brings us to the classical Hollywood cinema, which is predicated on the subject's unified body, the effacement of discourse in favor of story, and a trance-like spectatorial immersion in its world. "Classical" scoring has its own set of practices in accord with these principles. In chapter 4 I have synthesized a list of rules and principles for music composing, recording, and mixing in the classical narrative film. No one would wish to claim that Max Steiner's score for *Casablanca* works according to exactly the same model as Bernard Herrmann's *Vertigo* music or David Raksin's intriguing sounds for Abraham Polonsky's *Force of Evil*. My "degree zero" for the classical film score corresponds to the generalized paradigm of classical Hollywood film form of the thirties and forties[6]—a flexible model, or rather, a range of possibilities.

The reader will note frequent references to scores by Max Steiner in chapter 4's exposition of classical scoring principles. Steiner was surely one of the most melodramatic of Hollywood's great film composers. His pseudo-Wagnerian orchestrations and harmonies draw on a well-established reservoir of emotive signification. A Steiner score explicates, underscores, imitates, emphasizes narrative actions and moods wherever possible; it wears its heart on its sleeve, contributes toward the depiction of a dramatic universe whose sole transcendental morality might be that of emotion itself. If I have called upon Steiner's music to illustrate facets of the model of classical scoring, it is because, fundamentally, the classical Hollywood film *is* melodrama—a drama with music.

Finally, here is a list of some things this book is not:
1. A history of film music.
2. A study of representative film music composers.
3. A study of music in the following genres: the musical, the documentary, and experimental films.
4. A composer's-eye view of film music.

The annotated bibliography includes references for readers interested in the subjects above.

Part I
Music in the Narrative Cinema

CHAPTER I

Narratological Perspectives on Film Music

Underlying the particular relationships between music and the feature story film are theoretical and aesthetic problems that have intrigued scholars and critics for over half a century. What effects does the cinematic medium have on film music, and what effects does music have on cinema? What is the "correct" aesthetic balance between the two, and what makes good film music? What explains the persistence of music accompanying dramatic representation in general, and film in particular? And what justifies the study of film music at all—beyond understanding that music is sometimes informative, sometimes expressive, sometimes present merely to fill gaps in the soundtrack or slow moments in the narrative?

The moment we recognize to what degree film music shapes our perception of a narrative, we can no longer consider it incidental or innocent. Like lighting, free of verbal explicitness, music sets moods and tonalities in a film; it guides the spectator's vision both literally and figuratively. Having come to the cinema to experience a story, the spectator receives much more than that, situated by the connotative systems of camera placement, editing, lighting, acting . . . and music.

But music differs from lighting and other elements of film in several important ways. First, we hear it, we don't see it. Hearing is less direct than visual perception; to see something is to instantaneously identify the light rays with the object that reflects them; in hearing, we do not as automatically identify a sound with its source. Moreover, hearing requires a greater duration of the sound stimulus than vision requires of an image in order to be recognized. Thus hearing is at once more selective and lazier than vision; it "focuses" consciously on one or at best two auditory events at a time. Now, in watching a conventional film whose dialogues and visuals are telling a story, we devote our concentration to its successive events and the meanings that are constantly accruing to them. Most feature films relegate music to the viewer's sensory background, that area least susceptible to rigorous judgment and most susceptible to affective manipulation.

Consider this situation. You are listening to a Bach fugue on the radio, pleased that your attentiveness enables you to pick out some of the many complexities of the fugual structure. You note the subject (the melodic theme) as each voice successively announces it in a different register; you can also perceive and marvel at certain permutations of the subject as, for example, it is played at different rhythms and tempi while embedded in the ongoing fugue, or is played in melodic inversion while yet other voices play the subject in its more recognizable form; with each new phrase, the movement of still more musical material constantly transforms it. At the heart of the performance, a friend walks into your living room and asks your opinion on a timely political issue. You are suddenly faced with an either/or proposition: lose completely the threads of that magnificent fugue, or ignore the would-be interlocutor. In a film, where narrative is the excuse for, the cement of, and the raison d'être of the film's existence, we opt to focus attention on the narrative and visual realities on the screen before us, just as we probably will choose to concentrate on the political conversation and thereby cease following the fugue's rhetorical structures. We forsake contemplating that abstract arrangement and rearrangement of sound which is music, because it is nonrepresentational and nonnarrative and does not inhabit the perceptual foreground of the narrative film.

Let us further suppose that the interlocutor is attractive and you decide to put aside the Bach on the radio. While you discuss, the music continues. Absentmindedly you allow your hand to play with the radio dial; the station changes and your conversation is suddenly accompanied by some drunkenly, brazenly improvised sixties blues. This strikes you as inappropriate, "cheapening" the ambience of your tête-à-tête. You return quickly to the Baroque music station, redeemed by centuries of culture and dignity.

This example raises a point upon which most of film music's critics have not insisted.[1] To judge film music as one judges "pure" music is to ignore its status as a part of the collaboration that is the film. Ultimately it is the narrative context, the interrelations between music and the rest of the film's system, that determines the effectiveness of film music.

We may see music as "meaning," or organizing discourse, on three different levels in any film. First, if we listen to a Bach fugue, independently of any other activity, we are listening to the functioning of *pure musical codes*, generating musical discourse; music on this level refers to musical structure itself. Second, the Bach fugue playing pleasantly on the sound system of a coffeehouse where people discuss politics or play chess functions more in its cultural context; it refers to *cultural musical codes* (and elicits enculturated reactions). The music that plays while a film's credits unroll— jazz, pseudoclassical, Wagnerian, folk—activates these cultural codes, and can reveal beforehand a great deal about the style and subject of the narrative to come. Third, music in a film refers to the film—that is, it bears specific formal relationships to coexistent elements in the film. The various ways in which it does so shall be called *cinematic musical codes*, and this chapter will focus largely on the latter.

"Pure" Music vs. Film Narrative

There might be something inherently paradoxical about the presence of music in films, even as our experience as spectators seems to affirm that music quite "naturally" belongs on the soundtrack. The problem might be posed in this way: is not the rhetoric of filmic discourse (representational, "naturalistic," rhythmically irregular) incommensurate with the rhetoric of musical discourse (nonrepresentational, "lyrical," rhythmically regular)?

Music, indeed, is constantly engaged in an existential and aesthetic struggle with narrative representation. Proof of this music-film dialectic lies in examining films where the pure musical codes apparently dominate. Take for example a scene in Eric Rohmer's *Ma Nuit chez Maud* (1969), when protagonist Paul accompanies a friend to a concert. During the concert, the camera rests exclusively on the violinist (Leonid Kogan) for an entire movement of the sonata he plays. But narrative context wins out nonetheless. Even though the music claims the foreground, the spectator pays attention to it only incidentally, for two other factors preempt his/her interest. First, since previous shots have strongly suggested that the concert is seen from Paul's point of view—for example, the camera's direct upward glance at the concert hall chandelier—one tends to concentrate as much on the fact of Paul's spectatorial presence as on the explicit content of the scene (musicians and music). Second, one watches the violinist *perform*. In the act of placing its object in a frame, photography/cinematography encourages a special "aesthetic" mode of contemplating its content. Thus, in this supposedly purely musical scene, musical codes are still vying for attention over visual and narrative cinematic codes.

Jean-Marie Straub's *Chronicle of Anna Magdalena Bach* (1967) further illustrates the music-film dialectic. The film consists primarily of musical performances; any nonmusical elements are there to add authenticity and meaning to the Bach works performed. The actors deliver their lines in a flat monotone, constantly denying the viewer the pleasure of immersion in a fictional continuity. For this reason, *Chronicle* may require at least two viewings, so that the viewer learns to experience the music without insisting on cinematic (narrative) discourse. The camera is motivated by little but musical codes: it frames a medium close-up of "Bach" playing a harpsichord cadenza in the Fifth Brandenburg Concerto, and then pulls back suddenly into a general shot because the orchestra has entered for the movement's closing *tutti*.

Straub has said that his cinema is "free of language,"[2] that cinematic rhetoric would obscure the filmed reality. In *Chronicle*, he at least thinned the texture of cinematic language to a point where musical rhetoric can once more be recognized by spectators and enjoyed as such. The drastic degree of cinematic minimalization necessary in this enterprise attests eloquently to the enormity of the spectator's will—or conditioning—to impose narrative motivations in viewing a film. As an exception to the rule, *Chronicle* reconfirms the fact that musical meaning is subordinated to narrative meaning in the standard feature film.

This does not mean that there are no rules for musical syntax in cinema. In Jean-Luc Godard's *Vivre sa vie* (1962), music cues by Michel Legrand are often interrupted in mid-phrase, before the tonal resolution one expects of its pseudoclassical style. This technique of robbing the musical statement of its closure has the effect of drawing attention to the score. The standard feature film, on the other hand, is often characterized by music composed in short phrases; in addition, such compositional devices as modulations, *sostenuti*, and sequence-progressions guarantee a minimum adherence to musical syntax, with a maximum flexibility of resources, so that the score can accommodate itself to narrative events.

The Music/Scene Relationship (Nondiegetic Music)

Straub's *Chronicle of Anna Magdalena Bach* is an extreme example, well outside the conventions of classical narrative, to show that although film music undeniably possesses its own internal logic, it always bears a relationship to the film in which it appears. Our next task is to consider the possible interactions between music and the filmic narratives in which it "participates."

The restricted number of possible narrative/music relationships as discussed by most film scholars seems curiously primitive, limited largely to the concepts of *parallelism* and *counterpoint*. Either the music "resembles" or it "contradicts" the action or mood of what happens on the screen.[3] Siegfried Kracauer, for example, writes that counterpoint occurs when music and picture convey "different meanings" that meet in a montage effect: "Imagine the close-up of a sleeping face which appears to the rhythms of nightmarish music: it is all but inevitable that the intriguing discrepancy between these sounds and so peaceful a picture should puzzle us."[4]

Is there no other way to qualify film music that does not lie between these opposites but outside them? If we must summarize music-image and music-narrative relationships in two words or less, *mutual implication* is more accurate, especially with respect to films of any narrative complexity. The notions of parallel and counterpoint erroneously assume that the image is autonomous. Further, it is debatable that information conveyed by disparate media can justifiably be called the same or different. Kracauer's very examples show how music helps the viewer to define the images, themselves polysemic. Hanns Eisler and T. W. Adorno comment on the inadequacy of the parallelism category:

> From the aesthetic point of view, this relation is not one of similarity, but, as a rule, one of question and answer, affirmation and negation, appearance and essence. This is dictated by the divergence of the media in question and the specific nature of each.[5]

We may then ask: isn't any music usually sufficient to accompany a segment of film? In fact, the answer is yes. Whatever music is applied to a film segment will *do something*, will have an effect—just as whatever two words one puts together will produce a meaning different from that of each word separately, because the reader/spectator automatically imposes meaning on such combinations. Kracauer's reactions to a drunken movie-house pianist from his youth, whose inattention to the screen resulted in pleasingly unorthodox audiovisual combinations, recall the Surrealists' delight in discovery on every plane of life where there issued a "fortuitous encounter" between two unlikely entities. Jean Cocteau actually scored some of his films on the principle of what he called "accidental synchronization": he would take George Auric's music, carefully written for particular scenes in his film, and deliberately apply the wrong music to the wrong scenes. Sergei Eisenstein had pointed to music as one of the elements in montage construction. And whether a certain montage of elements is intended or not (surrealist word-games vs. traditional poetic activity, the drunken pianist vs. a score by John Williams), their corroboration will generate meaning. Image, sound effects, dialogue, and music-track are virtually inseparable during the viewing experience; they form a *combinatoire* of expression.

Any music will do (something), but the temporal coincidence of music and scene creates different effects according to the dynamics and structure of the music. Obviously, if instead of orchestrated folk music a sudden tense dissonance or Indian drumbeat were to "hit" the characters in John Ford's *Stagecoach* (1939) as they wend their way across Monument Valley, we would drastically revise our mental inventory of interpretations of the drama of the moment. In fact, as long as the general musical style is not completely at odds, whatever the music at the moment, the scene seems to justify it. To demonstrate the interdependence of music and filmic representation, we can borrow from linguistics the tool of commutation, taking any small segment of film and applying different types of music to it. The *Stagecoach* example already suggests the dramatic importance of tension-producing harmonies and pauses, as well as general style. Let us further investigate music's capacity to create rhythm, atmosphere, cinematic space, spectatorial distance, and point of view, by selecting a short segment from François Truffaut's *Jules and Jim* (1961).

In a sequence fairly early in the film, Catherine, Jules, and Jim bicycle down a country road in a sort of metonymical image of their own lives' trajectories. A long high-angle shot shows the bicyclers as little more than a trio of specks on their winding road, pedaling very regularly, embodying the dialectic of fate and free will that characteristically pervades Truffaut's films. The musical theme that plays consists of two neighboring notes alternating with each other for measures on end before resolving to a cadence.[6] Though it can hardly be called an interesting melody, Georges Delerue's delicate woodwind-and-string orchestration counteracts its basic dullness. Also, of course, there is its relationship to a particular set of images.

The regularity of the musical repetition emphasizes the regularity of the characters' pedaling motions. The allegretto tempo and the total lack of harmonic or rhythmic surprises only reinforce the diegetic pedaling rhythm. It is important to note that the rhythms are not one and the same: if each musical downbeat coincided exactly with each turn of the pedal shaft by each character, we would be affected strangely indeed, made conscious of a perversely manipulative narrator. Nevertheless, the music turns regularly, and although there is no question of identity between musical and diegetic rhythm, there does result a sensation of mechanicalness; the music is, in a not unpleasant way, reinforcing the detachment conveyed in the high-angle shot.

Let us now perform a commutation on the bicycling segment by changing the music on the soundtrack. First, if we put the music into a minor mode, a sadder, darker, more remote feeling comes upon the scene. Later in the film the melody does in fact appear in minor; and, especially by contrast to its previous statement in major, it gives all the more poignancy to the mood of its scene. Or we might change the tempo of the music. If played much faster, allegro staccato, this music will add an energy, an *allégresse* to the three characters' bicycling, and perhaps even an optimism not previously suggested in Delerue's score.

Further changes could be wrought on the theme in terms of instrumentation: imagine the difference in effect if the melody were performed on a solo violin (more pathos), a solo tuba (more humor), a large orchestra (overblown, Romantic excess). Imitative-denotative instrumentation ("mickey-mousing"), such as violins playing *col legno*, might also give a comedic touch. Changes in rhythm, as well as articulation (accents, phrasing), would each have corresponding effects on the way we receive the diegetic information.

These commutations elucidate some culturally coded connotations; further, cinematic musical codes can also come into play. We could, for example, replace the entire unit of music by another theme. In a later scene Catherine sings a song, "Le Tourbillon," that subsequently finds itself on the soundtrack as background music. The lyrics in the sung version—words that emphasize the character of life as a circular, repetitive series of meetings, affairs, and separations—are reinforced by a pleasantly repetitive tune. Wouldn't this tune work well as nondiegetic music for our bicycling theme? Yes. But a theme is by definition a musical element that is repeated during the course of a work; as such it picks up narrative associations, which, in turn, infuse themselves into each new thematic statement. If textual element X is repeated later in a text, it is not still merely X, but X plus an escort of accumulated meanings. "Le Tourbillon" is first performed in the film by Catherine (and by Albert, a secondary suitor). If this melody were to accompany the bicycling shots of the three protagonists, it would function in such a way as to put the weight on Catherine—to imply some manner of narrative focus on her or complicity with her. The melody which in fact accompanies the scene carries no such thematic baggage, for this is its first occurrence.

On the other hand (and returning to cultural codes), we may compose a piano boogie-woogie for the afternoon cyclists. This injects humor into the image, partly by virtue of the ungainly juxtaposition of rhythms it creates, and partly also because of the cultural associations of this musical style (historical period, class) that enter to color our perception of the threesome. Speaking of associations, we need only to commute a well-known piece of classical music—say, the opening of Beethoven's Fifth Symphony—to imagine its effect on the scene. Such a theme, in all its force, would lend uncalled-for epic grandeur to the poor trio of unsuspecting bicyclers. Moreover, since the filmgoer knows this musical warhorse, his/her pleasure in recognizing it in a new context threatens to interfere with "reading the story" of the film.

Silence

Since commutation focuses attention on the existing music versus the music that might have been, it brings out stylistic and cultural information that goes unrecognized in the usual processes of film viewing, and again suggests the breadth of the subliminal power that music exerts during the film experience. But there is another commutation yet to consider: silence.

The effect of the *absence* of musical sound must never be underestimated; filmmakers have, by and large, tended to ignore musical silences in mixing their soundtracks. "Above all, no gaps or holes, cry filmmakers with alarm. And if hole there be, plug it up with music." Henri Colpi voiced this criticism, picking up on Maurice Jaubert's complaint as early as 1936 that filmmakers call on composers only to underscore (constantly) the moods and actions of scenes and "boucher les trous sonores."[7]

What would a musical silence do to the bicyclers' promenade? Interestingly, this depends on what kind of silence is imposed. A *diegetic musical silence* might consist of the characters wending their way along the road to the sole sound of pedals and gears creaking. In this sort of scene, which conventionally demands background music, diegetic sound with no music can function effectively to make the diegetic space more immediate, more palpable, in the absence of that Muzak-like overlay so often thrust on the spectator's consciousness.[8] (It also emphasizes that the characters are not speaking, where there is no music to mitigate this verbal silence.) Conventional practice has made an anchor of background music, such that it dictates what the viewer's response to the images ought to be. Remove it from a scene whose emotional content is not explicit and you risk confronting the audience with an image they might fail to interpret.

For *nondiegetic silence*, the soundtrack is completely without sound. Dream sequences or other filmic depictions of intense mental activity sometimes run to a silent soundtrack. A complete nondiegetic silence would be extremely unlikely anywhere in *Jules and Jim*, let alone the bicycling segment. For if this silence seems oneiric, we might ask ourselves whose dream or memory we are watching, and why it is so dreamlike. (With Alain Resnais or Werner Herzog, these questions might be more appropriate.) The spirit of easy collectivity among Truffaut's characters would be altered if the music, taken from the soundtrack, left a void. Nondiegetic silence can also be put to "modernist" or comedic use, as in Godard's *Bande à part* (1964). When three characters in a cafe decide to stop talking and have "one minute of silence," Godard overdoes it by removing all sound for exactly a minute. Truffaut has also indulged in this type of self-reflexive playfulness, but no such joke is set up in the little bicycling sequence in *Jules and Jim.*

A *structural silence* occurs where sound previously present in a film is later absent at structurally corresponding points. The film thus encourages us to expect the (musical) sound as before, so that when in fact there is no music, we are aware of its absence. For example, *Public Enemy* (William Wellman, 1931) begins with a title shot, "1909," accompanied by busy, cheery music in a major key. The first sequence follows, introducing the two protagonists as young boys, playing boys' games—depicted as harmless—which involve various degrees of trickery and petty theft. The next sequence takes place six years later, when they have graduated into "real" crime. Its corresponding introductory title shot, "1915," is not accompanied by music. The silence suggests a loss of frivolity, a fall from the childhood games of innocence that had initiated the two into their lives as criminals.

A similarly somber use of absent music occurs in Federico Fellini's *Nights of Cabiria* (1957). In the opening scene, no music plays on the soundtrack, while on the screen an untrustworthy suitor shoves Cabiria into the river and runs off with her purse. An abundantly music-filled movie follows, until the final sequence is reached. Cabiria and her beloved husband-to-be walk atop a steep cliff overlooking a river; she has with her all her life's savings. Again, music leaves the soundtrack, and again, the man has deceived her. No music could be as eloquent as the lack of it here; and this silence points out a structural relation, showing, in a way, that the film has virtually created Cabiria as a woman to be deceived, robbed, and pushed into rivers by men.

Songs with Lyrics

We noted the possibility of accompanying the bicyclers with a song: but "Le Tourbillon" would already have gathered connotations by this point in the story. Further, if Catherine were the singer, the impression of a balanced trio of individuals would disappear. This would all but turn Catherine into a musical voiceover narrator, a voice of authority. The lyrics, too, would command attention in their own right, and oblige a particular reading of what would otherwise be an understatedly neutral image.

In scenes from dramatic films where a character sings a song—Rita Hayworth in *Gilda*, Marlene Dietrich in *Destry Rides Again*, numerous singing

cowboys in westerns (e.g., Ricky Nelson and Dean Martin in *Rio Bravo*)—
the action necessarily freezes for the duration of the song. Songs require
narrative to cede to spectacle, for it seems that lyrics and action compete
for attention. This is also true for songs sung nondiegetically, heard over the
film's images. "The Ballad of Chuck-a-luck" in Fritz Lang's *Rancho Notorious*
(1952) is heard over images of the western landscape and/or riders on horse-
back. Similarly, a male voice in Sam Fuller's *Forty Guns* (1957) croons "She's
a High Ridin' Woman With a Whip" over vistas of Barbara Stanwyck riding
with her hired men across the countryside. Rather than participating in the
action, these theme songs behave somewhat like a Greek chorus, com-
menting on a narrative temporarily frozen into spectacle. "Help Me Make
It Through the Night," sung at the opening of John Huston's *Fat City* (1972)
as the protagonist awakens in a dilapidated room, also serves as an anthem
setting the narrative stage.

The 1983 re-edition of Fritz Lang's *Metropolis* (1926), which features a
contemporary rock score by Giorgio Moroder, provides an interesting coun-
terexample of the standard practice of segregating song lyrics from dialogue
and significant action. During some "dialogue scenes" (intertitles were converted to subtitles for enhanced visual pacing), songs with lyrics, sung by
such stars as Pat Benatar, Adam Ant, and Billy Squier, are heard on the
soundtrack. They provide a choruslike commentary on what is seen, sometimes with brilliant irony. Some listeners, their primary attention divided
between the lyrics and the "dialogue," find this difficult to assimilate.

Song lyrics, then, threaten to offset the aesthetic balance between music
and narrative cinematic representation. The common solution taken by the
standard feature film is not to declare songs off limits—for they can give
pleasure of their own—but to defer significant action and dialogue during
their performance.

Narrative/Diegesis

Although by the 1920s the Russian Formalists had explored the basic
distinction between "fable" (the narrated story, the represented, the diegesis) and the "subject" (the textual treatment of the story, that is, its narrative representation), it was the French *filmologues* of the 1950s, headed
by Gilbert Cohen-Séat, who refined certain concepts and terminology that
paved the way for a systematic study of film narrative. Gérard Genette
defines the diegesis as "the spatiotemporal universe referred to by the pri-

mary narration."[9] Etienne Souriau, a *filmologue*, elaborated upon this definition in terms of cinema specifically:

> *Diegesis, diegetic*: all that belongs, "by inference,"[10] to the narrated story, to the world supposed or proposed by the film's fiction. Ex: (a) Two sequences projected consecutively can represent two scenes separated in the diegesis by a long interval (several hours or years of diegetic time). (b) Two adjoining studio sets can represent locations supposedly hundreds of feet apart in diegetic space. (c) Sometimes there are two actors (e.g. a child and an adult, or a star and a stuntman or double) to successively depict the same diegetic character.[11]

Genette's and Souriau's definitions would agree that the diegesis means the space-time universe and its inhabitants referred to by the principal filmic narration. Souriau's application to cinema brings out some important details. First, he takes care to furnish examples of both spatial and temporal diegetization of filmic elements. Second, he includes the phrase "by inference" ("dans l'intelligibilité"), whose importance will presently become clear. At this point, then, we may summarize and define "diegesis" as being the *narratively implied spatiotemporal world of the actions and characters.*

However, a problem arises in film study: how to pinpoint this *narrative implication.* What in a film makes it possible for us to infer that characters and space exist even when they do not appear on screen, to infer a logically continuous universe, when the film presents only a series of two-dimensional compositions—discrete and discontinuous shots? In other words, how do the perceived sounds and images, all edited and spliced together, give us the impression of some "real" world they are supposedly extracted from? We seem to have the psychological capacity to impose continuity on filmed images and sounds before us—a capacity to take Kuleshov's mini-sequence composed of a shot of a man's face followed by a shot of a bowl of soup followed by a shot of the man again, and to say that the man stands near the table and is looking at the food (even before jumping to the connotative level on which we perceive him expressing hunger). From three fragments of a supposed reality, we infer, reconstruct, the diegesis; all narrative representation presents us the subject from which we derive the fable.

At the same time, filmmakers have departed from strictly diegetic representation almost since the beginning of film itself. In the silents, visual metaphors commonly appeared (e.g., the cradle motif in D. W. Griffith's *Intolerance*). In the sound film, the use of visual metaphor strikes us as artificial, since the realistic integrity of the diegesis, seemingly enhanced by the lifelike presence of sounds and dialogue, is all the more violently perturbed by nondiegetic images. On the other hand, "metadiegetic" images—those supposedly narrated or imagined by a character in the film—persist. In addition to dreams, visions, fantasies, and the like, a whole flashback introduced by a character (who thereby becomes a secondary narrator) is a common element of film discourse.

It is not difficult to realize that the soundtrack takes many more liberties with the diegesis than does the image track. Voiceover commentaries and verbally narrated flashbacks, both nondiegetic, punctuate many film narratives. Sound effects, however, tend to remain diegetic (unless they accompany also nondiegetic images). One reason for this lies in the ambiguity of many sounds when presented out of the context of their sound source. Significantly, the only element of filmic discourse that appears extensively in nondiegetic as well as diegetic contexts, and often freely crosses the boundary line in between, is music. Once we understand the flexibility that music enjoys with respect to the film's diegesis, we begin to recognize how many different kinds of functions it can have: temporal, spatial, dramatic, structural, denotative, connotative—both in the diachronic flow of a film and at various interpretive levels simultaneously.

Diegetic Music

Definitions

Diegetic music: music that (apparently) issues from a source within the narrative. While most viewers will agree on whether a particular instance of film music issues from a diegetic source or not, a caveat—itself with rich consequences—is in order here. Fellini, for example, deliberately blurs the line between the diegetic and the nondiegetic, and he particularly loves to use music to serve this purpose.[12] As one of its most deeply entrenched conventions, the Hollywood musical also plays on the tensions that the musically diegetic/nondiegetic ambiguity creates. And Vigo, Clair, Duvivier, Grémillon, Resnais, Carné, Renoir, and a host of other French directors since 1930 participate in a strong Gallic tradition of exploiting the diegetic ambiguity inherent in film music.

If Genette has distinguished at least three levels of narration—the diegetic (arising from the primary narration), the extradiegetic (narrative intrusion upon the diegesis, and which I shall henceforth call nondiegetic), and the metadiegetic (pertaining to narration by a secondary narrator)—may we speak also of metadiegetic film music? A hypothetical instance: early in a film we witness the great romance of protagonist X, which ends tragically during the war. Years later, while X and his best friend Y sit in a bleak cafe discussing their irretrievable joys, Y brings up the name of X's lost love. This strikes a chord: a change comes over X's face, and music swells onto the soundtrack, the melody that had played early in the film on the night X had met her. On which narrative level do we read this music? It is certainly not diegetic, for the forty-piece orchestra that plays is nowhere to be seen, or inferred, in the filmic space of the cafe. In a certain sense, we may hear it as both nondiegetic—for its lack of a narrative source—and metadiegetic— since the scene's conversation seems to trigger X's memory of the romance and the song that went with it; wordlessly, he "takes over" part of the film's narration and we are privileged to read his musical thoughts.

Affective roles of diegetic music

The mood of any music on the soundtrack, be it diegetic or nondiegetic music, will be felt in association with diegetic events. Curiously, critics often make the error of classifying film music as either nondiegetic and therefore, they contend, capable of expression, or diegetic, "realistic," divorced from the tasks of articulating moods and dramatic tensions.[13] We need only think of countless nightclub scenes where countless couples declare their love to soft music: sometimes a (diegetic) orchestra or jukebox plays it, sometimes it plays nondiegetically on the soundtrack—with about the same expressive value.

What we may indeed remark about the special expressive effect of diegetic music is its capacity to create irony, in a more "natural" way than nondiegetic music. Imagine, for instance, that the heroine is enjoying herself at a party; people dance and shout to a lively jitterbug. Suddenly a message arrives for her, saying that her fiancé has just been killed. As a close-up shows us the note, the gay music continues to revel on the soundtrack, "unaware" of its ironic commentary on her lover's death. Now imagine the scene conceived differently. Instead of being at a party, the heroine sits at home chatting with a neighbor. The unfortunate telegram arrives, and a nondiegetic rendition of the jitterbug accompanies the close-up. Now this seems a shocking exercise in sheer style and narrative self-consciousness. Even though we know that the narrator has been equally responsible for the music/image irony in the party scene, "his" creative effrontery strikes us with greater force in the second case—even puzzlement. By taking music meant as extranarrative comment and rendering it diegetic in the first example, the narration motivates, naturalizes the music, makes its disparity with the filmed events acceptable. Alfred Hitchcock creates outlandish ironies using diegetic music in *The Man Who Knew Too Much* (1934): a man is murdered to the tune of dance music; an assassin fires a rifle at the climactic moment in a symphony concert; a church organ plays during a grim life-and-death brawl. In *North By Northwest* (1959), a violin and piano duet in the Plaza Hotel's cocktail lounge innocently plays "It's a Most Unusual Day" just as complacent business executive Roger Thornhill is being drawn into his nightmarish odyssey.

For French critic-musician Michel Chion, struck by narrative cinema's frequent use of diegetic music for ironic effects, such music is not only "unaware" of the dramatic situation, but "indifferent"—or, as he puts it, "anempathetic." Musical time is abstract time; once begun, a piece's musical logic demands to work itself through to the finish. This is what can put music at odds with dramatic human time, which is a less logically predictable time, more subject to the aleatory experiences of "real life." The Hitchcock examples testify to the power of this music which blissfully lacks awareness or empathy; its very emotionlessness, juxtaposed with ensuing human catastrophe, is what provokes our emotional response.

In standard narrative filmmaking, the rhythm and mood of diegetic music that "coincidentally" plays with a scene has been made to match the scene's mood and pace with an uncanny consistency. This practice in fact implies a departure of diegetic music from its naturalistic independence and a movement toward the action-imitating roles we might more readily expect of nondiegetic music. There are, of course, degrees of this improbable fusion of diegetic music with action. The most closely synchronized music-scene coordination is what I shall call "orchestration." In *Nights of Cabiria*, a rich actor, Lazzari, has brought protagonist Cabiria, a prostitute, to his home for the night. While they wait for the servant to bring dinner, Lazzari puts the second movement of Beethoven's Fifth Symphony on the record player. For the rest of the duration of the piece, or until Lazzari removes it from the turntable, Fellini paces the action to match exactly the movement of the symphony. At the point of a great crescendo and modulation, a servant wheels in a majestic tray loaded with food in silver serving dishes. The spectacular interplay continues: during a quiet, pensive moment in the Beethoven, Lazzari, having inspected the champagne and its vintage, repeats the year 1949 nostalgically, as if directed by the music to do so at that time and no other.

Fellini achieves a degree of stylization by manipulating the characters' actions so that they submit to musical division of time rather than dramatic or realistic time. The characters in the narrative film, whom we conventionally accept as subjects, become objects when their movements and speech coincide strictly with the music: for, again, musical rhythm—an abstract, mathematical, highly organized disposition of time—can be considered at odds with spontaneous, "real" time. We sense that the characters have been created, and they do not inspire us to identify with them. Contributing to a definite departure from psychological realism, the music employed acts ironically as a much stronger narrative intrusion, even though diegetic, than nondiegetic music.[14]

Diegetic music, sound space, temporal continuity

In a narrative film, diegetic music functions first and foremost as sound. Considering music this way, we are far from the concerns of pure musical codes; the issue is rather music's functioning in terms of cinematic space. Offscreen sound, for example, typically motivates camera movement and/or cutting to new quadrants of space. As the camera eye searches out the sound source, cinematic space "naturally" unfolds. Diegetic music fleshes out film space, and variables in recording, mixing, and volume levels further determine the quality, the "feel," or framed/lived space in a given film. In films with stereo sound, diegetic music—as well as dialogue and sound effects, of course—can articulate space with all the more directional precision.

Music can also create depth in space; its spatial properties became well established, and particularly codified in Hollywood, within a few years of the coming of sound. In *Public Enemy* (1931), Tom Powers and Matt Doyle stand outside the Red Oaks Club. A saloon piano plays "Hesitation Blues" faintly on the soundtrack. The boys open the saloon door and the music becomes louder. After a cut to the inside, the camera tracks by the Red Oaks' adolescent clientele and comes to rest on Putty-Nose, who is playing this song at the barroom piano. The music has of course played continuously across the cut and has grown louder until the medium close-up of Putty-Nose at the piano. The diegetic music in this scene has a double function. First, it provides temporal continuity to two spatially discontinuous shots, acting as a seamless auditory match. Second, it provides depth cues: since loud means near and soft means far (with corresponding levels of reverberation), a continuous progression from soft to loud means a continuous movement forward in cinematic space, toward the sound source.

The Blue Angel (1930) bases a whole scene on the power of the soundtrack to describe physical volumes. Professor Rath, somewhat embarrassed, is meeting Lola Lola backstage for the first time. Often at moments that add ironic punctuation to Rath's halting words, minor characters "happen" to enter by either of two doors through which escape sounds of laughter and sleazily played music from the girlie show. The expressive functions of diegetic music here are motivated by its spatial functions.

Since a piece of music has its own temporal structure, which may or may not coincide with the temporal structure of a narrative film sequence, it may have a variety of temporal functions in the narration. The example from *Public Enemy* shows how diegetic music playing continuously strongly reinforces our sense of the temporal and spatial contiguity of the discrete shots in a sequence. (This very point was lost at the beginning of Christian Metz's syntagmatic analysis of *Adieu Philippine*, by the way, for what he described as a "bracket syntagma" of musicians recording in a television studio during the opening credit sequence is actually a "scene," held together as one temporal unity by the single continuous tune the musicians are playing.)[15]

Montage sequences often use nondiegetic music to bridge gaps of diegetic time. The famed breakfast-table sequence in *Citizen Kane*, for example, showing Kane and his first wife sitting at progressively greater distances from each other as the years pass, visually signaling the emotional distance that grows between them, has a theme-and-variations music—as well as equally symmetrical shot compositions—to simultaneously bridge and demarcate the temporal discontinuities in the narrative.

One might continue to enumerate other types of continuity that music can promote: thematic, dramatic, rhythmic, structural, and so on. In each case music functions as connecting tissue, a nonrepresentational provider of relations, among all levels of the narration. One area that invites extensive exploration is the function of music with respect to point of view: for it can mark shifts in point of view, or it can assure a continuous, often narratively "illogical," progression from one viewpoint to another. In a key segment of Hitchcock's *Blackmail* (1929), for example, a continuously playing musical theme leads the filmic narration from the standard objective mode (as a male suitor plays the piano to the woman protagonist) to a guilt-ridden, subjective instance (as the woman walks the London streets having stabbed the man to death, and on the soundtrack an increasingly orchestrated and harmonically/acoustically altered version of the original diegetic piano theme is heard). The music's progression from diegetic to metadiegetic status, combined with Hitchcock's subjective camera techniques, leads us into identifying with a murderess.

Themes

A theme is defined as any music—melody, melody-fragment, or distinctive harmonic progression—heard more than once during the course of a film. This includes "theme songs," background instrumental motifs, tunes repeatedly performed by or associated with characters, and other recurring nondiegetic music. A theme can be extremely economical: having absorbed the diegetic associations of its first occurrence, its very repetition can subsequently recall that filmic context. This means that although music in itself is nonrepresentational, the repeated occurrence of a musical motif in conjunction with representational elements in a film (images, speech) can cause the music to carry representational meaning as well.

Themes accumulate meaning to varying degrees. The theme can be assigned a fixed function, constantly signaling the same character, locale, or situation each time it appears, or it can vary, nuance, play a part in the film's dynamic evolution.

A motif is a theme whose recurrences remain specifically directed and unchanged in their diegetic associations. When in *Stagecoach* Ford's camera pans across Monument Valley from the stagecoach to the Indians lying in wait, rhythmic "Indian music" is heard. The motif is redundant (redundancy is far from being a "bad" feature of this film, whose poetry of archetypes depends on repetition and reinforcement): a brief exercise in commutation shall explain why. Let us replace the existing motif, *A*, with another, *B*:

I have intentionally made *B*, a distinctively shaped melodic line, ambiguous in its emotive effect, by freeing it from traditional harmonic associations. In our hypothetical *Stagecoach*, this atonal melody occurs at first sight of the Indians and as yet has no solid thematic—and little emotive—function. When the Indians' next appearance is accompanied by *B*, a logical link between *B* and Indians begins to take root. A relationship of denotation develops from their ongoing coincidence. Have stagecoach driver Buck voice his fears about the Apaches, and a rendition of *B* now will seem entirely appropriate. By the time the travelers reach Apache Wells and find that the settlement has been razed, *B* will suffice to explain the tragedy even if no character utters a word. Independently of any inherent properties of the melody, meaning has been born. The relationship *B*-Indians is arbitrary, just as the word "dog" is to the animal it denotes.

Returning to *A*, the motif actually used in *Stagecoach*, we find that its redundancy is clear. Not only does the film assign *A* to each Indian reference, using the music as a denotative tag, but its cultural-musical properties— rhythmic repetition in groups of four with accented initial beat, and predominance of open intervals of perfect fourths and fifths—*already* signify "Indian" in the language of the American music industry. Two different levels of codification overlap to communicate the same message.

The critical writings of Richard Wagner, to a greater extent than any writings on film music per se, provide insights into the nature of thematic music in dramatic representational works. Wagner elaborated his ideas on motifs in *Opera and Drama* (1850–51) as part of a larger conceptual structure, justifying the importance of leitmotifs as elements essential to the total musical-dramatic work that his operas after *Lohengrin* were to exemplify. What he named "motifs of reminiscence" are of interest for film music. Jack M. Stein summarizes:

> . . . There often occur moments when the immediate expression is influenced by the thought of something lying in the past which continues to have an emotional effect on the speaker. The presence and consequently the influence of this reminiscence can be communicated by the repetition of the characteristic musical line which was part of the original musical expression. The melodic line alone, originally the musical counterpart of the idea contained in the verse, is sufficient to inject this idea as a conditioning element of reminiscence into the new situation. It thus appears as a realization and representation of what was just thought of by the character on the stage. Even when such a reminiscence occurs against the will of the character, the fact of its having conditioned his present reaction can be communicated in this way.[16]

Wagner's definition of these memory-motifs includes three features: the memory motif must first be stated in conjunction with a verbal text; it functions specifically to evoke a memory; and this memory belongs to a character in the drama.

That Wagner required each motif of reminiscence to originate from a melodic-poetic line (*Versmelodie*) means that he was concerned to root the motif in denotation. The melody would recur later in the orchestra, but its precise referent will have been set firmly by its verbal context. Thus, in the *Rhinegold*, we find in the Curse motif a clear example of the memory motif as Wagner intended it:

The melodic line which was originally united with the words, "Wie durch Fluch er mir geriet, verflucht sei dieser Ring!" [As by a curse it came into my power, cursed be this ring!] is repeated by the orchestra at moments throughout all the Ring dramas whenever reference to this curse is made, especially when its effects are seen in the subsequent catastrophes of the plot. Thus, when the two giants quarrel over possession of the ring and Fasolt is slain by Fafner, the motif is announced solemnly by the brass. The original curse is forcefully injected into the emotional picture by the motif's appearance. The original scene, the original words even, are recalled.[17]

Recalling Wagner's reason for the linguistic origin of the motif—denotation—we note that the cinema has other means at its disposal for establishing such denotation; aspects of framing, notably the close-up, can single out the referent to which the music will be associated. With the *Stagecoach* motif, the association between image and music is sufficient, independent of verbal language.

As it turns out, Wagner often disregarded his own precepts about musical denotation. Of the ninety motifs that run through the *Ring* dramas, over half do not originate in the melodic verse but in the orchestra instead. The audience is left to judge by dramatic context alone what the motifs stand for; it is not surprising that the names used to identify these motifs vary from critic to critic. These melodies are freer from unilinear identification; thus they are more expressive than referential. If a motif no longer refers to a specific object, it cannot very well operate to recall, either. Wagner's theoretical specifications in *Opera and Drama* give way in practice to leitmotifs as we know them, both denotative (Sword, Curse) and "floating" in characteristically suggestive ways.

Numerous film scores are built on one central theme, which may or may not accrue associations in the manner I have described. Alfred Newman's music for *All About Eve* (1950) provides a typical example:

Does this melody, first heard over the credits, and subsequently at most emotional moments where Eve (Anne Baxter) appears, signify Eve herself, or Eve's emotional impact on her "audiences" (the characters and filmviewers she manipulates), or is it simply a signature for the film *All About Eve*? In many cases, the theme's designation is so diffused that to call it a leitmotif contradicts Wagner's intention.

Summary

    Music behaves synergically in films. Change the score on the soundtrack, and the image-track can be transformed. Studying the functions of music in narrative cinema necessarily entails studying, as a first step, its relations with other elements in the textual system. Subsequently, we may learn more about film music through examining it in contextual systems that take history and conditions of spectatorship into account.

    Music in film *mediates*. Its nonverbal and nondenotative status allows it to cross all varieties of "borders": between levels of narration (diegetic/non-diegetic), between narrating agencies (objective/subjective narrators), between viewing time and psychological time, between points in diegetic space and time (as narrative transition).

    Finally, the connotative values which music carries, via cultural codes and also through textual repetition and variation, in conjunction with the rest of the film's soundtrack and visuals, largely determine atmosphere, shading, expression, and mood. What is mood? Certainly, a difficult point to interrogate without recourse to more exhaustive phenomenological description, historical investigation, and inquiry into the psychology of musical emotion. The question remains how to present cogent theoretical arguments on the subject: for mood—the most obvious and oft-mentioned function of film music—originates in the complex of all connotative elements in the filmic system and beyond, in the "texts" of the spectator's existence. Through close analysis of individual films, historical analysis of music in the silent and the sound cinema, and examining a variety of perspectives on the film spectator/auditor, we may approach a fuller understanding of how music works in creating meaning in tandem with cinematic narrative.

CHAPTER II

Why Music?
From Silents
to Sound

Posing the Question; Film Music's Discursive Status

The classical narrative sound film has been constituted in such a way that
the spectator does not normally (consciously) hear the film score. In the last
chapter, I offered some explanation of this phenomenon, based on the idea
that the spectator focuses attention on the narrative events in the film. Music
being nonnarrative and nonrepresentational takes a back seat, as it were, to
the viewer's principal object of attention—the story, the characters: the
diegesis. Composers, sound editors, and critics speak both descriptively and
prescriptively about film music's "subordination" to the story. The spectator
tends to be conscious of discourse (elements, including music, that enunciate
the story) only insofar as it "transgresses" or "interrupts" story (that which
is enunciated).

But the question why we don't hear film music (especially, but certainly
not exclusively, the music in commercial narrative films), and the question
of precisely what focusing attention means, lead to further questions. If we
don't necessarily hear it, in favor of following the story, why is music there?
Does it have similar discursive status to, say, camera movement or framing,
and if not, what is the nature of its relation to story, of its function with
regard to story? What might it globally signify? What good is it? What *business* does it have in cinema's psychic and narrative economy? This kind of
questioning reorients our inquiry a little less toward music's position in a

text—assumed as a coherent, self-enclosed semiotic system—and more toward the dynamics of the spectator's position in relation to this text.

Some observations are in order concerning the discursive status of film music. At first glance, we might wish to equate the function of film music with, say, that of the close-up or of the tracking shot: these elements of narration serve to intensify, isolate, specify, connect, or otherwise draw particular attention to something in the narrative. But soundtrack music does not bear this same relation to story at all. The close-up isolates an object, an action, inside diegetic space. Likewise, the tracking shot depicts and connects diegetic elements as it moves through diegetic space. Music need not denote anything in the represented space (although, of course, some music in a given score typically has this referential task—"South America," "wartime patriotism," motifs for characters). More typically, and unlike other elements of discourse, nondiegetic music does not denote anything in the represented space. Rather, it figures in the expression of mood, pace, feeling *in relation to* the represented space.

The musical score's rhythmic, textural, and harmonic qualities, expressive via cultural musical codes, emphasize latent or manifest narrative content through a synergetic relationship with the other channels of filmic discourse. In emphasizing moods or feelings, in specifying or delineating objects for the spectator's attention, music enforces an interpretation of the diegesis. Borrowing slightly out of context from Roland Barthes, let us say that music behaves as *"ancrage,"* anchoring the image more firmly in meaning.[1] Were we to seek a visual analogue of music's status as nondiegetic "interpreter" of diegetic events, we might think of the "poetic insert" (a nondiegetic shot that draws a comparison), which suggests a likeness to some quality of the diegetic signified. Silent cinema, from Griffith to the intellectual montage of Eisenstein, used nondiegetic inserts freely. In the sound cinema they have been rare. Fritz Lang's *Fury* (1936) inserts a shot of clucking hens into a montage of the gossiping women in the small town where Spencer Tracy's nightmarish story takes place. The hens are terms of a grotesquely humorous comparison between the women's gossipmongering and the reflexive cackling of barnyard animals. The insert interrupts the flow of the diegesis, and this may explain why it was already perceived in the mid-thirties as an "outdated" device for a narrative sound film.

A better visual analogy to music as nondiegetic "interpreter" might be a nondiegetic discursive element that does not interrupt the flow of the diegesis. Take for example the use of tinted film stock—printing the visuals on monochromatically dyed stocks. Tinted stock aided in the creation of mood (e.g., a melancholy scene in blue) and of verisimilitude (e.g., red tinting for a fire sequence). But again, the widespread practice of tinting sequences during the silent era had its demise in the latter twenties. Color tinting presumably met its end due to the development of more "realistic" color processes, or to more complex combinations of factors. Whatever the case, monochrome sequences occurred rarely after the transition to sound.

Viewed in this perspective, then, nondiegetic music is closer in discursive status to the nondiegetic insert, or to "nondiegetic color"[2] (neither of which survived the transition to sound) than to the close-up or moving shot. It denotes nothing in the story, only signifies in relation to the story. But on the other hand, we know that in standard narrative films, music seems to be as "natural," even as necessary, a discursive element as the close-up or tracking shot. The question remains: why did nondiegetic music persist into the sound film? Why does it not produce the effect of interruption as strongly as nondiegetic visuals or, for that matter, other nondiegetic sounds? If music, unlike the insert, has persisted into the diegetic sound film despite its non-diegetic status, then the payoff it brings to some psychological register, other than the strictly diegetic illusion, must be lucrative indeed. To trace the problem more accurately, let us first examine what roles music played in the silent cinema.

Music in Silent Films

The answers to the question "why music in silent cinema?" are situated on two levels we might call specific and global. Answers of the first kind focus on the specific ways music was employed to provide transitions, direct attention to details, establish atmosphere and mood, and so on. But these specific functions could just as well be served by other means already at the silent film's disposal—intertitles, color tinting, camerawork, acting, lighting. The global question "why music?"—its very presence in cinematic discourse, its overall signification—shall take precedence for the moment.

Historical arguments

A first category of responses is historical. Music and dramatic representation, as is often pointed out, have weathered many centuries as a team. Starting no doubt even before the Greeks, continuing through the Middle Ages and the Renaissance, and resurfacing to popularity in the late eighteenth-century French *mélodrame*, the tradition of accompanying drama with music simply passed along, into a variety of nineteenth-century forms of popular entertainment, and finally into the new cinematic medium. Roger Manvell and John Huntley find the immediate precursors to film music in the popular theater, notably in the elaborate restagings of Shakespeare (Mendelssohn's music for "A Midsummer Night's Dream," completed in 1843, is a famous example) and the new large-scale melodramas. Melodrama productions were enhanced by "the powerful emotional stimulant provided by what was called incidental music . . . by the time the cinema was born, the pianist and the orchestra had been long established in the living theatre."[3] Indeed, reviews of these elaborate productions read like descriptions of silent film spectaculars. An organ or orchestra was nearly always present for big-city productions, to set moods and underscore actions.

The melodrama aspired to pictorial illusion down to the minutest detail. For Irving, Belasco, and others, dialogue was *not* important (and thus, dialogue's absence in the cinema may not have felt as abnormal to audiences as numerous present-day critics have insisted)—even when it came to Shakespeare! By the time Henry Irving produced "Romeo and Juliet" in 1882 (with a special musical score composed by Sir Julius Benedict), "the words had lost their necessity. Everything had been done visually with pictorial settings, descriptive business, and mass tableaux."[4]

Melodrama called for music to mark entrances of characters, to provide interludes, and to give emotional coloring to dramatic climaxes and to scenes with rapid physical action. Musical cues appear abundantly in "acting editions" of British melodramas. From them we can see that the clichés of film music arose directly from those of melodrama, too. James L. Smith writes,

> Plaintive heroines flee to *tremolo* violins, bandits with cat-like tread prowl to *pizzicato* strings, and combatants in *The Dumb Maid of Genoa* time every blow with the orchestra, parrying to pirouettes and stabbing each other to strong chords. Chords also emphasize important facts. Everyone gets the message when *The Shade*, pointing to the ruined cloister, cries:
>
>> Blondel—there thy friend was foully murdered! (music in a terrific chord) Blood for blood! (chord more terrific) Revenge! (chord) Revenge! (chord) Revenge! (chord – thunder.)[5]

A 1910 article by British stage composer Norman O'Neill (1876–1934) gives valuable information about the use of incidental music in the British popular theater. O'Neill makes clear that music not only was played between segments of the drama, but also accompanied dialogue scenes. In his essay we sense an approach remarkably similar to prevailing practices in Hollywood a quarter century later: "The musical accompaniment to a speech should steal in and steal out so quietly, that the audience are no more aware of it than they are of some subtle change in the stage lighting. . . ."[6]

Peter Brooks emphasizes that music brought additional *legibility* to a dramatic form whose moral impulse is borne out by hyperexplicitness; melodrama gives a world in which "nothing is left unsaid":

> Not only is the very existence of melodrama as a distinct genre originally linked to its use of music, music is inherent in its representations, as to those of the cinema, its inheritor in this convention. Through the film and the pervasive exploitation of background music, we have become so accustomed to music used toward the dramatization of life that it is difficult for us to recapture its radical effect, to measure its determination of our reading of the representations before us.[7]

The physical context of the earliest cinema explains much about the immediate connection between movies and music. For the first decade and a half, movies were often shown in a theatrical setting, as part of an evening's live entertainment which featured vaudeville skits and musical numbers. Musicians already being present, it was natural that they accompany the moving picture section of the program, too. Subsequently, it still seemed natural that once the cinema separated off into its own theaters, its own evening's entertainment of feature-length films, its own "art form," musical accompaniment had become part of it and was there to stay. Max Winkler, Bert Ennis, and several others each take credit for having invented the cue sheet around 1911; this was a sort of quick-reference guide of a few well-known pieces to play at given points to accompany a particular movie. Cue sheets were widely popular through the teens, since they saved movie-house pianists much time and effort of preparation. Studios hired composers to write for them and to search the music literature for appropriate melodies, and the resulting sheets were distributed with new films each week.[8] With the postwar advent of picture palaces, and the institutionalization of the cinema as a middle-class entertainment, music became a dramatically more ambitious presence at the photoplay. The mighty Wurlitzer was an attraction all by itself in some theaters. In other urban palaces, entire orchestras played scores adroitly compiled by conductors or specially hired "music illustrators" from mood-music collections. Even before 1910, some films in Europe had specially through-composed scores written for them; in the United States, Griffith's spectacular *Birth of a Nation* (1914) had one of the earliest specially composed scores.[9]

Evolutionary or historical accounts of the continuity of musical accompaniment into the new theatrical tradition of cinema are compelling, but one should note that they answer the overall question only in part. "X is a thief because his father was, and his father's father before him": accepting the idea of a *tradition* can obscure why the tradition endures in the face of

change (sociological, economic, technological). The complex specific determinations of X's life, despite his thievish ancestry, could certainly lead him
into athletics, accounting, even police work.

Likewise, historical change has spawned wide variation in the nature and
deployment of music in drama. In some traditions music has played while
actors performed (miming, declaiming poetry, speaking in naturalistic prose);
while in many traditions it has served only as "between-the-acts music" and/
or during musical interludes dictated by the drama (e.g., a performance
within an Elizabethan play), if it was present at all. There is no "only natural"
which necessarily or wholly accounts for the persistence of musical accompaniment in the cinema of the teens and twenties. Like X, who could almost
as easily have become a policeman, the movies, a technologically new and
distinct medium, could just as well have been projected silent, or with some
other combination of audiovisual means[10].

It might also be argued (as Peter Brooks has suggested) that it was the
subject matter of the cinema's theatrical heritage, and not purely its form,
that demanded musical accompaniment. Melodrama—the very term marries
music and drama—opposed the classical stage's insistence on rationality and
moderation. The genre continued into the twentieth century to satisfy the
demand for spectacle. The cinema and its working-class mass audience welcomed melodrama as soon as it welcomed narrative on a large scale at all,
that is, around 1907–08; viewers flocked to the nickelodeons to see action,
drama, romance, excess. Family melodrama and adventure melodrama carried into the cinema of the teens with enormous popularity. Who could
imagine *The Perils of Pauline* without a tense, racing piano following the
adventurous heroine in danger, or a dulcet accompaniment to a romantic
scene?

Invoking dramatic traditions in general, and the melodramatic tradition
in particular, historical-evolutionary arguments, assuming the power of continuity of tradition, go a long way toward explaining the presence of musical
accompaniment in early cinema.

Pragmatic arguments

On the other hand, there are arguments based on the cinema's *technological specificity*. Most frequently, critics remind us that music had the
decidedly practical task of drowning out or covering up the mechanical clatter
of the movie-house projector.

> For in those times there were as yet no sound-absorbent walls between the
> projection machine and the auditorium. This painful noise disturbed visual

enjoyment to no small extent. Instinctively cinema proprietors had recourse to music, and it was the right way, using an agreeable sound to neutralize one less agreeable.[11]

This technologically based explanation, in turn, raises more questions. Once projection booths became a standard feature of the cinema, why did music continue? Another point of interrogation: what defined the status of music as less distracting than projection noise? (Both sounds, after all, are nondiegetic.) Viewers seemed to accept the most egregiously bad music, too, according to documents of the period—drunken musicians who paid no attention to the story on the screen and played comically inappropriate music, or small-town ensembles whose performances were far from reverie-inspiring. What makes screechy, out-of-tune music more desirable for film viewing than the regular hum and click of a projector?

A related musical practice, but on the production end rather than in the movie-house: hired musicians often played on the studio set during filming. Manvell and Huntley quote Maurice Elvey reminiscing on such use of music in the teens "to counteract the noise in the studios—after all, you often had two films being made on the same stage."[12] It helped the actors get into character despite the bustling activity around them (the set by no means quieted down when the mike-less cameras rolled), and helped them concentrate on the scene's rhythm and mood.

Aesthetic arguments

Two aesthetic explanations for the practice of film music also originate with the technological specificity of the film medium. The impression of reality gained from watching moving figures on the screen, a realness brought on by the cinema's origin in photography, made the actors' silence all the more notable and strange. Cinema also had the psychological effect, some argue, of flattening the real onto a two-dimensional plane. Thus, first, music came to replace, or at least compensate for the lack of, speech. Second, all sound exists in three dimensions; music as sound gave back, or at least compensated for the lack of, the spatial dimension of the reality so uncannily depicted in the new medium.

Leonid Sabaneev makes both these points in a rather curious formulation: music's "aesthetic function . . . was, *inter alia*, to fill up the tonal void which was an inherent feature of the silent film."[13] If title cards supplied the informational content of the missing speech, it was up to music to compensate for tones of voice, rhythms, inflections. Kurt London adds that "speech is the foundation of the whole of civilization"; and in the film, music took its place.[14] As for the role of music in restoring the spectator's sense of spatial depth, London posits that until music came to restore the dimensions of color and depth, "films, shown without a sound, on a plane, in a monotonous black and white, were in a manner of speaking dimensionless."[15] But, we may ask—even leaving aside the question of color—why would music affect the visual perception of depth? Traditional film music theories fail to account for this effect which they claim music exerts on the image, except to say that experiencing music in the three-dimensionality of sonic space somehow rubs off synaesthetically on our two-dimensional visual experience. (More on this later.)

For some authors, music was important for providing not only the dimension of depth, but rhythm as well. Sabaneev, London, Manvell and Huntley—and other writers into the seventies—invoke this problematical term to account for another phenomenon difficult to analyze. The regulated temporal movement of music seems to have something to do with the aesthetic justification of the pace of visual movement on the screen. For example, London says:

> The reason which is aesthetically and psychologically most essential to explain the need of music as an accompaniment of the silent film, is without doubt *the rhythm of the film as an art of movement.* We are not accustomed to apprehend movement as an artistic form without accompanying sounds, or at least audible rhythms.[16]

Jean Mitry maintains that the rhythm of music mediated between real time as experienced by the audience and the diegetic or psychological time adhered to by the film:

> Owing to its unrealistic nature, the silent film was incapable of making the spectator experience a real feeling of *duration.* The time lived by the characters of the drama, the temporal relations of the shots and sequences—all this was perfectly well *understood*—rather than *felt.* What was missing in the film was a sort of beat which could internally mark the psychological time of the drama in relation to the primary sensation of real time. In other words, what was missing was a beat capable of justifying cinematic rhythm and cadence. This beat, this "temporal content," was provided by music.[17]

Noël Burch, noting the "greater impression" which Fritz Lang's *Dr Mabuse der Spieler* made on him when he saw it with a musical accompaniment, also comments on music's function of temporal/rhythmic mediation: "it provides a time scale against which the 'rhythms' of the découpage become far more concrete."[18]

Psychological and anthropological arguments

Perhaps the richest and most controversial thesis comes from Hanns Eisler and Theodor W. Adorno. They agreed with those who stress music's compensatory or mediating function in the new technological circumstances of the cinematic spectacle. The argument runs that sound, in the form of music, gave back to those "dead" photographic images some of the life they lost in the process of mechanical reproduction. Words such as three-dimensionality, immediacy, reality, and, of course, life recur throughout film music criticism in its attempt to describe the effect and purpose of film music: "the very liveliness of the action in the primitive silent films appeared unnatural and ghostly without some form of sound corresponding to such visual vitality." Music seemed to help flesh out the shadows on the screen.[19] Eisler and Adorno went even further, describing in anthropological terms the need that brought music into cinema. Music took on a *magical* function, counteracting the lifelessness of the moving figures on the screen:

> The pure cinema must have had a ghostly effect like that of the shadow play—shadows and ghosts have always been associated. The magic function of music . . . probably consisted in appeasing the evil spirits unconsciously dreaded. Music was introduced as a kind of antidote against the picture. The need was felt to spare the spectator the unpleasantness involved in seeing effigies of living, acting, and even speaking persons, who were at the same time silent. The fact that they are living and nonliving at the same time is what constitutes their ghostly character, and music was introduced not to supply them with the life they lacked . . . but to exorcise fear or help the spectator absorb the shock.[20]

The fact that earlier critics described the film image as dead, empty, or unnatural, and saw music as providing life, immediacy, or a magical antidote to cinema's ghostliness, bears a striking kinship to Christian Metz's metapsychological account of the film experience in *The Imaginary Signifier* (1974). Metz characterizes the film image as signifying the "presence of an absence," being only the representation of what was present, not the thing itself. This absence or lack has something to do with what London, Eisler/Adorno, and others called flatness, emptiness, ghostliness. The film image signifies a lack, but filmic discourse has developed strategies to make good the lack. Such strategies restore belief (or suspend disbelief) in the immediacy and wholeness of the filmic events;[21] that is, they permit the viewing subject to identify with filmic discourse. Figures of editing, particularly the shot reverse-shot pattern (which "sutures" the spectator-subject into the filmic discourse), have been most thoroughly explored in this connection.

Clearly, though, film music scholars recognized in music a suturing device of capital importance.[22] Music permitted a deeper psychic investment in the grey, wordless, two-dimensional world of the silent film.

Eisler and Adorno hint at yet another compelling thesis. Taking a cue from earlier German musicologists, they raise the idea that music bears the sociological/psychological value of evoking the collective community. Ordinary music listening, they claim, is "archaic" in contrast to visual perception, upon which knowledge, at least in Western culture, is based. The visual is the register of systems of signification,[23] while aural perception "preserves comparably more traits of long bygone, pre-individualistic collectivities. . . . This direct relationship to a collectivity, intrinsic in the phenomenon itself, is probably connected with the sensations of spatial depth, inclusiveness, and absorption of individuality, which are common to all music."[24] Film music, like other forms of music in mass culture, taps in on this evocation of communality. Its social function is "that of a cement, which holds together elements that otherwise would oppose each other unrelated—the mechanical product and the spectators, and also the spectators themselves."[25] Music acts as a cement among "the spectators themselves"; it binds the audience together into a community of listener-participants. I shall pursue this idea at greater length in discussing music in the sound film.

In summary, critics and scholars have used a variety of perspectives to explain why music accompanied silent films. The art-historical approach links film music with the dramatic traditions (and "arts of movement") using incidental music. Pragmatists point to music's effectiveness in neutralizing the new medium's projector noise. Aestheticians insist on the way music *qua* rhythm motivated the visual and narrative rhythms of the silent screen. Others emphasize the imbalance created by this mechanical rendering of life; what it gained in realistic detail, it lost in the absence of speech and of spatial depth. Film music had a double function, as an aural language and as a spatial presence, to compensate for these "losses." Eisler and Adorno further claim that music had a magical function—as an antidote to the ghostliness of the cinematographic picture. As I have suggested, those who viewed music as addressing cinema's "loss" presaged recent psychoanalytic models of the cinematic experience. Finally, the psychologically and anthropologically derived notion of sound (particularly music) perception as "pre-individualistic" suggests that music played a particular role in the spectator's relation not only to the screen but to the surrounding community of spectators.

Some of these arguments clearly apply to the situation of the sound film. The art-historical "continuity of traditions" theme is stated and restated with variations throughout the literature on film music. Second, music in the sound film, even if it is no longer needed to replace speech or color, is felt to provide depth, rhythm, "life" to the picture. Theses regarding the magical or suturing functions, and Eisler/Adorno's notion of music's power to evoke the *collective* in the cinematic experience, also deserve the closest scrutiny in the context of sound film.

Silent vs. Sound Film: Some Distinctions

In considering music's survival across the transition to sound in the late twenties, it is imperative to acknowledge the differences between the silents and sound film which would affect the presence, behavior, and effects of music. The music played by live musicians during the silent era bore a different kind of relationship, not only to the narrative, but to the spectator, than does nondiegetic ("soundtrack") music in the sound film. Unlike live performances, nondiegetic music in the sound film is recorded. It is welded to the film text. Further, the miking, recording, and mixing of sound do not *reproduce* it: the mechanical and electronic processing of sound is arguably as much a *representation* and interpretation as is the visual representation of events in cinema. (Alan Williams has shown how the soundtrack positions the spectator-auditor as "auditory subject," placing him/her in an "ideal" listening position by technological means.)[26]

Perhaps most crucially, we must bear in mind that although the silent and sound cinemas' music may have many similar "underscoring" functions, music in the sound film does not occupy the soundtrack in isolation. Rather, background music shares the soundtrack with other acoustic phenomena (dialogue, effects, music) whose ostensible source is located in the diegetic space. The overwhelming "revolutionary" significance of the coming of sound lies in the power the cinema acquired to represent the human voice. The film industry would hardly have gone to the expense of reequipping all facets of production and exhibition had the enormous gain of the human voice not impelled it. The recorded voice fleshed out the human body on the screen, endowed it with a "surplus of reality." Recorded sound effects and music were implicated in the shift, following along in subordinate rank to the momentous arrival of the voice.

Briefly, some consequences: the fact that sound film music coexists with speech and other diegetic sound affects the spectator's relation to it. Since there is diegetic sound, this music is all the more clearly *outside* the story. Further, music does not play in a continuous stream as it did for silent cinema; the alternation between it and nonmusical sections allowed it to play, in Manvell and Huntley's words, "a much more intimate and much more emotionally effective part. . . . Music for the film, like the dialogue itself, needed to learn a new discipline, a new relation to the film drama."[27]

The addition of sound to the story film meant the consolidation of the narrative's sonic space. Diegetic sound posed problems that needed working through—problems of continuity, of auditory realism, of pacing, of spatial and temporal intelligibility. The silent cinema did not by any means codify diegetic space as strictly as, by necessity, the diegetic sound film. Nancy Wood, who traces the semiotics of the "sound shift" in Hollywood film, concludes:

> Compared to its silent counterpart, the talking cinema was considered an 'inflexible institution', above all because certain latitudes in spatial and temporal construction available to late silent narratives were not permitted in the early sound film. It was as if the introduction of sound caused an immediate 'densening' of the more permeable spatio-temporal field of the silent film, thereby requiring more concrete and exacting definitions of the spatial and temporal dimensions.[28]

Music consequently adapted to the new spatiotemporal regime of the sound film.

Is it possible to ignore or to minimize the significance of these distinctions, and to use the art-historical approach to explain music's persistence across the transition? That is, is it historically accurate to argue, as many have done, that the convention of music accompanying silent films, itself inherited from nineteenth-century stage conventions, passed uninterruptedly into the sound era—that *continuity of conventions* is a sufficient explanation for music carrying over into sound film?

The Transition to Sound (The Voice Arrives): Historical Considerations

The story is more complex than such an argument would suggest. Background music did *not* continue uninterruptedly into the sound era. For a period of half a decade, the state of sound technology, and perhaps the prevailing perceptions of what was realistic, did not allow for background music. Then, by 1932–1933, the background score reentered the (nonmusical) narrative film. So at least for several years, the "tradition" of musical accompaniment to the drama was interrupted, discontinuous.

Nor did background music necessarily return to the sound cinema for all the same reasons for which it had belonged to the silent film experience.

Understanding how music worked in the silent film does not by any means fully explain the continued presence of music in the sound era and into the diegetic sound film.

Between 1926 and 1934, the introduction of sound technology brought substantial changes in the relationship between spectator and cinematic event. If I momentarily digress from music in particular to sound in general, it is because we need to examine the *context* in which music figured in the emerging diegetic sound film, and to speculate on the spectator's relationship to its sonic world. If live musicians had provided the musical sound for silent films—to cover projector noise, to mediate between live audience and "dead" mechanically-produced shadows on the screen, to augment moods, to compensate for actors' lack of speech as dialogue intertitles were shown, to compensate for the screen's lack of spatial depth—how was the addition of the (recorded) human voice and sound effects going to affect the spectator's relationship to (belief in, distance from) the film story?

Comolli and "impression of reality"

Jean-Louis Comolli speaks of the relationship between spectator and filmic event as a kind of contract, a "disposition of representation," which at a given time ensures the spectator's impression of reality. Major terms of this contract had to be renegotiated during a period of normalization following the introduction of sound.[29] Comolli, proposing a materialist model of film history, and

> writing from an avowedly Marxist perspective, asserts . . . that a history of technology and technical forms is not enough. He does not reject technical explanations but calls for the analysis of a larger context which locates and determines ideology. This larger context is composed of two social demands—the ideological and the economic. Comolli states that "it is to the mutual reinforcement of an ideological demand ('to see life as it is') and the economic demand to make it a source of profit that cinema owes its being."[30]

Comolli discusses the coming of sound, when

> Speech and the speaking Subject come onto the scene. As soon as they are produced, sound and speech are commonly decreed the 'truth' which was lacking in the silent film . . . the truth which is suddenly noticed, not without alarm and resistance, as having been lacking in the silent film. And at once this truth renders no longer valid all films which do not possess it, which do not produce it. The decisive supplement, the 'ballast of reality' (Bazin) constituted by sound and speech intervenes straightaway, therefore, as perfecting and redefining of the impression of reality.[31]

Comolli's insistence on ideological demands and economic pressures goes beyond the technological, industrial, aesthetic, anecdotal, and idealist approaches that characterized film history for so long. His emphasis on dialectical, nonlinear movement in history, his insistence on cinema as a signifying practice related to other signifying practices, and its ideological determinations, have influenced the way film history is written. But in the interest of a larger question—the rapid changeover to sound—he does not examine the intermediate period of experimentation and readjustment. Comolli terms "alarm and resistance" (I assume he is referring to aestheticians and filmmakers such as Arnheim, Clair, and Chaplin) the movement by fits and starts, by trial and error, in the rhetorical, technical, and generic regimes of the nascent sound film. Also, in his brief treatment of sound he relies on the sole ideological demand of "realness," "truth," as that which governed the changes in disposition of representation. While not rejecting his "larger context" model, we need to explore more extensively why non-diegetic music—decidedly not a contributor to the impression of reality—returns to the newly "realistic" order of the diegetic sound film.

Novelty

Stephen Heath, Ed Branigan, and Kristin Thompson have pointed out—in historical inquiries on early cinema, color, and animated film, respectively[32]—that new technological developments in dominant cinematic representation do not contribute solely to greater "realistic effect." These inquiries suggest that it is the novelty of the technology that is celebrated for a while; its very presentation mystifies or makes a spectacle of the technology in question. Furthermore, we may add in the case of sound, it was the technology's "realness" that was first foregrounded as spectacle.[33] A typical ad in *Photoplay* (November 1928) reads:

> FAZIL is indeed an amazing picture to see! And—it is also an amazing picture to HEAR! In FAZIL you will hear that astonishing movie miracle—FOX MOVIETONE. It puts SOUND into movies—realistic, true-to-life sound!. . . . You hear the voices of the desert. You hear a full symphony orchestra, as though you were sitting in a great moving picture cathedral on Broadway. . . . You won't believe your own ears! It's as true to your ears as it is to your eyes—because the SOUND, like the scene, is PHOTO-GRAPHED. . . .[34]

A subsequent phase of integration promotes the technology not for the spectacle of its realness or immediacy, but *qua* dramatic, visual spectacle. An ad for *Hit the Deck*, from September 1929, whets the appetite for "Musical extravaganza. . . . Glorious scenes of the Chinese Revolution. . . . The rattle of distant gun-fire blends with lilting melodies. . . ." Only after these phases is the technology taken for granted—absorbed, from the spectator's point of view, into the invisibility of discourse that is a necessary condition for the full diegetic effect.[35] Finally, the "impression of reality" presumably reaches a new point of stability.

Historical specificity, impression of reality

It is necessary here to point out the similarity, but also the slippage, among some terms that various critics use to describe the suspension of disbelief, the spectator's psychic investment in a diegetic world presented by film: "realism," "impression of reality," "verisimilitude," "illusionism," "realistic-effect," and "diegetic effect." Since "realism" also designates a specific literary movement, and since film studies have given it a proliferation of meanings, I shall avoid it. The remaining terms stress not so much the "objective" verisimilitude of the film itself, but (realistic-*effect*, *impression of* reality) a *relation* between spectator and film, one that produces the level of belief or immersion in the diegesis. The degree to which the spectator identifies with the diegesis as his/her own hallucination fluctuates from spectator to spectator, from narrative moment to moment, from genre to genre. We may think of this variable as a distance. Beholding the song-and-dance number in a musical, in which everyone faces the camera (violating the convention that normally makes the spectator into a voyeur), the spectator is at a good remove; the realistic-effect or diegetic effect is weak. On the other hand, a love scene in intimate closeup, if it "works" at all, produces a strong diegetic effect.

In the history of sound film, the evolution toward a new point of stability in the "impression of reality" did not occur all at once. Hundreds of commercially distributed talking and musical shorts in the twenties, following upon similar efforts in the teens—indeed, efforts that originated before the birth of film in 1895—, began to introduce sound to moving pictures on a large scale. Lee De Forest's Photophone process was used in a thousand short sound films between 1923 and 1927. Warners' Vitaphone and, a year or two later, Fox's Movietone were turning out commercial sound shorts that were widely seen in programs along with live performing acts and/or silent features. These shorts consisted by and large of filmed performances of one kind or another: vaudeville, orchestral, operatic, or interviews or recitations.

Warners' first feature-length Vitaphone film, *Don Juan* (1926), a lavish costume drama starring John Barrymore, had a recorded musical soundtrack and no synchronous sound or dialogue, and thus displayed a fully silent-film mentality. Warner Brothers had introduced Vitaphone, in fact, with the sole intention of using it to provide recorded musical accompaniment; the idea of making "talkie" features did not arise until later. Aside from absenting the orchestra from the spectacle (and a phonograph often accompanied silent films, at that), *Don Juan* did not appreciably innovate any changes in the disposition of representation (although one of the shorts that preceded it on the program, in which Will Hays spoke directly into the camera and mike, audibly proclaiming "the beginning of a new era in music and motion pictures," received much admiring acclaim). Through 1928, numerous feature films of its kind, with a canned music soundtrack, appeared. Fox joined in with orchestral tracks for *What Price Glory* (January 1927) and *Seventh Heaven* (May 1927). William Wellman's *Wings* (Paramount, August 1927), shot silent, was released with a soundtrack that included sound effects as well as music, and many other films followed suit through 1930.

The Jazz Singer (Warners, October 1927) is famous in the discourse of film history, not only because of its enormous popular success, but precisely because of a primary reason for its success. It inaugurated a dramatically new relationship between spectator and film. While its soundtrack consists mostly of the *Don Juan* type of recorded continuous silent-film musical accompaniment,[36] it occasionally breaks into synch sound in the manner of the Vitaphone and Movietone shorts. During four sequences, the microphone records Al Jolson's Jack Robin speaking and performing musical numbers. For the first time in a feature story film, the voice—Jack's monologue in a nightclub, a hyperkinetic chat at home with his mother—contributes toward the constitution of a diegetic space.

Let us recall that the overwhelming majority of sound shorts in the twenties introduced the voice for its documentary value: recitations, songs, nonnarrative performances, interviews. Therefore, the recorded voice already had its conventions in the cinema: one could argue that it signaled a *supplement of reality*. Now, here was the voice in a *fiction* film. It is not difficult to imagine the enormous increment of verisimilitude, a surplus of both realism- and spectacle-value, that Jolson's speaking voice brought to the story film.

David Cook writes, "Suddenly . . . here was Jolson not only singing and dancing but speaking informally and spontaneously to other persons in the film as someone might do in reality. The effect," he claims, "was not so much of *hearing* Jolson speak as of *overhearing* him speak, and it thrilled audiences bored with the conventions of silent cinema and increasingly indifferent to the canned performances of the Vitaphone shorts."[37] "*As someone*

The Jazz Singer. Jakie Rabinowitz/Jack Robin talks to his mother and then breaks into a jazzy version of "Blue Skies." *Courtesy of Warner Brothers.*

might do in reality": a Vitaphone recitation looks and sounds canned (not unreal, but certainly not spontaneous), whereas the Jolson outbursts no doubt seemed spontaneous, realistic, to those who watched *The Jazz Singer* in its first run.

We need also to reemphasize a distinction between "silent film mentality" (e.g., *Don Juan*) and "fully diegetic sound film",[38] and the fact that there was an (uneven) historical development, during the late twenties and early thirties, from one to the other. Within this perspective it seems hardly accurate to call the bulk of *The Jazz Singer*'s score *nondiegetic*, since the film constructs no consistent diegetic sound space to which to oppose non-diegetic music. Scenes that do have synch sound clearly take place on a sound stage as *performances*. As Jack sings "My Mammy" to a theater audience, or "Blue Skies" to his mother at home, he is performing, within the fiction; but even in the dialogue with his mother (prior to "Blue Skies") one senses clearly that Jolson is "performing," on a metafictional level, before the microphone on the set. The novelty of sound surely made the monologues exciting to watch and hear—and Cook is no doubt right that the 1927 audience felt it was "overhearing" these speeches—but new phases of the impression of reality were to follow quickly.

Alexander Walker, in his book *The Shattered Silents*, distinguishes between declaimed or recited dialogue, and a more intimate, illusionistic mode of dialogue. In Walker's view, the latter becomes discernible, at the earliest, in late 1928, in such 100 percent talking films as *Interference*, Paramount's first talkie. Walker quotes a reviewer of November 1928 who praises the dialogue in *Interference* as

> retaining the status of conversation as confidential exchange. . . . Their words put over the meaning. . . . All the time the film is unreeling we see the figures of the characters moving slowly through their scenes and hear the low tones of their voices, a slight noise as a door is closed, and a faint tinkle when a phone bell rings.[39]

This language suggests a new stage in the successive renewals of the impression of reality on the dialogue soundtrack. Conversation is confidential, in low tones; the reviewer is describing the effect of imaginary fourth-wall illusionist theater as opposed to the kind of spectacle staged for (acknowledging) the audience. What one means by realistic at any time is determined by a complex historical confluence of convention, technology, and larger social and representational contexts. A closely detailed study of the rapidly changing codes of spectatorship during this period would be desirable for us to understand better the dynamic interrelationships between technological innovation, historical specificity of the audience, and cinematic rhetoric and technique.

Following the successes of *The Jazz Singer*, *Lights of New York*, *The Singing Fool*, *Broadway Melody*, and many other part- and all-talkies of 1927–1930, the industry vigorously explored avenues of textualizing sound technology according to demands for realism and spectacle. In a milieu financially sensitive to public response, technical and stylistic innovations followed one another with amazing rapidity.[40] Contemporary critical and trade discourse provides intriguing hints about the nature of these waves of novelty and fatigue. Apparently, at first it was enough to hear sound, speech—to hear the stars talk. Then the reviews clamored for greater accuracy of sound reproduction, and for actors whose voices were better "suited" to the microphone. Then the psychological verisimilitude of the dialogue and acting, and later the mutual adjustments and accommodation of genre, plot, and sound technique, became foci of critical and (presumably) popular demand.

The well-known case of John Gilbert illustrates how these technological and stylistic changes produced large shifts in codes of producing and reading cinematic representation. Gilbert, celebrated for the intensity of his amorous passion in silent screen romances, embarrassed rather than enraptured moviegoers in his first dialogue appearance (*His Glorious Night*, October 1929). In his previous silent roles, he had mouthed "I love you, I love you, I love you . . ." to his spectators' romantic pleasure. But when he actually articulated those lines on the soundtrack, audiences reacted with derisive laughter. In all likelihood the problem did not lie exclusively with the physical quality of his voice (its squeakiness did not befit his roles),[41] as most critics write. The wooden acting by the female lead (Katherine Dale Owen), juxtaposed with his physical grace and urgency, certainly contributed to the film's downfall. But also, the new medium of the sound film revealed the uncensored, inarticulate baldness of his lines. *Variety*'s review:

> A few more talker productions like this and John Gilbert will be able to change places with Harry Langdon. His prowess at love-making which has held the stones breathless takes on a comedy aspect . . . that gets [them] tittering at first and then laughing outright at the very first ring of the couple of dozen "I love you" phrases designed to climax . . . the thrill of the Gilbert lines.[42]

The addition of recorded sound, in this case laying bare not only voice quality but semantic properties of spoken language itself, was necessitating shifts in the content of movies and ways in which they were consumed. Technology, text, and reading were implicated together in mutual readjustment.

Sound and time

Recorded sound also changed the temporal experience of images on the screen. The silent cinema, as we know, worked according to a more or less flexible sense of time, a time that could be motivated as much by a scene's emotive tone, or by its "rhythm" (that ubiquitous word in aesthetic discourses on silent film), as by the story's "realistic" dictates. Time could be elastic and even reversible without upsetting narrative conventions. Think of the long close-ups of faces in a Stroheim film, prolonging a dialogue or action beyond what the sound film would find an acceptable duration. Recall Eisenstein's freedom to fragment and analyze not only space but time on the Odessa steps. Consider the parallel editing in a Griffith film which shows on one hand the heroine selecting a (poisoned) chocolate and putting it to her lips, intercut with, on the other hand, the hero careening through several miles of space to save her in the nick of—a very unequal—time.

Michel Chion suggests that if we see a silent shot of a house, it is temporally indeterminate. If we add to it the sound of a dog barking or a passing car, the sound creates in the image a sense of lived duration. In this sense, diegetic sound therefore heralded a supplement of temporal reality—a precise, linear temporality—but at the same time it would more strictly *limit* filmic representation to this linear temporality.

Genre and technology

By 1929 the sound film had temporarily settled into several newly favored film genres, including musicals in large numbers, courtroom and other melodramas, elegant drawing-room dramás, comedies, and westerns. Films had one of several possible soundtrack "dispositions": silent films (amounting to roughly 25 percent of total production), silent films with music (and sometimes sound effects) on the soundtrack, part-talkies (with some purely musical selections),[43] and the 100 percent all-talkie, which might have "background music" (mostly during scene transitions) or which could be completely without music. Older accounts explaining why some 100 percent talkies wholly eliminated soundtrack music are inconsistent; one likely explanation is that by 1929 some studios considered music antithetical to screen realism.[44] Indeed, realism itself, in spatial and temporal terms and in terms of what counted as credible and acceptable plot and dialogue, was in the process of undergoing redefinition.

But there are additional factors—namely, technological—to consider in addition to these—even if ultimately with Comolli we consider technological determinism inadequate in itself. The constant changes in disposition of dialogue, sound effects, and music, *in the short term* were largely determined by what the technology allowed at particular studios at particular times. For example, before 1929–1930, sound had to be recorded simultaneously with the filming. As a rule, if a star's voice had to be "doubled" by a singer for a musical sequence, the double would sing into a microphone just off the set with his/her eye on the lip movement of the star being filmed. By early 1929 some studios used an alternative technique of dubbing for musicals: the double could post-record the song, following along with the actor's lip movements as projected.

Ernst Lubitsch attracted attention in November 1929 for his ingenuity in filming a musical number for *The Love Parade*. Although other sequences did use dubbing, this particular number ("Isn't It Romantic?") called for elaborate logistics of mise-en-scène and shooting. The servant pair (Lupino Lane and Lillian Roth) sang on an exterior set while the patrician couple (Maurice Chevalier and Jeannette MacDonald) sang on an adjoining interior set, since the music had to be recorded all in continuity:

The script and score of the production called for a double duet by these four principals, and Herr Lubitsch was forced to devise ways and means for directing two sets of actors with one wave of the wand. So he had his hirelings erect the two sets cheek to cheek . . . [the orchestra was present, too, out of camera range]. Our hardworking directors may soon be expected to direct three scenes, juggle four pool balls, eat a bacon and tomato sandwich and sing "Mammy" simultaneously.[45]

But in general, technological limitations before 1931 put restrictions on two overall areas of the diegetic sound film as we know it. First, in all but exceptionally inventive productions, synch sound visually rooted actors to the spot, and limited the possibilities of exploring space within a scene (although multiple-camera shooting was used in an effort to counteract these restrictions). Actors were obliged to remain close to the microphones, which (as comically illustrated in *Singin' In the Rain*) were hidden behind props; early mikes not only had poor sensitivity to voices but paradoxically seemed to pick up every other stray sound on the set. The camera, imprisoned in its soundproofed booth, would not generally regain freedom of movement until the development of the blimp and rolling camera carriages in 1930–1931 (although Mamoulian proved in his 1929 *Applause* that nothing could stop a determined director from moving the camera even in its bulky housing).

Second, early sound-film editing tended to be "transitional" only, due to technical limitations. It was virtually impossible to edit a soundtrack that had been recorded and synchronized simultaneously with the images. Single-system sound-on-film (i.e., Movietone, 1927–1929), whose sound was recorded onto the same strip of celluloid as the image, posed the inconvenience of the twenty-frame displacement between sound and corresponding picture. The editor had to make the cut twenty frames (about a second) ahead of the action in order not to lose dialogue. The result was that if the images were cut, soundtrack continuity suffered; cutting occurred mainly during the absence of any sound on the set. Thus, editing as well as camera movement was sorely limited. Studios that converted to sound in mid-1929 went directly to double-system sound-on-film, which separated the sound strip from the image.[46]

In terms of film music, it was impossible to have a sustained, edited synch-dialogue scene with background underscoring. Not until 1930 or 1931 did background music during a talking scene make, in Nancy Wood's words, a "discreet entry."[47] Some Laurel and Hardy films of 1930 have underscoring, but good-quality dialogue-music mixing would not be generally adopted until 1932, when the industry took the necessary step of recording separate tracks for speech, music, and effects. *King Kong* (1933) was a showcase for state-of-the-art sound techniques, including a lush score by Max Steiner which brought the great special-effects ape alive.

By 1930 sound technology had come to stay. International agreements standardized sound equipment. The development of the boom mike, of more movable soundproofed cameras, of multiple-channel recording,[48] and finally of dubbing and postproduction mixing afforded increasingly more control over the synthesis of audiovisual space in the nonmusical film. Mixing entailed a giant step forward. Interestingly, post-dubbing and mixing in practice *separated* sound and image production; filmmakers had the flexibility to record, rerecord, mix, and then restore soundtrack to image in a "unified" whole. By 1933 or 1934, via the detours of the all-talking film on one hand and the musical on the other, the fully diegetic sound film, with more or less stabilized regimes of "realism" (according to various genre conventions) consolidated its codes of audiovisual narration.

By 1933–1934, then, characters could speak "in their own voices." The human body and the space in which it moved had been endowed with sound; sound in turn reinforced the reality-effect of those bodies and spaces.

CHAPTER III

Why Music?
The Sound Film
and Its Spectator

Let us sum up the arguments we have examined so far. According to different writers, music was used to accompany films in the silent era because:

1. It had accompanied other forms of spectacle before, and was a convention that successfully persisted.

2. It covered the distracting noise of the movie projector.

3. It had important semiotic functions in the narrative: encoded according to late nineteenth-century conventions, it provided historical, geographical, and atmospheric setting, it helped depict and identify characters and qualify actions. Along with intertitles, its semiotic functions compensated for the characters' lack of speech.

4. It provided a rhythmic "beat" to complement, or impel, the rhythms of editing and movement on the screen.

5. As sound in the auditorium, its spatial dimension compensated for the flatness of the screen.

6. Like magic, it was an antidote to the technologically derived "ghostliness" of the images.

7. As music, it bonded spectators together.

In this chapter we shall consider which of these arguments help us understand the persistence of music into the narrative sound film—or whether the sound film has its own distinct reasons for using music. The nagging question remains: what might help to explain the return of background music to the soundtrack of a cinema whose diegetic codes had become strongly consolidated? Nondiegetic music simply does not logically belong in a diegetic film. Max Steiner states that sound film producers before 1932 considered background music unacceptable, fearing that spectators would demand to know where the music was coming from. French cine-semiotician Michel Marie likewise points out the "radically" nonrealistic nature of soundtrack music:

> Film music is the only sound that does not issue from the visually produced diegesis, but the film's spectator conventionally accepts it. Its arbitrary manifestation is radical. This naturalized arbitrariness is particularly revealing of the degree of convention the spectator will accept, and it structures all the rules that determine the functioning of filmic listening.[1]

In the preceding chapter, I traced the multifaceted evolution of cinema during the transition to sound in order to show that (1) demands for both illusionism and spectacle underwent rapid changes; (2) the introduction of sound effected shifts in what was read as "realistic"; (3) background music was implicated in those shifts.

Thus, while it is necessary, it is not sufficient to recognize that the musical score persisted as a convention because it had been there before. The continuity-of-conventions thesis cannot stand alone. A specious argument in illustration: if all could be explained by continuity of conventions, we might also expect intertitles (other than dialogue titles) to persist too. After all, both titles and music have informative and expressive functions, and, historically, both titles and music did persist into the era of the part-talkies.

The continuity-of-conventions thesis may be inadequate, but even worse, Comolli's ideological model, as it stands, avoids the issue entirely. He mentions the role of music in silent films as sonic compensation for lack of actual diegetic sound; but he does not return to the problem of nondiegetic music in the sound film, whose presence can no longer be explained as a substitute for sound and speech. In fact, virtually all theorists of sound cinema—with rare exceptions such as Marie—disavow the nondiegetic music problem, limiting their concerns to diegetic sound and, occasionally, the voiceover.

Let us briefly probe a bit deeper into the John Gilbert phenomenon mentioned in the preceding chapter. Articles and reviews published in 1928–1929 indicate that not only Gilbert in his first sound feature but others as well—for example, Charles Farrell, in *Sunny Side Up* (October 1929)—were being received with whistles and laughter (signs of male embarrassment?) for love scenes whose dialogue was overly "mushy." In fact, placing it in historical context, we may surmise that this "overexplicit" dialogue violated the viewing contract then in effect. Instead of heightening a spectator's involvement in the story, it only threatened to break the contractual terms that made involvement possible in the first place. It is almost as if the silence of intertitles had acted as a form of psychic censorship, and reintroducing the spoken word itself was too concrete an outlet of libidinal energy. A *Variety* review of Autumn 1929 takes up the issue of some dialogue films' treatment of romantic love:

> Studios have found that the hooey going over in [inter-] titles won't go over in talkers. Someone in the audience titters and it's all off. Hereafter the love passages will be suggested with the romantic note conveyed by properly pitched music. Metro, the first to learn by experience, is heading that way: others will follow for their own protection.[2]

What precise terms of the filmic viewing contract might this anonymous reviewer be suggesting? Either he advocates a recorded music sequence (in the style of *Don Juan*) acting as a dialogue "overlay"—a part-talkie solution—or he might be proposing that the characters not directly declare their passion in their dialogue, and that simultaneously playing nondiegetic music should indicate this passion instead (a solution, we recall, that was not technically feasible until 1931 or 1932). Whatever the reviewer has in mind, his example illustrates features central to film music accompanying emotional scenes. Music removes barriers to belief; it bonds spectator to spectacle, it envelops spectator and spectacle in a harmonious space. Like hypnosis, it silences the spectator's censor. It is suggestive; if it's working right, it makes us a little less critical and a little more prone to dream.

Music has persisted as an integral part of the sound film because it accomplishes so many things at once. Its freedom from the explicitness of language or photographic images, its useful denotative and expressive values easily comprehended by listeners raised in the nineteenth-century orchestral tradition, its malleability, its spatial, rhythmic, and temporal values, give it a special and complex status in the narrative film experience. If the advent of diegetic sound narrowed the possibilities of temporality into a sort of relentless linearity, music could return as the one sound element capable of freeing up that temporal representation (thus music normally accompanies montage and slow-motion sequences, initiates flashbacks, and so on). Film music is at once a gel, a space, a language, a cradle, a beat, a signifier of internal depth and emotion as well as a provider of emphasis on visual movement and spectacle. It bonds: shot to shot, narrative event to meaning, spectator to narrative, spectator to audience. In the rest of this chapter I shall discuss these aspects of music's behavior in film. Overall, the two overarching roles of background music may be characterized as semiotic (as *ancrage*) and psychological (as suture or *bonding*).

Functional Music

While film music functions differently from autonomous music, it is commonly held that well-conceived and well-written music for film will be better than "hack" scores, all other things being equal. This position, tenable as it might be, often leads scholars to dismiss serious consideration of the utilitarian functions of film music. After all, it is more acceptable to write about the work of such film composers as Sergei Prokofiev, George Antheil, Arthur Honegger, Hanns Eisler, and Bernard Herrmann than to tackle the question of the efficacy of sweet violins during a romantic scene or bass pizzicati mickey-mousing the footsteps of a thief through an abandoned warehouse.

For the moment, though, let us consider some purely functional aspects of music as it is set in the classical narrative film, by comparing film music to an extreme case, the most functional kind of music—background or "easy-listening" music. The age of mechanical/electronic reproduction, and of the commodification of music, has fundamentally changed the meaning of music, the ways in which we listen to it and hear it.[3] It is impossible to ignore that film music also participates in this transformation of listening.

Film music and easy-listening music have much in common. They are both utilitarian; both are received in a larger, nonmusical context; neither is designed to be closely attended to. (This latter feature does not obviate the possibility of their having "inherent" aesthetic worth. A Bach harpsichord sonata piped in through loudspeakers to a pastry and espresso shop is functioning as easy-listening music, as is rock or country music on the car radio as one drives along a city freeway.)

Easy-listening music is electronically regulated in its recording and in its consumption. It is commodified and quantifiable; more or less of it is consumed, depending on the contextual demand for it. It may nominally signify. By this I mean that the casual listener will recognize a studio orchestra's rendition of the Beatles' "I Wanna Hold Your Hand," and certainly the exceptionally attentive listener may follow an entire piece through, attending to the syntax of its musical discourse; but as often as not, musical signification is not essential to easy-listening. Nor is musical form. The piped-in music in a discount store may be interrupted at any moment to make way for a live voice that announces a special sale or the name of a child separated from its mother. One may turn the car radio on and off (and up and down in volume), not in function of the musical form, but of the duration of the drive or the rhythm of conversation with passengers. In its consumption, functional music subordinates its *form* and *volume* to the context in which it is deployed.

The calculated use of functional music for purposes of social control seems to have gotten its start during World War II. Wartime publications by an optimistic U.S. government and by ASCAP (the composers' and music publishers' union) document and prescribe its use in industry to boost morale and productivity. An ASCAP pamphlet proffers this advice:

> In selecting music for industry, remember that it is something which is intended for background. Do not choose the pieces which assert a constant demand on attention by having tricky instrumental effects, prolonged vocals, or changes of key in the middle of a chorus. . . . It is a customary practice to start the morning off with about ten minutes of march music while the shift is coming on. Military marches are generally the rule, but some plants have discovered that the associative effects can cause a psychological breakdown, particularly if large numbers of women are employed. Therefore, it is wise to be cautious . . . try a college march. . . . For the sake of variation, you might also insert a fast fox trot or a polka. In any event, what you are striving for at this point is to wipe the gloom off the faces of the incoming employees and perhaps to instill a little esprit de corps into the whole group.[4]

What does this utilitarian music do? It relieves anxiety, irritability, tension.[5] Music is good in traffic and on long drives. In the waiting room it allays fears about the imminent drilling or pulling of teeth, or the airplane's departure. It loosens shoppers' purse strings. For such reasons, music has been inserted into every public place where it is economically advantageous to alleviate consumer anxiety. It fills silences (or covers other sounds) that would allow us to dwell on such anxiety, or the "pain of existence" itself.[6]

Easy-listening music at its most standardized is barely discernible as music, and does not call attention to itself with surprising harmonies or dynamics. Extremes of volume or instrumentation, any departure from the most conventional harmony and the most regular rhythm, detract from the "ease" of listening. Such music signifies little but a general *pleasantness*. It has as its purpose to lull the individual into being an *untroublesome social subject*.

As I have suggested, the parallels to be drawn between easy-listening and film music are numerous. Music in film is electronically regulated, and generally rendered subservient to the denotatively signifying elements of narrative discourse. Its effectiveness often depends upon its not being listened to. While certainly not always signifying "pleasantness," it is nonetheless programmed to match the mood or feelings of the narrative scene of which it is a part, to bathe it in affect. Unlike the dentist's office, though, the narrative cinema (and the concert, too, for that matter)[7] is an institution that channels psychic energies in patterns of tension and relaxation; *the way* to the satisfaction of narrative closure (or musical resolution) is paved with anticipation and conflict. Thus the expressive range of functional music is broader in a film score. All the same, the overall purpose of film music is very much like easy-listening music: it functions to lull the spectator into being an *untroublesome* (less critical, less wary) *viewing subject*. Utilitarian music may be seen as an "intellectual or cerebral anesthetic." "Music will always have this influence," asserts Roger Tallon, "because it does not pass through the same control circuits, because it is almost directly plugged into the psyche."[8]

Easy-listening reduces the displeasure engendered by the economic tensions of shopping and the physical fear of dentists' drills. Film music also helps to ward off displeasure—a displeasure of two sorts connected with the film experience.

First—and we have mentioned this in other contexts—music serves to ward off the displeasure of uncertain signification. The particular kind of music used in dominant feature films has connotative values so strongly codified that it can bear a similar relation to the images as a caption to a news photograph. It *interprets* the image, pinpoints and channels the "correct" meaning of the narrative events depicted. It supplies information to complement the potentially ambiguous diegetic images and sounds. It cues the viewer in to narrational positions: for example, the menacing "shark" theme, heard even before the camera in *Jaws* reveals the deadly shark closing in on the unsuspecting swimmers, gives the viewer advance knowledge of the narrative threat. It creates on one hand an ironic distance between viewer and characters, and, on the other, a complicity with the film's narrative voice.

Further, standard film music efficiently establishes historical and geographical setting, and atmosphere, through the high degree of its cultural coding. The *signification* attained through the use of this music (freshness of springtime, the seventeenth century, menacing evil) wards off the displeasure of the image's potential ambiguity, which Barthes characterized "the terror of uncertain signs." This primarily semiotic functioning of music, then, is what Barthes called *ancrage* in connection with the photograph caption. Music, like the caption, anchors the image in meaning, throws a net around the floating visual signifier, assures the viewer of a safely channeled signified.

A second kind of displeasure that music helps to ward off is the spectator's potential recognition of the technological basis of filmic articulation.[9] Gaps, cuts, the frame itself, silences in the soundtrack—any reminders of cinema's materiality which jeopardize the formation of subjectivity—the process whereby the viewer identifies as subject of filmic discourse—are smoothed over, or "spirited away" (recall Eisler and Adorno's view of music as magical "antidote to the picture") by the carefully regulated operations of film music.

(In this light, it is possible to see that both "parallel" and "counterpoint" aesthetics of film music ultimately serve the same impulse, i.e., to have the spectator identify as subject with a certain production of meaning and expression.) The loss of identification which filmic discourse constantly threatens, via the very means that carry the narrative (cutting, the frame, etc.)—this loss of pleasure is countered in part by the particular ways in which the classical film takes advantage of music.

Needless to say, background music functions according to a larger sphere of reference than musical syntax itself. Like the supermarket music whose volume drops in deference to an announcement, film music is normally subordinated to more "directly" significant sounds on the soundtrack, and to the demands of "the narrative itself." Soundtrack music will drop in volume when characters speak, because the intelligibility of dialogue is more important in the narrational hierarchy. Likewise, musical form is normally subject to the temporal and dramatic conditions of narrative segmentation. The bath or gel of affect in which music immerses film narrative is like easy-listening music in that it rounds out the sharp edges, smooths roughnesses, masks contradictions, and masks spatial or temporal discontinuity with its own sonic and harmonic continuity. Film music lessens awareness of the frame, of discontinuity; it draws the spectator further into the diegetic illusion. The playwright Elmer Rice characterized this effect of movie music quite vividly—in fact he emphasized its oneiric power to the point of caricature—in his novel *Voyage to Purilia*, which originally appeared in *The New Yorker* during 1929. Here he describes the planet Purilia, a thinly disguised conceit of movieland:

> It is difficult to convey to the terrestrial reader, to whom music is an accidental and occasional phenomenon, the effect of living and moving in a world in which melody is as much a condition of life as are light and air. But let the reader try to fancy himself lapped every moment of his existence, waking or sleeping, in liquid, swooning sound, for ever rising and falling, falling and rising, and wrapping itself about him like a caressing garment. The effect is indescribable. It is like the semi-stupor of an habitual intoxication: an inebriety without intervals of either sobriety or complete unconsciousness. . . . the sensitive reader will catch echoes and overtones of that omnipresent harmony; now pathetic, now gay, now ominous, now martial, now tender, but always awakening familiar memories, always swellingly mellifluous, and always surcharged with a slight but unmistakable tremolo.[10]

Rice's satire may not be much of an exaggeration. Psychoanalytic critics, as we shall see, would agree with his view of music as a sort of sonic/psychic bridge between "sobriety" and "unconsciousness," being tied in with "familiar memories."

Music and Pleasure

> Describing [film music's] functions is
> rather like describing a beautiful woman—
> there's no way of doing it adequately.[11]

Underlying the arguments I have put forth are notions, taken from aestheticians and scholars of music and film, that music enjoys a direct line to the "soul." Exactly what this soul is, and why music has privileged access to it, has long inspired debate. Clearly music consists of a discourse—an organized series of units understood (in some way or other) by human beings, and involving the transfer or circulation of energy, of tension and release. But it is a discourse without a clear referent, and certainly a nonrepresentational discourse; consequently, its affective powers and its association with pleasure have remained elusive.

Theories abound regarding why music gives pleasure and emotion. Plato, in prescribing the study of harmony to liberate the soul from the tyranny of the senses, inaugurated a major line of thought which holds that musical pleasure depends on an intellectual ability to perceive structure. Most traditional aestheticians do not venture much beyond describing the satisfaction gained from witnessing music's organic unity and form. An opposing aesthetic argument roots musical pleasure precisely in the senses, claiming that rhythm, harmony, and melodic movement stimulate sensual responses which we call aesthetic experience.

In this century, structuralism has flirted with the issue; Claude Lévi-Strauss himself likened the role of music to—what else?—myth:

> A myth coded in sounds instead of words, the musical work furnishes a grid of signification, a matrix of relationships which filters and organizes lived experience; it substitutes for experience and produces the pleasurable illusion that contradictions can be overcome, and difficulties resolved.[12]

For their part, some Freudians point out homologies between the structure and processes of the unconscious and those of musical discourse: both are sites where energies circulate and whose manifestations are regulated by a limited number of processes—for example, condensation and displacement characterize both—and whose overall guide is the pleasure principle (the resolution of tension). Others emphasize that music is a nonreferential language which stimulates a temporary regression; it is a "safe" language in evading verbal logic and articulation, and it short-circuits the defenses and thus gains access to deep emotions.[13] Some claim that we may speak of a sort of "music-work" analogous to the dream-work, whereby melodic, rhythmic, and harmonic structures embody the manifest content of the composer's (and the responding listener's) unconscious desires.

These theories do little to shed light on the emotive effects of music *in film*, however. The pleasure they describe is based on the notion of formal structure, of a "whole" piece of music with no reference outside itself. Narrative film music often lacks this closed and sustained formal structure, but even in its "formlessness," it obviously has emotive effects (in fact, these effects are the major part of its mission).

In nineteenth-century Germany, Helmholz and Fechner were among the first to attempt to bring physics, physiology, and aesthetics together to understand responses to the basic musical elements. Such work blossomed into a century of empirical research on the psychology of music. For many psychologists, "musical emotion" is due to physiological responses to pitch, rhythm, tempo, timbre, and so on. This approach might be seen as a scientific extension of the traditional sensualist aesthetic. Today, researchers in this area regard pleasure in terms of arousal of the autonomic nervous system, and measurable via heart rate, EEG readings of brain waves, and respiration. Others, however, prefer to view musical emotion purely as the effect of repetition and association in culture; maintaining that it consists largely of a set of learned responses, they study tonal memory and the effects of repetition.[14]

Psychoanalytic theory provides a particularly compelling framework for considering not only musical emotion and pleasure, but the oft-cited quality of "depth," "inner feeling," the "dramatic truth" which music brings to the film scene. Psychoanalysts studying music tend to agree that musical response is related to the very earliest periods of development. Some comment on the "oceanic feeling" experienced by the music listener—feeling that the sounds of music come not only from outside but from within their own emotions—and trace it to the pre-Oedipal, preverbal period when the boundary between self and other does not exist. As early as 1917, Frieda Teller wrote that for the adult listener, music "causes the censor to weaken;"[15] it breaks down normal ego defenses and makes the listener more receptive to phantasy. Other writers have elaborated on the ideas that music relaxes the censor and has a hypnotic effect, and that it causes a temporary, benign regression, transporting the subject to the pleasurable realm of early phantasies.

More recent psychoanalytic work on the auditory dimension in general which has contributed to the understanding of film sound may also shed some light on film music. Guy Rosolato and Didier Anzieu theorize the role of sound in the development of the subject.[16] Auditory space, they claim, is the first psychic space. Even before birth, sounds such as the mother's heartbeat, digestion, and voice—and why not voices outside the mother's body?—constitute the sonic environment. Anzieu speaks of a "sonorous envelope" in which the infant exists, "bathed in sounds," and as yet unaware of distinctions between self and other or inside/outside the body. The sonorous envelope consists of sounds originating both in the infant and in its environment. One may reasonably link the melodic bath of the sonorous envelope to the oft-cited oceanic feeling of adult musical listening; this pleasure of music invokes the (auditory) imaginary.

Rosolato attributes prime importance to the formulation of originary phantasies based on auditory perceptions. "Sonorous omnipotence": the infant's psychic auditory space does not know the limits to be imposed later by the realities of psychomotor development; it can project its voice into space, it can hear and be heard in the dark, through walls and around corners. Also, the voice is both emitted and heard, sent and received, by the same body. This reciprocal movement carries with it the potential for a confusion of exit and entry, of exterior and interior.

> Because one can hear sounds behind oneself as well as those with sources inside the body (sounds of digestion, circulation, respiration, etc.), two sets of terms are placed in opposition: exterior/front/sight and interior/back/hearing. And "Hallucinations are determined by an imaginary structuration of the body according to these oppositions. . . ."[17]

The imaginary longing for bodily fusion with the mother is never erased; the terms of the original illusion of fusion are largely defined by the voice. Thus for Rosolato, Anzieu, and others, the voice of the mother is fundamental to the later development of the auditory unconscious; it is understood psychoanalytically as an "interface of imaginary and symbolic, pulling at once toward the signifying organization of language and its reduction of the range of vocal sounds to those it binds and codifies, and toward original and imaginary attachments."[18] In an earlier phase it is the rise and fall of her voice, its rhythm and timbre, that is a "good object" for the child as yet uninitiated into language.

> At the same time that she nurtures, the mother speaks, a speech charged with rhythm, pitch, timbre, tempo, and intensity, an imprint; word/sounds anchored to her body like the mouth to the breast. . . . Thus the amazement,

the incomprehension colored with anxiety, then the still doubting integration by a 15-month-old who discovers, in the morning, the word for a fly (*mouche*), and who in the evening hears mother say "Come let mommy wipe your nose (viens que maman te *mouche*)". Speech from which, if you take away the signified, you get *music*—which holds there the acoustical image, before 'language restores in the universal [the child's] function of subject.'[19]

The mother's voice is central in constituting the auditory imaginary, before and also after the child's entry into the symbolic. From this—and from even earlier auditory perceptions and hallucinations—musical pleasure may be explained. Of course, music is subsequently a highly coded and organized discourse; but its freedom from linguistic signification and from representation of any kind preserve it as a more desirable, or less unpleasurable discourse. It is therefore a "safe" language, it circumvents defenses and provides easier access to the unconscious (see Coriat, 1945). Dominique Avron reiterates this view:

> in the case of music, the organism is exposed to external excitations with whose direction and nature it is acquainted. It can let them penetrate to the deepest layers of the psychic apparatus without risk of feeling attacked. . . . This opportunity to let oneself be invaded in all safety figures into our pleasure in listening to music. As in the very beginning, the good thing is to be swallowed. Introjection of the good object; "good" less in the sense of its aesthetic qualities than its nonthreatening character.[20]

Rosolato, for his part, suggests that the pleasure of musical harmony is itself a nostalgia for the original imaginary fusion with the mother's body. "It is therefore the entire dramatization of separated bodies and their reunion which harmony supports."[21]

Bonding

For Jean-Louis Baudry the classical cinema is an institution that places its spectator-subject in a state of regression. The film spectator is like the dreamer in the dark, in a submotor, hyperreceptive state. During the course of a narrative film the spectator occupies a psychic register which mimes infantile and dream states. The classical narrative film encourages the film subject's return to a primitive narcissism, in which there are no boundaries between active and passive, body and environment, self and other. This cinema simulates not reality but *a condition of the subject*. In fact, Baudry makes the crucial point that the cinematic apparatus simulates a *subject-effect* of regression and identification, not *reality*:[22]

> The impression of reality that the spectator has in the cinema, and the consequent form of identification, has less to do with a successful rendering of the real than with the reproduction and repetition of a particular condition, a 'fantasmatization of the subject.'[23]

Nancy Wood develops Baudry's thesis to argue that the auditory realm as well as the visual is caught up in the circle of desire, which derives from the earliest memories of auditory pleasure. Cinema brings an artificial regression to a narcissistic hallucination wherein the subject was "bathed in sounds."

From these considerations the pervasive role not only of the voice, but, even more, of music in films, becomes clear. The underlying pleasure of music can be traced to originary hallucinations of bodily fusion with the mother, of nonseparation prior to the Oedipal crisis of language and interdiction. If music plays in a film—"secondarily" to the register of language, of narrative—if it is in the background, it works on the spectator-subject most effectively, fusing subject to film body, bypassing the usual censors of the preconscious. In practical terms this means a deeper sleep, a lowered threshold of belief, a greater predisposition for the subject to accept the film's pseudo-perceptions as his/her own.

During the course of a fiction film, the belief in the fiction, or to use Baudry's term, the subject-effect, ebbs and flows. Metz notes that the degree of this diegetic effect "is inversely proportional to that of wakefulness." Music, at least in some cases we shall examine, lessens the spectator's degree of wakefulness. Were the subject to be aware (fully conscious) of its presence as part of the film's discourse, the game would be all over. Just as the subject who resists being hypnotized might find the hypnotist's soothing language silly or excessive, the detached film spectator will notice the oversweet violin music in a romantic scene. Like the good hypnotic subject, on the other hand, the cinematic subject receptive to the film's fantasy will tend not to notice the manipulations of the background score.

Film music makes a second kind of bonding possible as well—defined in terms not so much of the film body, but of the body of the audience. Recall Eisler and Adorno's reference to the bonding power of music among members of a group; anthropology stresses the importance of music in ritual and group identity. The two kinds of bonding fostered by film music are complementary and often coexist in a film. The first bonding function we shall call "identification," the second "spectacle."

Identification

> "Films are fantasy—and fantasy needs music."
>
> JACK L. WARNER

Let us recall that our 1929 *Variety* reviewer advocated "properly pitched music" to make intimate, sentimental dialogue more acceptable. Here I shall illustrate, through examining a few seconds of a conventional melodrama of 1940, what became of his impulse to use background music to solve the problem of emotional dialogue that threatened to distanciate spectators.

Following an ocean cruise in *Now, Voyager*, Jerry (Paul Henreid), after much proper gentlemanly resistance owing to the fact that he is married, declares his love to the self-effacing Charlotte (Bette Davis). (Increasingly romantic violin music accompanies his subdued declaration.) But Charlotte does not commit herself to him during the scene. The question nominally remains whether she reciprocates Jerry's attraction, or whether her reserve accurately reflects a lack of feeling for him. The answer comes soon thereafter, in a scene set on a hotel balcony overlooking Buenos Aires at night. Background music plays plentifully throughout the scene, inflecting each revelation, each movement of emotion between the two characters.

The conversation has turned to kinds of happiness, and Jerry gives examples:

[JERRY:] . . . Having fun together. Getting a kick out of simple little things . . . out of beauty like this [they both glance toward balcony] . . . sharing confidences you wouldn't share with anybody else in all the world. [Cut to Charlotte-centered MCU.] Charlotte, won't you be honest and tell me that you're happy too? [Cut to tight CU of both.] Since that night on the boat when you told me about your illness, I . . . I can't get you out of my mind. Or out of my heart, either. [Charlotte's theme song is heard, woven into the music which plays throughout sequence.] If I were free, there would be only one thing I want to do: prove you're not immune to happiness. Would you want me to prove it, Charlotte? [Cut to CU, profile of Charlotte against Jerry's chest.] Tell me you would. Then I'll go. [Charlotte turns slightly toward camera. Her theme plays in a higher key.] Why, darling . . . you're crying! [They embrace.]
[CHARLOTTE:] I'm such a fool . . . such an old fool. These are only tears of gratitude . . . an old maid's gratitude for the crumbs offered.
[JERRY:] Don't talk like that.
[CHARLOTTE:] You see, no one ever called me darling before. [They kiss.] Let me go . . . [They kiss again. Fadeout.]

Hollywood composers, soundmen, directors, and critics constantly refer to scenes "needing" or "requiring" music. A studio composer could not conceive the above scene without musical accompaniment, which acts as a psychological condition for accepting the dialogue. Such melodramatic excess is representable only in conjunction with appropriate background scoring—in this case, Max Steiner's theme music. In fact, the nineteenth-century tonalities and instrumentation contribute to the excess, in accord with a particular strategy: "artificially prolonging the emergence of the phantasy [in this case, the temporary consummation of Jerry's desire—learning the "truth" of Charlotte's desire for him] for a few additional moments, thanks to a rhetorical and narrative amplification."[24] The entire treatment of the mutual declaration of love exemplifies the tactics of delay and amplification. The declarations have been staggered over several days of story time. In the scene at hand, a series of delays put off the climactic moment—first, Jerry's speech; then, certain camera angles (we cannot see Charlotte's face); then, Jerry's ability to see something we cannot see ("Why, darling, you're crying!"); then, Charlotte's self-deprecation instead of uttering the words we desire; and finally even her last sentence ("Let me go") before her surrender, which is shown to us in full, the culmination of Jerry's/our desire, after which there is nothing for the scene to do but end.

The scene is built according to a principle of *prying*, of constantly closer camera reframings on Charlotte on one hand, and constantly shifting, more insistent verbal rhetoric from Jerry. It begins with discreet medium or medium-long shots, and ends—Charlotte's resistance having been conquered—on a tight close-up of Charlotte's face against Jerry's chest. The job of the music is to help gain access to the "truth." First it provides mellifluous continuity, stating Charlotte's romantic theme in ever-higher registers of the string orchestra; but at the same time it inflects each dialogue line with meaning, depth, and drama.

Its tasks run from the easily connotative to the general level of identifying filmic subject with filmic narration. The connotative: earlier in the scene, as Jerry asks Charlotte if she believes in immortality, Steiner actually inserts two churchbell-like notes on chimes. Then with Jerry's "If I were free," Charlotte's theme returns to a solo violin playing sweetly against the background of strings. At the moment of the revelation ("Why, darling, you're crying!"), her theme recommences, now an interval of a third higher; following a couple of bars of musical filler, it repeats.

The emotive excess of the narrative moment puts identification in a precarious position. One filmgoer—according to psychic needs, receptivity, personal constitution, and so on—might respond by "letting out all the stops," letting the free uninterrupted play of the imaginary sweep him/her up into the fiction. Another, however, might erect defenses that would work to destroy the diegetic illusion: call it "hooey," schmaltzy, embarrassing, react with the motor outlet of guffawing or "tittering," or otherwise become bored or alienated. The 1929 *Variety* reviewer, tending toward the latter end of the spectrum of response, advocates "properly pitched music" as a solution.

"Music supplies a perceptual-psychological human 'depth' which augments the literal immediacy of the pictorial illusion of reality," states Philip Rosen in his essay on Adorno.[25] It provides a depth above and beyond the literally spatial depth which Adorno and Eisler claim music restores to the two-dimensional photographic image. Psychological human depth; plenitude; the sonorous envelope; the auditory imaginary tipping the scales away from language. Witnessing Jerry and Charlotte's conversation, we might feel that the threat to our belief is not its overexplicitness, but rather its *underexplicitness*, its inadequacy to represent their words' "truth." As a voyeur of two people declaring their love, as an outsider, I am incapable of grasping the meaningful density of this moment for them. This is because the signifiers of this moment are "merely" gestures and dialogue (in addition, cinematic discourse moves me somewhat closer; the close-ups give an intimacy and intensity unavailable in, say, theater). Music enters to satisfy a need to compensate for, fill in, the emotional depth not verbally representable. Bernard Herrmann: "The real reason for music is that a piece of film, by its nature, lacks a certain ability to convey emotional overtones. Many times in many films, dialogue may not give a clue to the feelings of a character. . . ."[26] All music, say Eisler and Adorno, "belongs primarily to the sphere of subjective inwardness."[27] It thus supplies that dimension to the film-perceptual fantasy which is felt as lacking, and whose lack could pose a problem at particularly pregnant moments of the story's unfolding. To the "objectivity" of image and dialogue answers the subjectivity, interiority, depth, of nondiegetic music. Mary Ann Doane shows how bourgeois ideology splits the concept of knowledge into oppositions: between the intelligible and the sensible, intellect and emotion, reason and intuition.

> The ineffable, intangible quality of sound—its lack of the concreteness which is conducive to an ideology of empiricism—requires that it be placed on the side of the emotional or the intuitive. . . . If the ideology of the visible demands that the spectator understand the image as a truthful representation of reality, the ideology of the audible demands that there exist simultaneously a different truth and another order of reality for the subject to grasp.[28]

The highly codified styles and figures of dominant cinema music provide generally unambiguous musical signs in conjunction with the images. We see how music's *ancrage* function (as interpretation) meets up with these emotive functions in an efficient positioning of the spectator-subject before the filmic illusion.

Spectacle

There is a second kind of bonding or subjective positioning to which background music acts as an accessory. Think of the orchestral grandeur of the theme in *Star Wars* that plays as spaceships speed through the galaxy. Or how behind Mildred Pierce, silent in close-up as we ponder her tear-stained trajectory, we hear her lush theme. Dmitri Tiomkin's orchestral cues punctuate successive stages of the arduous cattle drive in *Red River*. The music playing in each case invites the spectator to contemplate; it is helping to *make a spectacle* of the images it accompanies; it lends an epic quality to the diegetic events. It evokes a larger-than-life dimension which, rather than involving us *in* the narrative, places us in contemplation *of* it. Intimate "identification" music (e.g., for the *Now, Voyager* dialogue) and epic "spectacle" music have different codes and functions. The former works to draw the spectator in, and not to be heard; while the spectator is more apt to notice the latter kind, which punctuates a pause in narrative movement in order to externalize, make a commentary on it, and bond the spectator not to the feelings of the characters but to his/her fellow spectators. (This second function is presumably what Eisler and Adorno mean when they call film music "universalized between-the-acts music.") In standard narrative films the audience can (and does) slip in and out of "spectacle" and "narrative identification" music fairly readily.

Summary

In addition to historical explanations for the presence and workings of background music in narrative films, this chapter has offered some arguments that take into account psychoanalytically and ideologically oriented theories of the film spectator/subject's positioning.

In the process of questioning why one does not normally notice background music in films, we ought to bear in mind that the work of cinematic discourse *in general* is to efface itself, in the service of "the narrative," as Christian Metz stated in *The Imaginary Signifier*:

The fiction film is the film in which the cinematic signifier does not work on its own account but is employed entirely to remove the traces of its own steps, to open immediately on to the transparency of a signified, of a story, which is in reality manufactured by it but which it pretends merely to 'illustrate', to transmit to us after the event, as if it had existed previously (= referential illusion): another example of a product which is its own production in reverse. . . . [T]he fiction film represents both the negation of the signifier (an attempt to have it forgotten) and a certain working regime of that signifier, a very precise one, just the one that is required to get it forgotten (more or less forgotten, according to whether the film is more or less submerged in its script). Hence what distinguishes fiction films is not the 'absence' of any specific work of the signifier; but its *presence in the mode of denegation*, and it is well known that this type of presence is one of the strongest there are. . . .[29]

Background music *should* be less invisible than other registers of the cinematic signifier, since it is not as directly a part of the fictional world. The returns on the investment of a musical score are enormous, considering that the film normally "gets it forgotten." Music greases the wheels of the cinematic pleasure machine by easing the spectator's passage into subjectivity.

Narrative cinema's "dispositions of representation" fluctuate constantly; the contractual terms setting the ratio between identification and spectacle change according to genre, directorial style, and a host of historical conditions. But globally speaking, music remains in the dramatic film as the hypnotic voice bidding the spectator to believe, focus, behold, identify, consume. One could imagine a narrative cinema that did not deploy music, but would it be as successful on all fronts?

CHAPTER IV

Classical Hollywood Practice: The Model of Max Steiner

Chapter 1 explored the ways in which music can function formally and narratively in a film. Chapters 2 and 3 examined aesthetic, historical, technological, and psychoanalytically oriented explanations for the development
and functioning of nondiegetic music in dominant (Hollywood) narrative
cinema. In this chapter I shall describe the actual form music takes in Hollywood films, and the principles determining it. First, however, we must
situate our investigation in the context of the "classical model" of narrative
cinema in general, for the codification of mainstream film has everything to
do with the musical language that goes with it.

To use the term "classical cinema" means understanding this cinema as
an institution, and a class of texts which this institution produces. The classical film text (which at its most specific is a Hollywood feature film of the
thirties and forties) is a conjuncture of several economies, a narrative discourse determined by the organization of labor and money in the cinema
industry, by/in ideology, and by the mechanisms of pleasure operating on
subjects in this culture. Christian Metz reminds us of these interconnected
aspects of the system:

> It is not enough for the studios to hand over a polished little mechanism
> labelled 'fiction film'; the play of elements still has to be realised . . . it has

to *take place*. And this place is inside each one of us, in an economic arrangement which history has shaped at the same time as it was shaping the film industry.[1]

What are these texts produced by the classical cinematic institution? In the sense that we cannot identify *the one* prototypical classical film, no one textual model exists. Rather, there exists a pool of conventions, of options, whose combination and recombination constitutes an easily recognized discursive field. We know that even allowing for a wide diversity of genres and studio and authorial styles, there is something identifiable as classical Hollywood cinema, an implicit model that determines the duration of a film, the possibilities of its narrative structure, and its organization of spatiotemporal dimensions via mise-en-scène, cinematography, editing (that is, the "continuity system"), and sound recording and mixing.

André Bazin's influential essay "The Evolution of the Language of Cinema" identified the classical age of the sound film as the late thirties.

> By 1938 or 1939 the talking film, particularly in France and in the United States, had reached a level of classical perfection as a result, on one hand, of the maturing of different kinds of drama developed in part over the past ten years and in part inherited from the silent film, and, on the other, of the stabilization of technical progress.[2]

Bazin likens the state of cinematic form to the equilibrium profile of a riverbed: just as geological equilibrium results from "the requisite amount of erosion," film genres and narrating techniques reached a new stability a decade after the coming of sound. He describes 1938–1939 as a moment of "classical perfection" of the feature film, exemplified by *Stagecoach, Jezebel*, and *Le Jour se lève*. What typifies the classical mode of narrative discourse? For Bazin, storytelling in this cinema is characterized by an editing whose purpose is *analytic, dramatic*, and *psychological*. The classical film ordinarily unfolds in several hundred shots, but these shots do not build up a narrative in the synthetic language of Soviet montage. Classical decoupage presupposes a unified scenic space. It renders this space via "establishing" (long) shots and subsequent breakdown; spatial intelligibility is safeguarded by such devices as the 180-degree rule, the eyeline match, and the shot reverse-shot pattern. Further, cutting is motivated by dramatic and/or psychological logic, accommodating to the spectator's need to see details of narrative importance.

Since Bazin, work on such films as *Stagecoach* (1939), *Young Mr. Lincoln* (1939), *The Big Sleep* (1946), *Suspicion* (1941), *Mildred Pierce* (1945), and *The Maltese Falcon* (1941) has studied features of editing and narration in the context of Hollywood's strongly consolidated "classical" system. These interrelated "classical" features predominate in cinema as far back as the teens and into the commercial cinema of the present, as well as in commercial cinemas of many other countries.

Recent film scholarship has recast the Bazinian description of the classical filmic system in two major ways. First, his phenomenological conceptualization of the spectator as an autonomous perceiving subject—who "wants" to see dramatically important details, and whose perceptual demands cinema satisfies—has given way to an anti-idealist stance which regards as crucial the film's ideological and psychical positioning of its viewing subject. The film positions the spectator; it does the looking and listening for the spectator. Classical editing has been reconsidered and understood in light of its particularly compelling strategies of channeling the spectator's desires, giving the "impression of reality," and encouraging imaginary identification with the film.

The second change in critical emphasis goes hand in hand with the first. If story refers to the narrative world and what happens in it, and if discourse refers to all the means of articulating the story, classical Hollywood film works toward the goal of a transparent or invisible discourse, and promoting fullest involvement in the story. For instance, cutting is a potentially disruptive characteristic of filmic discourse; Hollywood "effaces" the discontinuity that is part and parcel of cutting by means of continuity editing. Continuity editing is a kind of work that masks its own traces, a highly coded symbolic discourse permitting the spectator's fullest identification with the film, as Metz explains:

> [T]he basic characteristic of this kind of discourse, and the very principle of its effectiveness as discourse, is precisely that it obliterates all traces of the enunciation, and masquerades as story. . . . a fundamental disavowal [the film "knows" and at the same time "doesn't know" it is being watched] has guided the whole of classical cinema into the paths of 'story', relentlessly erasing its discursive basis . . .[3]

Now, as part of this discourse, background music clearly constitutes a major element of the classical narrative filmic system. It persists across most genres, from musicals to detective films, science fiction, war, and adventure films, from screwball comedies to domestic melodrama. The very fact that theoreticians of classical filmic discourse, even those who write about the soundtrack, have slighted the specific uses of music in this cinema attests to the strength of music's resistance to analysis. Nonetheless, principles similar to those articulated with respect to classical editing (and other subsystems of Hollywood narrative film) underlie the composition, mixing, and audiovisual editing of film music. Manuals and articles on sound recording and mixing, and aesthetic and practical writings on music composition and mixing, as well as the films themselves, provide access to these principles.

What follows, then, is a synthetic outline of the principles of music composition, mixing, and editing in the classical narrative film. It describes a discursive field rather than a monolithic system with inviolable rules. While I shall not argue for equilibrium profiles or ripeness, I shall emphasize the period of the late thirties into the forties, in order to contribute to an established and growing body of knowledge about the field of classical cinema. Examples shall be drawn in particular from scores by Max Steiner—not to establish his work as a paradigm, but because of his voluminous presence and influence in the classical period. That many of the films he scored have been the object of analysis by contemporary film scholars also renders him central to the study of Hollywood's film music norms.

Classical Film Music: Principles of Composition, Mixing, and Editing

I. *Invisibility*: the technical apparatus of nondiegetic music must not be visible.

II. *"Inaudibility"*: Music is not meant to be heard consciously. As such it should subordinate itself to dialogue, to visuals—i.e., to the primary vehicles of the narrative.

III. *Signifier of emotion*: Soundtrack music may set specific moods and emphasize particular emotions suggested in the narrative (cf. #IV), but first and foremost, it is a signifier of emotion itself.

IV. *Narrative cueing*:

—*referential/narrative*: music gives referential and narrative cues, e.g., indicating point of view, supplying formal demarcations, and establishing setting and characters.

—*connotative*: music "interprets" and "illustrates" narrative events.

V. *Continuity*: music provides formal and rhythmic continuity—between shots, in transitions between scenes, by filling "gaps."

VI. *Unity*: via repetition and variation of musical material and instrumentation, music aids in the construction of formal and narrative unity.

VII. A given film score may violate any of the principles above, providing the violation is at the service of the other principles.

I. Invisibility

The physical apparatus of film music (orchestra, microphones, etc.), like the film's other technological apparatus, such as the camera, must under most circumstances not be visible on the screen. In an article on film sound technology, Charles F. Altman asserts,

> The assumption that all sound-collection devices must be hidden from the camera is . . .—along with the complementary notion that all image-collection noises (camera sounds, arc lamps, the director's voice, etc.) must be hidden from the sound track—the very founding gesture of the talkies.[4]

It is revealing to examine RKO's *King Kong* (1933, score by Max Steiner) with respect to the "rules" being formulated here. For *Kong* was one of the early 100 percent talkies to have a sustained dramatic score, and the very places in which it exhibits awkwardnesses help us recognize, in retrospect, what would soon become the smoothed-out version of classical film scoring and editing. Early in the film, when adventure filmmaker Carl Denham and a half dozen companions go ashore to investigate Skull Island, the principle of invisibility receives an interesting treatment.

A tribe of natives is staging a spectacular ritual at the foot of the enormous wall that separates the island's human denizens from its monstrous ones. Some natives, dressed in ape gear, dance. Others are draping flower garlands onto a native virgin girl; we will learn that they are preparing her for sacrifice to appease the great ape Kong. Denham masses his companions behind some foliage and, as if plants could really hide him, stands behind a small palm; he parts some palm fronds to look. "Holy mackerel, what a show!" he exclaims. The spectacle, the excitement, the rising frenzy of the exhibition (natives) and the voyeurism (Denham & co.) build in tandem with the music. —What music? Well, indeed, music is overwhelming the soundtrack at this point. We can hear the tribal chanting and drum-beating, which we accept as diegetic—as well as the RKO studio orchestra (to be considered nondiegetic) playing a rhythmically repetitious figure in accompaniment.

Movie mogul Denham can't stand to "lose" this spectacle. He hauls his movie camera out into the open and starts cranking. The visual apparatus is exposed, made visible. The tribal chief sees that he's being filmed (or something like that; he has presumably never seen a movie camera). Like a huge black feathered orchestra conductor, the chief gives an imperious cutoff signal. The heretofore unselfconscious dancing, chanting, drumming, and nondiegetic orchestra stop abruptly.

Something—the force of convention, perhaps—made it acceptable for Denham to part the palm fronds, creating a keyhole through which to gaze (and hear) unseen (and unheard). But one cannot move one's kino-eye out into the open without being seen, without "breaking the diegetic illusion" (to make a parallel between the film spectator and the native folk). But the case of sound technology that *King Kong* puts forth is even more mystifying.

Are we to believe that Denham is shooting a *silent* film of all this dancing, chanting, drumming? No sound recording apparatus gets caught *in flagrante delicto* along with the camera. If a microphone and a soundman were accompanying Denham, what would the mike pick up? Would it record the drumming, the chanting, and the RKO orchestra? We know the "obvious" answer to this question, but this scene seems to test its very obviousness in eliminating, on the diegetic level, a soundman along with Denham and his camera. It is as if sound in a film has no technological base, involves no work, is natural, and will simply "show up," just like the spectacle Denham witnesses. Further, the classical paradigm would have us believe that no work has gone into the sound of what *we* witness. Sound is just there, oozing from the images we see. The principle of *invisibility of the sound-collecting apparatus* is inscribed more deeply into the fictional text than the corresponding visual principle of the camera's invisibility.

Some further remarks on the principle of invisibility are in order.

a. When the musical apparatus is visible, the music is "naturalized" as diegetic.[5] Exceptions tend to prove the rule. Eric Rohmer's *Perceval* (1978) shows us other possibilities, as medieval musicians are seen in frame accompanying the stylized actions. *Perceval* does not actually break the rule, as it is not by and large attempting to be a diegetic Hollywood film, but, to the contrary, is approximating conventions of medieval dramatic performance. Another exception occurs when the Godard of *Prénom: Carmen* (1984) intercuts segments showing a string quartet rehearsing Beethoven, with the fiction story of bank-robber Carmen and her companion. The quartet is situated problematically in the fiction via the female violinist who appears once or twice in minor scenes of the principal narrative. Otherwise, these shots of musicians have a wholly ambivalent status: are they nondiegetic (outside the "story") or not? A third kind of example is often found in Hollywood film comedy and musicals: Mel Brooks and Woody Allen have made comic use of "diegetizing" background music by placing musicians in an unlikely mise-en-scène (e.g., Count Basie's jazz orchestra on the western plains of *Blazing Saddles*).

b. Ordinarily, then, the visual representation of music making signals a totally different narrative order, that is, the diegetic, governed by conventions of verisimilitude (e.g., a dance band playing in a nightclub scene). And this, even when the visual representation is not really the source of the music we hear. When Stefan, the Louis Jourdan character in *Letter from an Unknown Woman*, plays the piano, Louis Jourdan is not playing the piano;

piano music has been dubbed onto the soundtrack to produce the illusion. A Hollywood music editor lays bare the artificiality of most diegetic music when he tries to describe a typical playback session on a set (where actors are filmed to synch with prerecorded "diegetic" music):

> You need also to watch for sideline musicians. They are actual musicians who are used in scenes where they are supposed to be playing, but like other performers they are just doing a playback. They may actually play at the same time but such a rendition is not recorded nor used.[6]

II. "Inaudibility"

I have set the term in quotes because, of course, film music can always be heard. However—and somewhat analogously to the "invisibility" of continuity editing on the image track—a set of conventional practices (discursive practices and viewing/listening habits) has evolved which result in the spectator not normally hearing it or attending to it consciously. Its volume, mood, and rhythm must be subordinated to the dramatic and emotional dictates of the film narrative. Leonid Sabaneev (or perhaps his translator) expresses this principle in particularly telling language:

> In general, music should understand that in the cinema it should nearly always remain in the background: it is, so to speak, a tonal figuration, the "left hand" of the melody on the screen, and it is a bad business when this left hand begins to creep into the foreground and obscure the melody.[7]

Bad business, precisely, for it is good business to give ticket-buyers what they have come for, namely a story, not a concert. This story is the right-hand melody, the focus of attention and desire; film music supports it with "harmony"—in fact, gives it signifying resonance.

Here are some practices dictated by the principle of inaudibility.

a. Musical form is generally determined by or subordinated to narrative form. The duration of a music cue is determined by the duration of a visually represented action or a sequence. Thus Sabaneev gives much practical advice about how to compose flexible and neutral music that may be stretched or trimmed, in the likely case that the studio should lengthen or shorten scenes in the final cut. "One might call it elastic or extensile music." He encourages composers to build pauses and sustained notes into the music, for one can draw them out further if the sequence is lengthened with added shots. The composer should write in short musical phrases, also for ease of cutting. Sequential progressions are convenient and therefore encouraged. And "it will be well for the composer to have small pieces of neutral music ready for any emergency—sustained notes on various instruments, rolls on the drum or the cymbals, string pizzicati, chords of a recitatival type."[8]

King Kong's score is largely constructed in this way, especially the central section where Denham, Jack Driscoll, and other crew members, themselves pursued by the island's fancifully created monsters, are attempting to find Ann and rescue her from Kong's clutches. Sequential progressions—each restatement of a motive beginning a step or a third higher than the last—build tension incessantly and relentlessly, and at the same time surely proved adaptable in fitting with the final cutting of the images. Steiner here anticipates Sabaneev's prescription for elastic, extensile film music, and this predilection for sequential repetition is a hallmark of his style throughout his career.

b. *Subordination to the voice.* "It should always be remembered, as a first principle of the aesthetics of music in the cinema, that logic requires music to give way to dialogue."[9] Sabaneev means narrative logic. Dialogue, or any narratively significant sounds for that matter, must receive first priority in the soundtrack mix, as composer Ernest Gold learned:

> What fiendish tortures await the composer at [dubbing] sessions! That tender cello solo, his favourite part of the entire score, lies completely obliterated by a siren which the director decided was necessary at that exact spot in order properly to motivate the reaction on the hero's face! Or that splendid orchestral climax . . . held down to a soft *pp* because of a line of narration that had to be added at the last moment in order to clarify an important story point.[10]

Pursuing the notion that music must not drown out speech, Sabaneev, already out-of-date by Hollywood standards, recommends in 1934 the total cessation of music while there is dialogue on the soundtrack, to rule out any aural "competition" and to ensure the dialogue's clarity. In the United States, the practice of lowering the volume of music behind dialogue, rather than eliminating it, was already *de rigueur*. A machine nicknamed the "up-and-downer," developed as early as 1934, had as its purpose to regulate music automatically. When dialogue signals entered the soundtrack, the up-and-downer reduced the music signal.[11] In an article about the up-and-downer, soundman Edward Kellogg gives a psychological rationale for the music-dimming practice it automated, claiming that it approximated the perceptual activity of attention:

> The system employed here attempts practically to imitate by changes of relative intensity the psychological effect of switching attention from one sound to another. In actual life we can usually take advantage of differences of direction in order to concentrate attention upon a particular sound. The result

of concentrating upon one sound is, of course, not to make the sound louder; but with our directive sense to help, we can largely forget the other sounds, which accomplishes the same purpose as making them actually fainter. Since, in the present case [i.e., a film soundtrack with more than one type of sound], all the sound comes from one direction, and our directive sense cannot be brought into play, the suppression of the sounds in which the listener is less interested is accomplished by making them fainter.[12]

The thirties also saw the development of guidelines for composing and orchestrating music to be placed behind dialogue. Musicians and soundmen felt that woodwinds create unnecessary conflict with human voices, and they stated a preference for strings. They concurred on questions of range, too: even in the seventies Laurence Rosenthal advised "keeping the orchestra well away from the pitch-range of the speaker—low instruments against high voices, and vice versa,"[13] although other composers note that combining voice and orchestra in the same register can sometimes be a creative move, if a sort of indistinguishable tone color is desirable.

c. For editing, certain points are "better" than others at which music may stop or start, for "music has its inertia: it forms a certain background in the subconsciousness of the listening spectator, and its sudden cessation gives rise to a feeling of aesthetic perplexity."[14] Typically, within a scene, music enters or exits on actions (an actor's movement, the closing of a door) or on sound events (a doorbell, a telephone ring). It may also begin or end by sneaking in or out under dialogue, or at the moment of a decisive rhythmic or emotional change in a scene. It goes relatively unnoticed in these cases because the spectator's attention focuses on the action, the sound, or the very narrative change the music is helping to dramatize. Finally, starting the music cue is considered more difficult than ending it; an entrance seems to be more conspicuous than an exit. Thus music almost never enters simultaneously with the entrance of a voice on the soundtrack, since it would drown out the words.

d. The music's mood must be "appropriate to the scene." Classical composers avoid writing music that might distract the viewer from his/her oneiric state of involvement in the story; the point is rather to provide a musical parallel to the action to reinforce the mood or tempo. A fast horse chase needs fast "Ride of the Valkyries" music; a death scene needs slow, somber music. Counterexamples—music inappropriate to the mood or pace—are usually comedic or self-reflexively modernist. In Godard's *Bande à part* (1964), a film abounding with Hollywood genre expectations gone wrong, brass instruments pleasantly execute a waltz as two would-be robbers tensely attempt to break into a house via a ladder to the upper floor.

Incidentally, this is one reason why the nineteenth-century Romantic orchestral idiom of Wagner and Strauss predominated for so long in classical cinema. It was (and is) tonal and familiar, with easily understood connotative values.[15] The gradual introduction of jazz and popular music to scores in the fifties and sixties provides further evidence of the stylistic conservatism of background music. A musical idiom must be thoroughly familiar, its connotations virtually reflexive knowledge, for it to serve "correctly," invisibly, in classical filmic discourse.

III. Emotion

Music appears in classical cinema as a signifier of emotion. Sabaneev describes the image-track, dialogue, and sound effects as "the purely photographic," objective elements of film, to which music brings a necessary emotional, irrational, romantic, or intuitive dimension. Music is seen as augmenting the external representation, the objectivity of the image-track, with its inner truth. We know that composers add enthralling music to a chase scene to heighten its excitement, and a string orchestra inflects each vow of devotion in a romantic tryst to move spectators more deeply, and so on. Above and beyond such specific emotional connotations, though, music itself signifies emotion, depth, the obverse of logic.

Music and representation of the irrational. Following *King Kong's* opening titles, music leaves the soundtrack altogether for a while. The film presents entrepreneur Denham and his "moving picture ship" making preparations to set sail. Denham makes a last trip into town, meets impoverished Ann Darrow, and hires her on for the mysterious and exciting adventure. The ship leaves; it crosses the ocean. On board, Denham administers to Ann her screen test/scream test, in apt foreshadowing of her rendezvous with Kong. All this expository material, from the opening shots to the ship's arrival at Skull Island, transpires with no background music.

Music finally appears with a fade-in to a shot of the ship approaching mist-enshrouded Skull Island. A harp in the low register plunks a tonally vague, repetitious motif, over sustained chords of a string orchestra. The music initiates us into the fantasy world, the world where giant apes are conceivable, the underside of the world of reason. It helps to hypnotize the spectator, bring down defenses that could be erected against this realm of monsters, tribesmen, jungles, violence. This association of music and the irrational predominates throughout the genres of horror, science fiction, and fantasy, as a catalyst in the textual process of slipping in and out of the discourse of realism. Max Steiner avers: "Some pictures require a lot of music and some of them *are so realistic that music would only hurt and interfere.*"[16] Thus, background music aligns with the paradigm of the right-hand column:

Logic	The Irrational
Everyday Reality	Dream
Control	Loss of Control

Music and representation of Woman. A film of the forties is airing on television. Even though you're in the next room, you are likely to find that a certain kind of music will cue you in correctly to the presence of Woman on screen. It is as if the emotional excess of this presence must find its outlet in the euphony of a string orchestra. I refer here to Woman as romantic Good Object, and not to old women, or humorous or chatty women, or femmes fatales (who possess their own musical conventions—jazz, brass, woodwinds . . .).[17] Sabaneev states categorically that films "with love episodes, would find it difficult to dispense with music."[18]

One finds an early—and curious—illustration of this principle in *King Kong.* The ship is anchored off Skull Island; it is evening. Alongside the ship's railing, Jack declares his love to Ann, while Denham and the skipper converse on the ship's bridge. Crosscutting between the two locales occurs as follows:

> [JACK, to Ann, concerned about her participation in the dangerous adventures on the island:] "I'm scared for you. . . . I'm sort of scared *of* you, too. [Melodic background music, in strings and harp, through this monologue, which cuts once to a CU of Ann, then back to Jack.] Ann, uh . . . I . . . uh . . . uh . . . Say, I guess I love you."
> [SKIPPER, in 2-shot with Denham on bridge:] "Mr. Driscoll: are you on deck?" [No music during this shot.]
> [JACK, embracing Ann:] "Yes, *sir!*" [Music plays.]
> [SKIPPER:] "Then please come up on the bridge." [No music.]

Jack and Ann engage in romance; close-ups highlight them against the dark night sky. Denham and the skipper seem to be engaging in a discourse of work; medium-long shots show them in an evenly lit interior. The score reinforces the contrast: violins play sweetly behind the romantic duo's shots, while no music plays with the shots on the bridge. This auditory alternation, strictly aligned with the visual cutting, proves quite disconcerting. The score distinctly ends up violating the "inaudibility" and "continuity" principles in its intended mission to accompany/illustrate the presence of Woman. (Abrupt stops and starts of music become rare after 1934. For a sequence like this, the composer would henceforth choose either a sustained musical cue throughout—its volume subdued as the men on the bridge are seen—or the less likely solution of eliminating music altogether.) The set of oppositions in this case can be drawn as follows:

Man	Woman
Objectivity	Subjectivity
Work	Leisure
Reason	Emotion
Realism	Romantic Fantasy

Music and epic feeling. Music, especially lushly scored late Romantic music, can trigger a response of "epic feeling." In tandem with the visual film narrative, it elevates the individuality of the represented characters to universal significance, makes them bigger than life, suggests transcendence, destiny. This phenomenon seems to point back to anthropological analyses of the ritual functions of rhythm and song in human groups. The sense of common destiny which fans at a football game might have as, "of one voice," they sing the national anthem or chant a slogan in support of the home team has something to do with the emotions inspired by group identity-inducing rituals in more primitive (or, as Eisler and Adorno put it, precapitalistic) groups.

In dominant cinema, this capacity of music to refer to commonality, destiny, and the like, is exploited for producing emotion and pleasure. The appropriate music will elevate the story of a man to the story of Man. When Mildred Pierce is stunned by a cruel argument with her ungrateful daughter, the reaction shot of her (a close-up in which she looks offscreen, suffering), backed by a loud and tragic rendition of the first three notes of her theme, becomes a statement not only of the condition of Mildred, but of the condition of Woman as Mother. At the film's end, as Mildred is reunited with her husband and walking from the police station into the sunrise, a full orchestra, with chimes and dominated by the brasses, restates her theme in a major key. Not only has the couple been reunited, but, in the words of Pam Cook, the patriarchal system (which the plot had threatened to dismantle) has been reconstructed, and "under the aegis of the Law . . . ambiguity is resolved and the shadows dispersed by the light of the new day."[19] I would suggest, again, that music has played a considerable role in the process.

John Ford's historical films provide numerous examples of a related strategy, using music to give a fictional scene mythical significance. The editors of *Cahiers du cinéma* demonstrated how dialogue, cinematography, mise-en-scène, narrative, and the audience's retrospective "knowledge of history" mythify the protagonist's smallest actions in *Young Mr. Lincoln.* Music contributes significantly to this. The final scene, for example, has Lincoln alone, "going on a piece—maybe to the top of that hill." The camera's low angle, the painterly grandeur of the landscape—*and* the Battle Hymn of the Republic on the soundtrack—transform Lincoln's little walk (his constitutional?) to a prefigurement of his destiny as Civil War president. (While virtually any Romantic orchestral music might help here in transforming the everyday to the mythic, the additional reference of the Battle Hymn serves to pinpoint the character's destiny.)

Thus a third large category of "emotion" signified by classical film music can be charted in the following way, with music contributing to the values on the right.

The Particular	The Universal
The Prosaic	The Poetic
The Present	Mythic Time
The Literal	The Symbolic

IV. Narrative cueing

We may divide the semiotic duties of music in classical film into two categories: (1) it refers the spectator to demarcations and levels of the narration; (2) it illustrates, emphasizes, underlines, and points, via what we shall call connotative cueing. Let us first consider some cases of the first type.

1a. *Beginnings and endings.* Music normally accompanies opening and end titles of a feature film. As background for opening titles, it defines the genre (*Mildred Pierce's* title music signals a melodrama); and it sets a general mood (for *Mildred Pierce*, sweepingly emotional, tragic perhaps, as it plays over images of waves washing up on shore). Further, it often states one or more themes to be heard later accompanying the story; the distinctness of the melody can cue even the nonmusical listener into this promissory function, setting up expectations of the narrative events to follow. Finally, opening-title music signals that the story is about to begin, bids us to settle into our seats, stop chatting with fellow moviegoers, and drift into its daydream. Conventionally for melodramas, adventure films, and comedies, composers wrote opening music "full of joy and gladness." (Dimitri Tiomkin reveals that some studios actually forbade the use of minor keys for opening titles, "their reasoning being that 'minor' meant sad and 'major' denoted happiness.")[20]

Ending music tends to strike up in the final scene and continues (or modulates) behind the end credits. Musical recapitulation and closure reinforces the film's narrative and formal closure. Often, it consists of an orchestral swelling with tonal resolution, sometimes involving a final statement of the score's main theme. At any rate, it typically provides a "rising crescendo," "loud and definite."[21]

1b. *Time, place, and stock characterization.* Music, via the well-established conventions, contributes to the narrative's geographical and temporal setting, at the beginning of a film or during a scene within it. The first diegetic shots of *Casablanca* are accompanied by a vaguely Middle-Eastern cue (a clarinet plays a minor-key melody with much ornamentation), to supply the impression of the exotic streets and markets of Casablanca, as if to situate *us* in *it* (when really it's the other way around), to create the sense of a world, even though no one in that world is (diegetically) playing the music.

Strongly codified Hollywood harmonies, melodic patterns, rhythms, and habits of orchestration are employed as a matter of course in classical cinema for establishing setting. A 4/4 allegretto drumbeat (or pizzicato in bass viols), the first beat emphatically accented, with a simple minor-modal tune played by high woodwinds or strings, signifies "Indian territory." A rumba rhythm and major melody played by either trumpet or instruments in the marimba family signifies Latin America. Xylophones and woodblocks, playing simple minor melodies in 4/4, evoke Japan or China. If one hears Strauss-like waltzes in the strings, it must be turn-of-the-century Vienna. Accordions are associated with Rome and Paris; harps often introduce us to medieval, Renaissance, or heavenly settings. The hustle and bustle of the big city, especially New York, is signified by rhythmic support of a jazzy or slightly discordant major theme played by brass instruments or strings, interrupted now and then by a brass automobile-horn imitation. Character types, too, have typical musical signifiers. The girl next door is graced with a sentimental tune in a major key; the seductress is often accompanied by a cocktail-lounge jazz clarinet or saxophone. Max Steiner gives virtually the same rhythmic, open-fifths theme to the Seminoles in Key Largo as he does to Apaches and Cheyennes out west. Woodwinds or xylophones often introduce comic characters in a major key with occasional "wrong"-sounding notes. The code and its constituent signs are well known to American filmgoers. Quincy Jones fantasizes the impossible (except in a comedy): "I've always wanted to see a juxtaposition of a Victorian setting with modern soul music. It would really crack me up to find, in the middle of scene out of Dickens, James Brown screaming away as the town crier."[22]

1c. *Point of view.* The classical film may deploy music to create or emphasize a particular character's subjectivity. Several devices cue the spectator: the association of the music with the sight of the character in a shot, a thematic association repeated and solidified during the course of the narrative, orchestration of music that was previously sung by or to the character, and the marked addition of reverberation for suggesting strongly subjective experiences.

Steiner's score for *Of Human Bondage* (1933) provides some striking examples of early point-of-view music in film. The educated, upper-class, club-footed protagonist Philip Carey (played by Leslie Howard) develops a romantic obsession for the prosaic, uninterested cockney waitress Mildred (Bette Davis). He takes her to dine at a restaurant, where an offscreen piano, violin, and cello trio plays a waltz. Philip's line, "I love that music: it makes me think of you," consolidates this as the Philip-thinking-about-Mildred theme. The nondiegetic rendering of this waltz will henceforth signify a romantic complicity with Philip's love/obsession for Mildred. This is not simply the Mildred theme. Significantly, it does *not* nondiegetically accompany scenes where Mildred actually is present: the cold reality of her emotional disinterest in Philip thus becomes clear, at some level, for the spectator.

Sometimes this musical theme turns into an index of strongly subjective point-of-view. As Philip takes a medical school examination, he absent-mindedly looks at a skeleton at the head of the classroom. A dissolve turns the skeleton into the shapely form of Mildred, and as it does, the scene's background music, a possibly diegetic calliope (outside the window?) playing the Mildred waltz, gives way to the waltz now played by a cello and string orchestra and recorded with an inordinate amount of reverberation. (This reverb contrasts markedly with the "dead" sound of the diegetic rendition in the restaurant.) One of Philip's classmates notices his distracted reverie, and as he coughs to bring Philip back to the business of exam-writing, the calliope tune returns to the auditory background. Earlier in the film he dreams of Mildred: they dance, he without his clubfoot, and they talk gaily, she without her nasal working-class accent. During this wish-fulfillment dream a string orchestra plays the familiar theme with a high degree of reverb.

2. *Connotative cueing.* Narrative film music "anchors" the image in meaning. It expresses moods and connotations which, in conjunction with the images and other sounds, aid in interpreting narrative events and indicating moral/class/ethnic values of characters. Further, attributes of melody, instrumentation, and rhythm imitate or illustrate physical events on the screen. Classical cinema, predicated as it is on telling a story with the greatest possible transparency, overdetermines these connotative values. Soundtrack music reinforces what is (usually) already signified by dialogue, gestures, lighting, color, tempo of figure movement and editing, and so forth.

Caged, a 1950 "realistic" prison melodrama, begins as a police van brings young and innocent Marie Allen (Eleanor Parker) to the women's prison to which she has been unjustly sentenced. As they are herded toward the door, another prisoner tells her to "grab your last look at freeside, kid." Marie turns around, and a last lingering shot follows of the "normal" world outside the prison gate: a city street, a building, a church spire, a few automobiles. At the film's end, a hardened Marie, headed for a criminal life, emerges from the prison door and takes her first look at "freeside" in over a year. Over the same shot—traffic, church—we now hear jazzy, sultry music on trumpet and saxophone. The whole meaning of the "normal" outside world has changed for her, and Steiner's score conveys this efficiently via musical conventions.

2a. Music has tremendous power to influence mood. The commutation experiment undertaken in chapter 1 with a small segment of *Jules and Jim* establishes—albeit in a simplistic way comparable to Kuleshov's short editing experiments—that different music will cue the viewer to different interpretations of an image or scene. The associations that (Hollywood's, Tin Pan Alley's) conventions attach to particular musical instruments, rhythms, melody types, and harmony, form a veritable lexicon of musical connotation which the studio music department exploits.

Even before 1925, film-music lexicons (e.g., Giuseppe Becce's 1919 *Kinobibliothek*), which aided in compiling cue sheets for individual films, enjoyed popularity and profit; indeed, they became instrumental to the efficient functioning of the musical staff of movie houses. Musical "meaning" was codified and institutionalized well before the coming of sound. In turn, these meanings were inherited from a long European tradition whose most recent forebears included theatrical, operatic, and popular music of the latter nineteenth century. Erno Rapee compiled the definitive lexicon of film-musical connotation in 1924, the *Motion Picture Moods for Pianists and Organists: A Rapid Reference Collection of Selected Pieces Adapted to Fifty-Two Moods and Situations*. The fifty-two subjects ranged from Aeroplane, Band, Battle, Birds, Calls, and Chase, through National, Neutral, Orgies, and Oriental, to Sea-Storm, Sinister, Wedding, and Western. The accompanist needing to supply "Sadness" during a film projection could select from among ten pieces, which included the first movement of Beethoven's Sonata no.2 (Op.27), Chopin Preludes 4 or 20 (Op. 28), Grieg's "Elegie" (Op. 47), and Gaston Borch's "Andante Patetico e Doloroso." The three selections available for wedding scenes were Mendelssohn's wedding march, Wagner's wedding march from *Lohengrin*, and "O Promise Me."

Classical film music scores that deviate from the standard stylistic repertoire—scores using jazz or electronic music, for example—end up participating in signification just as fully as scores written in the familiar Hollywood-Wagnerian idiom. The expression and connotation in Miklos Rozsa's electronic music in *Spellbound* (1945) might be a bit more difficult to characterize in words, but any moviegoer will tell you how eerie or spooky it sounds.

This is precisely as it should be, since the electronic music cues accompany dream sequences, events in the film that bring the murky unconscious into play.[23] Likewise, jazz during the studio era often conveyed connotations such as sophistication, urban culture, nightlife, decadence.[24] In general, any musical language, other than the major nineteenth-century one, itself carried connotations simply by virtue of being unusual. Even music that attempts to subvert the principles of classical scoring will connote *something* when played with narrative images; and the reading position of spectators in the thirties and forties was so thoroughly defined by the classical norm that the rare music composed with subversive intentions was most probably perceived as conforming, by and large, to the established canon.[25]

Without trying to cover the entire range of standard connotation, which also includes conventions of range, of tempo, and of rhythm, let us at least consider two categories.

Conventions of orchestration. Film music calls upon traditional connotative associations evoked by instrumental colors. Eric Sarnette, in his book *Music for the Microphone*, gives examples.

> When the picture of an irate man appears, brass trumpets are heard; chubby-faced bassoons, when a fat man is seen coming along; oboes, when a quiet valley with cattle is shown on the screen; plaintive violins to accompany a picture of a pair of lovers, more like a sentimental postcard than anything else. . . .[26]

Eisler and Adorno identify many other conventions of instrumentation in their delightfully grumpy first chapter, which zeroes in on Hollywood's "Prejudices and Bad Habits." They assert that "mountain peaks invariably invoke string tremolos punctuated by a signal-like horn motif." In another context, "The tremolo on the bridge of the violin, which thirty years ago was intended even in serious music to produce a feeling of uncanny suspense and to express an unreal atmosphere, today has become common currency."[27]

Melodic conventions. Certain melodic types characterize Westerns: either based on Western ballads, or the typical calls of bugles in the case of cavalry films, or "Western frontier" melodies in major keys with skips of perfect fourths and fifths, connoting the grandeur of the frontier landscape. Other melodic types illustrate another kind of "nature," the kind with birds, serene lakes, and virgin forests; these often present a stylization of bird calls or the major-key pastoral pleasantness of the first measures of Beethoven's Sixth Symphony.

Some Hollywood composers also made frequent use of stock music, musical clichés instantly recognizable by filmgoers and directly inherited from the lexicons. In *Of Human Bondage*, for example, a montage conveys Philip's confusion in London as his rival marries Mildred. When during the montage a single shot of the wedding is seen, the ongoing background score is briefly punctuated by a few seconds of Mendelssohn's wedding march—after which the music returns to its normal nondescript lushness. Eisler and Adorno again:

> . . . the scene of a moonlight night is accompanied by the first movement of the *Moonlight Sonata*. . . . For thunderstorms, the overture to *William Tell* is used; for weddings, the march from *Lohengrin* or Mendelssohn's wedding march. These practices—incidentally, they are on the wane and are retained only in cheap pictures—correspond to the popularity of trademarked pieces in classical music, such as Beethoven's E-flat Concerto, which has attained an almost fatal popularity under the apocryphal title *The Emperor*, or Schubert's *Unfinished Symphony*. . . .[28]

Sound film composers also quickly developed musical phrases, some extremely brief, to illustrate actions on the screen. For example, *King Kong* contains a scene in which Kong shakes several men off a large log, like so many ants, and sends them down a ravine to their death. From a niche in a wall of rock, hero Jack Driscoll manages to prick Kong's finger a couple of times with his knife. Kong's reaction, as he looks a bit sadly at his tiny wound, is accompanied by a pathetic-sounding violin glissando downward.

2b. *Illustration.* To a greater extent than other major Hollywood composers, Max Steiner synchronized musical effects closely with events on the screen. As one writer puts it, Steiner is legendary for a film-musical style intent on "*catching* everything." A Steiner score accompanying an eventful sequence can sound like a hodgepodge of mixed thematic material, rapidly changing dynamics and orchestral texture, and rapid modulations, in its tendency to provide hyperexplicit, moment-by-moment musical illustration.

Witness this description of a brief but busy sequence from *The Adventures of Don Juan* (1948):

> While reminiscing with one of his past amours, Don Juan discovers to his horror that he has no real idea where and when he became acquainted with the lady. She is furious when she realizes this, but then determines to win his affections all over again. At this point her father and fiancé enter and confront the couple. Don Juan flees. The scene dissolves as he ponders his predicament, concluding, "Woman, thy name is trouble."
> Steiner's accompaniment for this scene consists of a series of rapid-fire quotations of all the motifs identified with the various characters. The young woman's outburst of temper is accompanied by a woodwind glissando. When she exclaims, "This time you won't forget me," Steiner quotes the roguish,

sauntering melody that serves as the Don Juan love theme. As the philanderer tries to disengage himself from her embrace, she calls to her father, "I'm trying to get away from him, but he's so strong." When Don Juan identifies himself, the composer quickly quotes the Don Juan hero motif. The girl pouts, "Stop being so Spanish!" Immediately, we hear a tambourine, castanets, and Castilian rhythms. Don Juan's rapid departure is accompanied by a typical Spanish march. The principal theme is stated as a lyrical melody when he contemplates his fate, and resolves in the stirring hero motif again. Hardly any of these themes lasts more than a few seconds; the entire scene is only 3 1/2 minutes long.[29]

To achieve to-the-second synchronization of score and film, Steiner adopted the click-track technique early in the thirties. This was developed for the animated cartoon: even before 1930, Disney's Silly Symphonies used the device for exact timing of music with images. The click-track consists of holes which the studio's music editor punches into the soundtrack at the edge of the film for the purpose of matching metronomic tempo to that of the projected film. As it is projected during a music dubbing session, the conductor and recording musicians hear these clicks through their headphones, and they record their music to its beat. The music editor can create a rhythmically regular click-track, or one to match rhythmically irregular actions on the screen (such as a character's uneven steps), should the composer wish to match the music exactly with the visuals.

So while illustration to the minutest detail was a hallmark of Steiner's style in particular, our overall model of classical-era film music also must include the general tendency toward musical illustration. Two frequently used dramaturgical techniques of illustration are mickey-mousing and the stinger.

Mickey-mousing. Music making actions on the screen explicit—"imitating" their direction or rhythm—is called mickey-mousing (after musical practices used in the early Disney sound cartoons). Click-tracks made this effective as early as *Of Human Bondage* (the "clubfooted" limping theme of Philp Carey) and *King Kong* (the tribal chief walking over to parlay with Denham). Music mickey-mouses the gait of Gypo Nolan in *The Informer.* Near the beginning of *Casablanca*, as an Allied resistance fighter is shot, the score imitates his fall to the ground. Near the opening of *The Big Sleep*, a harp glissando helps to mickey-mouse the feigned collapse of spoiled Carmen Sternwood into the arms of Philip Marlowe.

The stinger. A musical *sforzando* used to illustrate sudden dramatic tension is called a stinger. A couple of examples from *Mildred Pierce*—a melodrama virtually built upon stinging revelations to its suffering protagonist, and therefore replete with Steinerian stingers—will suffice. As newly successful restaurateur Mildred embraces playboy Monte Beragon after hours,

Monte's theme appropriately plays in the background. Mildred's estranged husband Bert walks in on the scene; the sound of his closing the door, a cut to the startled couple, and a stinger in the score all coincide. Second, toward the end of the film, Mildred runs downstairs in Monte's beach house, and into a close-up showing her stunned revelation: as the orchestra does a glissando to a stinger chord, we cut to a medium close-up profile of her daughter Veda in an embrace with Monte.

Silence can also "sting." Mildred pays a visit to her daughter Veda, having learned of her desire to marry the rich young bachelor Ted Forrester. She asks whether family friend Wally knows that Veda wants to marry Ted. A big close-up frames Veda as she says, " . . . *want* to get married? We *are* married." The film cuts at that moment to a close-up of Mildred's stunned reaction; also at that moment the background music ends on a quick crescendo to a high, dissonant chord. The stinger in this case is the silence that abruptly follows.

V. Formal and rhythmic continuity

"At its most general functional level, film music serves as a kind of cohesive, filling in empty spaces in the action or the dialogue."[30] Virtually everyone who has written about standard film music agrees that music "fills the tonal spaces and annihilates the silences without attracting special attention to itself" (Sabaneev). Anti-Hollywood composers (e.g., Maurice Jaubert, Hanns Eisler) harp on this feature of classical film scores: the studio brings the composer in to "plug up the holes" in the soundtrack. Perhaps they are right: that the impulse behind using music this way arises from a fear of silence or of visual stasis, a fear that equates such absence with death. In soundmen's and musicians' discourse, music gives the soundtrack "life," "warmth," "color." Hollywood's narratives tend to be based on action, not reflection.[31] The classical film brings music into its service in particular ways we will now enumerate.

Music smooths discontinuities of editing within scenes and sequences. The discontinuity of a cheat cut or a temporal ellipse will be slightly less jarring or noticeable because of music, this flexible and pleasurable auditory substance (this "cohesive") in the background. As an auditory continuity it seems to mitigate visual, spatial, or temporal discontinuity. Montage sequences—calendar pages flipping, newspaper headlines spanning a period of time, citizen Kane and his wife growing apart at the breakfast table over the years—are almost invariably accompanied by music.

Music also bridges gaps between scenes or segments; the classical film uses it for transitions. Typically, music might begin shortly before the end of scene *A* and continue over into scene *B*. Or perhaps, scene *A*'s music will modulate into a new key as scene *B* begins. The beginning of *The Big Sleep* demonstrates how music functions as spatiotemporal connective tissue. Marlowe leaves the Sternwood mansion after having met Carmen, Colonel Sternwood, and Vivian in three successive conversations. Music strikes up as the butler escorts him to the door. The film cuts to a shot of a plaque that reads "Hollywood Public Library," then to a close-up of the documents Marlowe is taking notes on; then to longer shots reestablishing that Marlowe is doing research in the library. Steiner's transition music has no particularly musical form of its own, since it must obey the rhythm of the editing and the rapid change of locations it is illustrating and connoting. It modulates frequently, but it is still one uncut piece of music, a continuous substance that compensates for the spatiotemporal discontinuities—necessary for narrative coherence, efficiently getting Marlowe from one place to another.

In the *King Kong* sequence that crosscuts between Ann and Jack's romantic dialogue on one hand and Denham and the skipper's "work talk" on the other, the presence of music signifies emotion. But it doesn't "work" there, precisely, because it violates the need for auditory continuity in which music is usually caught up. Strictly aligning music (or its absence) with the crosscut scenes only emphasizes a discontinuity which runs counter to classical soundtrack construction.

VI. Unity

Classical cinema, predicated as it is on formal and narrative unity, deploys music to reinforce this unity. We have already seen that opening and closing music encloses the film within a musical envelope, announcing genre, mood, and setting, and then providing musical recapitulation and closure to reinforce narrative closure.

Tonal relationships in the score are also managed so as to contribute to a sense of the film's unity. Sabaneev gives a typical rule of thumb: if music has been absent for more than fifteen seconds, the composer is free to start a new music cue in a different and even unrelated key, since the spectator/auditor will have sufficiently forgotten the previous cue's tonality. But if the gap has lasted less than the requisite time, the new cue must start in the same key (or a closely related one).

The major unifying force in Hollywood scoring is the use of musical themes, although it is by no means accurate to claim that all classical scores rely on themes. Max Steiner's film-composing method, however, relied on thematic structuring. After watching the rough cut, he devised the principal character and idea motifs, and then elaborated the score from there. The thematic score provides a built-in unity of statement and variation, as well as a semiotic subsystem. The repetition, interaction, and variation of musical themes throughout a film contributes much to the clarity of its dramaturgy and to the clarity of its formal structures.

VII. Breaking the rules

The principles of Hollywood scoring I have enumerated should not be considered as hard-and-fast rules. Enjoying a special status between conscious and unconscious perception, sometimes between diegetic, nondiegetic, and metadiegetic fictional levels, and between formal and narrative rhythms, music as a nonrepresentational "cohesive" mediates among many types of textual contradictions and itself participates in them. Thus, for instance, in its illustrative function (IV), mickey-mousing music often becomes noticeable, violating the principle of inaudibility (II). This is to say that certain conditions (the specificity of the text itself, the composer's personal style, the studio's practices of orchestrating, mixing, and editing, historical factors) may require one principle to take precedence over another.

Steiner's Score for *Mildred Pierce*

Let us examine the "classical" principles as they operate in *Mildred Pierce*. Having provided numerous examples of principles I through V, I will now emphasize the "unity" principle by exploring the film's use of musical themes in the context of its narrative. I will also suggest ways in which Steiner's compositional style, above and beyond its adequacy to the classical Hollywood model, is paradigmatic for melodrama in particular.

By the time he composed the score for *Mildred Pierce*, Max Steiner was a veteran of film music, at the height of a career that would include more than three hundred film scores over a period of thirty-five years. Head of the music department at RKO from 1930 to 1936, and a chief composer at Warner Brothers thereafter, Steiner's influence on the procedures and style of film composing during the studio years was enormous. Whether avidly pro- or anti-Steiner, film music's critics have characterized Steiner's work along fairly consistent lines. Some refer to his music as "pure schmaltz";[32] all agree on his "heavy-handed emphasis on large-scale symphonic composition;" his "sweeping melodic lyricism" is "nostalgic, emotional, and sentimental."[33] The tendency of a Steiner score to accompany as much of the film as possible led Henri Colpi to assert—a bit unreasonably—that this

Form E-3—20M—K-I-J Co. 6-33

R K O STUDIOS, IN
Inter-Department Communication

Messrs: KAHANE
        BERMAN   WHITE
        O'HERON ABBOTT
To............... NOLAN............WILKINSON.......

Date......September 29, 1934.......

From......MAX STEINER...........................

Subject....OFFICE HOURS..................

<u>TO ALL LOVERS OF NIGHT SHIFTS!</u>

        Effective Monday morning, October First,
I can be found at the Studio during the hours:
9:00am to 12:30pm; and from 1:30pm to 6:00pm,
every day except Sundays and Holidays. However,
I WILL NOT be found, any longer, during the
hours from 6:00pm to 9:00am next morning, as
in the past.

        Should this not be satisfactory to anyone,
I shall be only too happy to cancel my contract.

        Furthermore, I just received an offer
from the President of the May Company, Eighth
at Broadway, Los Angeles, California, who wants
to obtain my services, on a long term contract,
as a "BED-TRYER" and that looks awfully good
to me.

                                     Max Steiner

MS/h

A 1934 memo from the much-in-demand Max Steiner to his colleagues in the
RKO Music Department. *Courtesy of RKO Pictures, Inc.*

composer was "no doubt frightened by silence."[34] Mark Evans views Steiner's tendency to state and restate themes, and insert illustrative music at the slightest narrative provocation, as a compulsion to "catch everything," as we have seen.

At Warners, Steiner put to frequent use his lush symphonic style and his predilection for minute coordination of music with narration. Among his scores for melodramatic pictures of those years were *Jezebel, Dark Victory, Gone with the Wind, All This and Heaven Too, The Letter, The Great Lie, Casablanca, In This Our Life, Since You Went Away,* and *Now, Voyager.* In light of recent reevaluation of women's pictures and the melodramatic in film, it seems fitting and necessary to investigate what this most prolific composer brought to the genre. How is the function of music for melodrama served out in specifically cinematic terms?

Very few readers could spontaneously recall the musical motif assigned to *Mildred Pierce's* protagonist—which is repeated fifty to a hundred times— although many who have seen the film can accurately quote lines of dialogue or describe shot compositions. Only in actively deciding to listen for the music will we realize how structured and repetitive it is, and how central to our emotional reception of the narrated events.

The score of *Mildred Pierce* has five major themes. These we may identify easily by examining what musical lines are associated with what characters or events. The main theme (A) belongs to Mildred.

A

One comes gradually to associate Mildred with this music. First, as waves wash over the film's opening credits, the piece is heard. Then, when in the fifth diegetic shot a man falls to the floor, his dying word, "Mildred," is followed by a rendition, in minor, of A. Three shots later, a woman—soon to be identified as Mildred—walks onto a pier, as on the soundtrack the first three notes of melody A are repeated and varied in accompaniment to Joan Crawford's mysterious half-hearted attempt to commit suicide.[35] The theme is next heard in its entirety—still in minor—when Mildred pulls up to her mansion at night, before a pair of detectives take her to police headquarters. Not until well into her flashback narration of her separation from husband Bert and the beginning of her restaurant career do we hear the melody in its full major-key statement. Bert has left; alone, late at night, Mildred reviews her finances as her voiceover says, "It didn't take me long to figure out that I was dead broke." Thus the first major statement of A is reserved for the protagonist at a point when a quick exposition has removed her husband—economic and emotional support—and put her at the beginning of her road of work, sacrifice, and suffering. Mildred's theme will henceforth occur on a multitude of occasions, always associated with the character Mildred.

Another of the score's major themes belongs to Bert.

B

The association between this motif (B) and its character is established rapidly. In the sequence where Bert is introduced, leaving his real estate office, his theme plays through. After the argument that culminates in their decision to separate, Bert's theme plays slowly, in minor, by a plaintive oboe, as a few last hesitating words pass between him and Mildred. Later repetitions of B are heard as Bert comes to grant Mildred a divorce, as he comes to visit her after her marriage to Monte, and as Mildred thanks him for reuniting her with her prodigal daughter Veda.

A third theme (C) belongs to both daughters, Veda and Kay—a rather curious designation, since each daughter is not only strongly differentiated, but is virtually the opposite of the other in terms of values in the mother-daughter constellation that the film assigns to them. In melodramatic terms, Kay is the good daughter and Veda the evil one. How, then, can the score use one theme for the two of them?

C   Allegretto

The earlier part of the story concentrates not so much on Veda's evil traits as on the breakup of Mildred's marriage, and the development of her career, all necessitated by her "putting the children first." Mildred bakes pies and cakes for neighborhood customers so that both Veda and Kay may have expensive music and dance lessons. The daughters function as a unit, the vessel into which Mildred's sacrifice and hard work are poured. Only later—precisely, the night of Kay's death—is Monte Beragon introduced into the constellation of sexuality which will culminate in the Mildred/Veda/Monte Oedipal triangle; this sexual dimension really brings Veda's evil and competitive attributes into narrative play. Thus, the very night when the Oedipal (strictly speaking, Electra) plot is initiated by the introduction of Monte as

Mildred's lover, Kay is dying; after her death, the daughters' musical theme will only be needed for Veda anyway.

A fourth theme (D) is a jaunty melody associated with Mildred's restaurant business and with the growth of her social and financial status.

D

It is first heard early in Mildred's waitress career. When Mildred starts her own restaurant, this melody regularly accompanies the narration of the growth of the business. Finally, we also hear *D* in connection with a newspaper article about Mildred's impending marriage to Monte. In contrast to the sinister behind-the-scenes conditions of the marriage, the shot of the newspaper's wedding announcement, especially with *D* playing on the soundtrack, creates an ironically pleasant nuance. It shows the public face of this union as opposed to what we know to be its seedy motives of mutual exploitation.

A final major theme (E) refers to the romance between Monte and Mildred.

E

This is the only theme which the film presents both diegetically and non-diegetically. When Monte first seduces Mildred at his beach house, he has put on a record of mood music (E). "Monte . . . the record," says an offscreen Mildred weakly, as the sight and sound of the scratching phonograph needle acts as a metonymical figure of the seduction. Tune *E* is heard several more times in the film, nondiegetically, always referring to the romance between the two.

The lion's share of *Mildred Pierce*'s score consists of statements or variations of these five themes. The melodies are treated in conventional ways to fit each narrative context in which they appear. Variations in tonality, register, harmonic accompaniment, time signature, rhythm, and instrumentation alter their sound and mood. The first few treatments of Kay and Veda's theme will amply illustrate the expressive range Steiner derives from such variation.

The first statement of *C* coincides with the film's first shot of Veda and Kay. Especially following the film's *noir* opening and then the oppressively claustrophobic look of the scene of Mildred's quarrel with Bert, the even exterior lighting and compositional simplicity of the initial shot of the girls strikes the viewer as virtually from another world, another film, simpler and cheerier. Likewise, the soundtrack bursts in with violins introducing theme C in ⁴⁄₄, forte, allegro, in A-flat major. As they talk on their way home, Kay, the younger, unselfconsciously turns, dances, and skips as she goes; accordingly the tempo of the music shifts to ¾ to accentuate—to mickey-mouse— her dancing.

A few scenes later, Veda tries on the new dress that had given rise to the argument and separation of her parents. At the moment when Veda says "I wouldn't be seen dead in this," a reaction shot shows a stunned Mildred in the hall having overheard. Now theme C plays in a minor key, in a lower register, and much more slowly—conventional ways of inflecting a melody with darker or sadder connotations.

Elsewhere: Bert meets Mildred outside the house in the rain, on the night of her tryst with Monte. Bert gravely tells Mildred that Kay has pneumonia. As she says "Oh, no," we hear bass viols, unaccompanied, state theme C slowly in minor. After Kay has died at Mrs. Biederhof's, a viola plays C with much vibrato, connoting mournful sadness and nostalgia. Steiner is certain, however, to have Mildred share the stage with Kay even as Kay dies— milking the spectator for mother's grief by presenting Mildred's theme A at the moment the doctor says he couldn't save the child. A close-up of Mildred grieving over the little body, accompanied by A, thus shifts the focus of sympathy to the protagonist. Only several shots later does the score return properly to mourn the dead, sounding Kay's theme as the doctor says that he brought her into the world.

Once Kay is out of the picture, the theme belongs to Veda. Now a successful restaurateur with a socialite daughter, Mildred gives Veda a car for her birthday; theme C plays rhythmically and jauntily. When Veda goes for a first drive, it continues to play, though more amorphously and with no rhythmic accentuation, as Monte and Mildred discuss their differences over Veda. The music serves at least a double function here, as it does throughout the score. The theme itself designates that Veda is the subject of narrative focus; it directs attention to this character. The musical *treatment* of the theme, especially in contrast to the bouncy rendition seconds before, expressively underscores the scene's narrative conflict, Mildred telling Monte to stay away from Veda. I. A. Richards might say that these two functions of themes in classical Hollywood scores are the referential (C denotes or directs attention to Veda) and the emotive (a particular musical treatment of C yields a certain range of expressive connotations); my overall category of narrative cueing includes both these functions.

The score continues to use C whenever Veda appears. When as prodigal daughter she returns to Mildred, who now lives in a mansion and is married to Monte, a richly and warmly orchestrated version of Veda's theme plays through the scene. By means of a final example, I wish to point out the increasing harmonic "distortion" the theme undergoes toward the film's end. Mildred discovers Veda in an embrace with Monte; a fragment of C plays repeatedly, each repetition a step up from the last. The tension evoked by this ascending stepwise repetition, and by the progressively closer shots of Veda's face in alternation with reaction shots of a shocked, disbelieving Mildred, has a double culmination: musically in a dreadful silence, and in Veda's line: ". . . and there's nothing you can do about it."

The cursory examination of this theme and its elaborations shows that the relation between the theme and its referent is extremely clearly articulated—often to the point of redundancy—and that little but the standard late-nineteenth-century conventions of tempo, instrumentation, and tonality are employed to give the theme its emotive values at given points along the narration. Steiner was not interested in subtlety. In his own words:

> The danger is that music can be so bad, or so good, that it distracts and takes away from the action. And beware of embellishments; it's hard enough to understand a melody behind dialogue, let alone complicated orchestrations. If it gets too decorative, it loses its emotional appeal. I've always tried to subordinate myself to the picture. A lot of composers make the mistake of thinking that the film is a platform for showing how clever they are. This is not the place for it.[36]

Thus Steiner clearly bore in mind the difference between the referential function of a musical theme, "understanding a melody," and the theme's emotive function: "if it gets too decorative, it loses its emotional appeal." It almost goes without saying that both functions of themes in the film score are "subordinated . . . to the picture," to the narrative discourse.

Steiner's music often sacrifices its musical coherence to effects gained in coordinating with diegetic action. The formlessness and fragmentary nature of musical statements in his scores are perhaps the most easily recognizable mark of his style. More mickey-mousing occurs, for instance, early in the film when Mildred attempts to frame Wally by locking him in the beach house with Monte's body. The musical score rhythmically apes Wally's increasingly harried steps as he walks from door to door searching for an exit. I see Steiner's fondness for such rhythmic redundancy as being closely linked with the "melodramatic spirit"—a desire to externalize and explicate all inflections of action, from emotional values in a scene to the very rhythms of physical movement.

On several levels, then, the musical score exhibits a pronounced tendency toward hyperexplication. Steiner's intrusively lush dramatic music has an interesting effect—an effect common to all "realist" Hollywood cinema but which is especially prominent here. The music is an element of discourse that magnifies, heightens, intensifies the emotional values suggested by the story. Just as melodrama displays a tendency to use the close-up on the female star's face—and just as the close-ups in *Mildred Pierce* have caused critics to comment on the revelation of every twitch and wide-eyed stare in Crawford's small inventory of expressions—Steiner's music has a similar effect. The close-up of Crawford, bigger than life, parallels this musical score, which also renders bigger than life James M. Cain's tawdry story. Like melodrama in general, *Mildred Pierce* "allows us the pleasures of self-pity and the experience of wholeness brought by the identification with 'mono-pathic' emotion."[37] The background score has a key function of guiding the spectator-auditor unambiguously into this particularly compelling identification.

CHAPTER V

Eisler/Adorno's Critique

Critics and musicians have opined on various aspects of the implicit "classical" film music model since it emerged in the thirties. By and large, personal taste has prevailed as the dominant criterion for evaluating film scores and scoring practices.[1] No one has attempted a rigorous, consistent, global critique of the classical model other than Hanns Eisler and Theodor Adorno, whose landmark *Composing for the Films* (1947) is grounded in the Frankfurt School's neo-Marxist theoretical debates on culture and society. Eisler and Adorno's analysis of dominant film music in the framework of the "culture industry," and their proposals for an oppositional practice, stand out so strikingly against the general background of impressionistic film music criticism that any subsequent responsible work on music in film must take stock of their book.[2] Though certainly the authors' proposals for alternatives to the classical model deserve serious critical attention, here I shall only present their critique of the classical model itself.

Composing for the Films represents a collaboration between a composer (Eisler) and a social philosopher and music critic (Adorno).[3] The two authors had much in common. Both studied music in the Vienna school of composition (Eisler with Arnold Schoenberg, Adorno with Alban Berg); the passionate antifascism of both during the tumultuous prewar years in Weimar Germany found a theoretical basis in Marxism; and both wrote and taught in Europe and, during the war, in the United States. Their thinking differed in this major respect: Eisler, closer to Brecht, believed in the possibility of

direct intervention through art, in "agit-prop" consciousness-raising of the
working masses; Adorno's famous pessimism regarding the status of human
in advanced capitalist society virtually ruled out the hope of "awakening"
the alienated majority.

Eisler, who along with Berg and Webern was one of Schoenberg's star
composition protégés in the early twenties, moved in 1924 to Berlin. The
radical political and social climate there led him to the arduous process of
integrating politics with his art. Rejecting the hermetic intellectual isolation
of Schoenberg's musical work, he composed political ballads and revolutionary workers' songs (along with concert songs, children's songs, cantatas,
oratorios, and symphonic and chamber works), becoming closely involved
with the workers' movement. In fact, when his oratorio-style didactic play
Die Massnahme was first performed in 1930, this "first great master of revolutionary proletarian music" was to be found singing in the choir.[4] His creative partnership with Bertolt Brecht commenced in 1928. With the
"bourgeois esthetic" as their common enemy, they collaborated on songs
and dramatic works, including *Die Massnahme* (*The Measures Taken*, a political "oratorio," 1930), *Kuhle Wampe* (a film championing worker solidarity,
directed by Slatan Dudow, 1932), *Mother* (Brechtian "epic theater" adapted
from Gorki, 1932), and collections of political songs and other choral works
using texts by Brecht. From 1931 on, Eisler composed scores for politically
progressive documentary films in several countries including France and the
Soviet Union. Like Brecht he developed compositional methods designed
to break the audience's identification and immediate rapport with musical
sonority, "in order to re-experience consciously the music and the text. By
reaching the mind via the route of emotion, music must help clarify the
passions without which political revolutions are impossible."[5]

Living in the United States from 1938 through the war necessarily subdued
Eisler's radicalism. Since immigration restrictions prevented him from writing topical music overtly for the class struggle, he composed concert music,
song cycles, and scores for independent and commercial films.[6] Like many
fellow Europeans, he taught at the New School for Social Research (dubbed
"the university in exile") in New York. A Rockefeller grant in the early forties
funded his work on theory and practice of film music,[7] work that resulted
eventually in the publication of *Composing for the Films*.

The specific theoretical underpinnings of Eisler and Adorno's book, notably in its critique of the culture industry, clearly point to Adorno's influence. Throughout the corpus of his writings, Adorno was concerned with
the fate of knowledge under advanced capitalism. He expressed a pessimism
uncharacteristic of the cultural Marxists, claiming that capitalist society exerts

on its subjects an inescapable ideological stranglehold. The regimentation and forms of deception it assumes have altered human consciousness in such a way that this ideological domination can only continue to refine itself in an irreversible process. Adorno painted his grim picture of the effects of modernization and industrialization on capitalist society by drawing from the work of Max Weber and the young Georg Lukacs. His arguments arose from the notion that not just the economic but all spheres of social life, including the cultural, have been penetrated by a single logic of *formal rationality*— having grown out of the Enlightenment ideal of reason into a sort of Taylorism operating on every level of the social formation. This logic in modern society "is defined by the principle of orientation of human action to abstract, quantifiable and calculable, and instrumentally utilizable formal rules and norms."[8]

Advanced capitalism has spawned a burgeoning bureaucracy to manage material production. "Mental labor," too, has been overtaken by the bureaucratized state. The administrative rationalization of culture has led to the standardizing of cultural production: works produced in this system share a "sameness" as they serve and affirm the existing order. Through capitalist technology, through mass production and reproduction by the culture industry (Adorno's term), the administrative cultural order exerts more and more complete social control. The culture industry produces standardized works for mass consumption, materials that serve as "entertainment." The artwork has become a product, a commodity, and its value is judged solely in terms of its exchange-value.

> All the other films and products of the entertainment industry which [spectators] have seen have taught them what to expect; they react automatically. The might of industrial society is lodged in men's minds. The entertainments manufacturers know that their products will be consumed with alertness even when the customer is distraught, for each of them is a model of the huge economic machinery which has always sustained the masses, whether at work or at leisure—which is akin to work.[9]

The culture industry produces objects—films, phonograph records, radio programs, and so on; these objects' industrial/technological character by definition rules out spontaneity or immediacy with the audience. There cannot be direct interaction between the works and the consumer—spatially, temporally, or in terms of the ideology they represent. The media, in other words, are profoundly mediated. On this unbridgeable remoteness between work and spectator in the cinema in particular, Eisler and Adorno write:

"SO WELL REMEMBERED"

PRODUCTION #2069

"POSTER MONTAGE"

REEL 6 - M:63

NOTE: ᵀhis crossed out of M:61 cue.

START MUSIC ON THE THIRD X-MARK, MIDDLE OF THE DISSOLVE TO ..   .00
GEORGE WORKING THE PRINTING MACHINE.

WE HEAR THE NOISE OF THE MACHINE IN ACTION AT 00 2/3

THE CAMERA STARTS TO PAN TO THE RIGHT FOLLOWING THE 04 1/3
MOVEMENT OF THE MACHINE -- A VERY SLOW PAN.

END OF THE CAMERA PAN AND WE ARE ON A CLOSE SHOT OF THE .....   .10 1/3 —
POSTERS THAT ARE ~~TURNICEX~~ TURNED OUT OF THE PRINTING MACHINE
AND IT READS: "DIPHTHERIA KILLS! GO TO THE CLINIC NOW."

MIDDLE OF THE DISSOLVE TO AN EXTERIOR TENEMENT HOUSE AND 13
WE SEE MOTHERS AND THEIR CHILDREN COMING OUT.

NOTE: ᵀhey come out and cross the street.

END OF THE NOISE AT 13 1/3

CUT TO A SHOT OF A WOMAN WITH HER BABY IN HER ARMS 20 1/3
CLIMBING THE STAIRS TO THE CLINIC --- CAMERA PANS WITH HER.

SHE REACHES THE TOP OF THE STAIRS AND AS SHE WALKS OUT 25 1/3
OF THE SCENE WE SEE THAT SHE HAS PASSED THE DIPHTHERIA POSTER.

NOTE: ᵀhe camera remains on this poster.

MIDDLE OF THE DISSOLVE TO THE INTERIOR CLINIC AND 29 2/3
WE LOSE MUSIC UNDER THE SOUND OF THE CRYING YOUNGSTERS.

Music cue sheet for a 30-second sequence in *So Well Remembered* (RKO
Pictures, 1947). The cue sheet, prepared by the sound editor after the composer's preliminary screening of the film, succinctly describes all visual and
sound events that may be relevant for composing the music. Measurements
at right are in seconds. *Courtesy of RKO Pictures, Inc.*

Original draft of Hanns Eisler's music for the sequence in *So Well Remembered*
described on the cue sheet. Change of tone color at measure 32—from short
notes in upper strings to more sustained notes played in octaves in lower
strings—starts at the 13-second mark and introduces the montage of shots of
mothers and children. Note Eisler's economy of instrumentation and of musical
material: extremely spare harmony, and play of duple and triple rhythms. Note
also Eisler's effort toward "non-standardized" dynamics and precision: triple-
forte and even quadruple-forte indications, and the note at the end to RKO
Music Director Constantin Bakaleinikoff. *Courtesy of RKO Pictures, Inc.*

No. 81

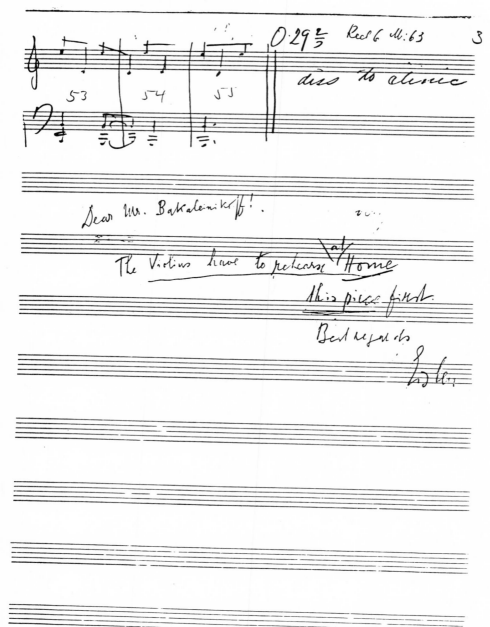

The motion pictures are made to measure for their customers, planned according to their real or supposed needs, and reproduce these needs. But at the same time the products that are most widespread, and therefore closest to the public, are objectively more remote from the public, as regards the methods by which they are produced and the interests they represent. Motion-picture production is entirely divorced from that living contact with the audience, which is still operative in every stage performance; the alleged will of the public is manifested only indirectly, through the box-office receipts, that is to say, in a completely reified form. [10]

A contradiction inheres in the cinema: between the remoteness of its mass production, and the immediate, "here and now" quality if its images. The studio further plans a film not for the meaning of its component details in the film's formal whole, but for their immediate audience effects. Cultural values, not the filmic form, mediate textual details. It is presumed that audiences desire formulas and tried-and-proven effects: details that bear instant, automatic signification and which may be "read," and thus consumed, with ease and passivity.

The Hollywood film is accordingly shot through with the "pretense to immediacy"—a strategy designed to prevent the spectator from understanding the extent of his/her alienated condition. The pretense to immediacy—textual strategies for involving the spectator, grasping him/her in a hold of imaginary identification—obscures the contradictions inherent in film (its administrative remoteness, its technological nature).

Given this perspective, it is clear why Eisler and Adorno launch an all-out attack on standard film music, which epitomizes the ideological efficacy of the culture industry and a degenerated aesthetics. First, such music aims directly at "suturing" (immediacy) effects, along with other standard devices such as the close-up, the matching of sound and image, and continuity editing. Music aids and abets the standard film's illusion of reality, of immediate life—the illusion that we are not mechanized. It

brings the picture close to the public, just as the picture brings itself close to it by means of the close-up. It attempts to interpose a human coating between the reeled-off pictures and the spectators. [p. 59]

Eisler would wish for a film-musical practice that would lay bare the image's mediated nature; instead, the classical film masks it.

Second, especially in subordinating itself to a (narrative) textual system outside itself, standard film music offers the very opposite of the authors' aesthetic standard of generating musical meaning. It has no autonomy, no form that determines the function of its component details. Instead, it is "advertising" for the very film it appears in.[11] Clichés of fragmented cultural signification "program" the audience, and rely on conditioned reflexes and automatic responses; this constitutes an extreme case of the degradation of musical listening Adorno identified in modern popular music in general.[12] Adorno and Eisler find in standard film music, calculated and planned for effects of immediacy, a prime example of the culture industry's objectification of subjectivity and rationalization of the irrational.

The standard practices the authors attack are precisely those that arise from principles of "classical" scoring.

1. *The leitmotif,* whose function in film "has been reduced to the level of a musical lackey, who announces his master with an important air even though the eminent personage is clearly recognizable to everyone" [p. 6].

2. *Melody and euphony,* which bourgeois culture has designated as "natural," and whose "poetic" associations and melodic symmetry belie the objective technological and asymmetrical character of the film it accompanies.

3. *Unobtrusiveness,* based on "a vague notion that music should have a subordinate role in relation to the picture" [p. 9].

4. *Visual justification,* the common practice of rendering diegetic any music which is needed for mood and pacing (it is portrayed as coming out of a radio, for example; this "justifies" its usage).

5. *Illustration,* the use of music to express or underline meanings already expressed in the images. Music either "directly imitating" screen events (mickey-mousing) or using instrumental and melodic clichés for moods, reinforces automatism in listening.

6. *Geography and history* (i.e., music for cueing the spectator to the narrative's setting): "The absurdity of such 'applied art' arrangements is glaring in contrast with the technique of the film, which is of necessity modern" [p. 15].

7. *Stock music*: accompanying film sequences with the Moonlight Sonata and the William Tell Overture robs such overworked pieces of any of their original meaning or *éclat*; they act as mere signposts to accompany stock dramatic events.

8. *Clichés*: like other details in a film ("typical situations, ever-recurring emotional crises, and standardized methods of arousing suspense"), these musical conventions are deplorable because of their false claim to uniqueness and authenticity.

9. *Standardized interpretation,* resulting in one-dimensionality of dynamics on one hand and illusory individualization of performance on the other. (Eisler and Adorno use the term "pseudo-individualization" much as Walter

Benjamin might speak of "false aura": by this they mean endowing a work with signs of authenticity, uniqueness, and spontaneity. "Pseudo-individu-alization is what fools us about predigestion.")[13]

Further, the authors comment astutely on the way the classical film uses music to signify emotion. Hearing, they maintain,

> has not adapted itself to the bourgeois rational . . . order as readily as the eye, which has become accustomed to conceiving reality as made up of separate things, commodities, objects that can be modified by practical activity. Or-dinary listening, as compared to seeing, is 'archaic'; it has not kept pace with technological progress. . . . [A]coustical perception preserves comparably more traits of long bygone, pre-individualistic collectivities than optical per-ception. . . . This direct relationship to a collectivity, intrinsic in the phe-nomenon itself, is probably connected with the sensations of spatial depth, inclusiveness, and absorption of individuality, which are common to all music. But this very ingredient of collectivity, because of its essentially amorphous nature, leads itself to deliberate misuse for ideological purposes. [pp. 20–21]

The swell of emotion music can provoke, the epic dimension it can con-tribute to the experience of the narrative event, is put to calculated use in Hollywood. This use masks a contradiction: between music's "direct rela-tionship to a collectivity," and its rationalized, technified deployment in commercial film. Music's lyrical and emotional basis "can be made to serve regression 'psychotechnically' . . . as it deceives its listeners in regard to the reality of everyday existence" [p. 22].

As we have seen, the classical film score encourages identification: emo-tional proximity through the use of culturally familiar musical language and through a matching, an identity of sound and image which masks contra-dictions and posits a wholeness with which to identify unproblematically as subject. It is this situation that Adorno and Eisler criticize most insistently. Elsewhere Adorno puts such music in its place:

> Identification with it compensates for the universal defeat that is the law of each individual life. Just as poor old women shed tears at a wedding of strangers, the consumed music is the eternal strangers' wedding for all.[14]

Composing for the Films is a remarkable work on the ideological situation of standard film music, written a quarter century in advance of mainstream film theory's parallel concerns with the cinematic apparatus. Its weaknesses, although minor, need to be addressed.

The first problem arises from an inconsistency between Eisler's and Ador-no's positions. Briefly stated, Adorno advocates making of the artwork a *mediated totality*: Schoenberg's music, for example, refuses all identification (except in a negative sense) with cultural signification outside it; the form itself mediates all the elements, constructs its meaning. The artwork must be autonomous. Film music, on the other hand, is essentially Muzak, background music; rather than directing attention to its formal logic, it is fragmented, and therefore degraded, commodified. Adorno's bitter nostalgia for an edenic state of music—of which film music is the antithesis—is a highly problematic point of departure.

The strength of the argument resides in stressing that film music encourages *identification*, on a level that has little to do with musical aesthetics and meaning (pure musical codes); it leads to identification with a "false" subjectivity that denies individual freedom. Eisler/Adorno seem little concerned with the historical development of such functional music; it is unclear what would be their thesis regarding incidental music for earlier forms of drama, for example.

Second, when the book discusses a progressive film music practice, the authors' insistence that there can be no formulas leaves the reader perplexed regarding what this practice can be, aside from cliché-free. Adorno's theoretical argument is lost, in favor of a pragmatic approach clearly arising from Eisler's experience. Ironically at times the authors suggest precisely what Hollywood composers suggest: compose in short and flexible phrases to accommodate to the images, and so forth.

Finally, and most crucially, *Composing for the Films* leaves one with the impression that film music can have an emancipatory effect on the narrative film in which it is set, and that this is the reason for its opening critique. Note that Eisler as film composer chose his collaborators well: documentarists on the left, and intellectuals such as Odets, Renoir, Lang, and Sirk. But what could Eisler have done in scoring *Mildred Pierce*? *Mildred Pierce* is a whole textual *system*, signifying through the conjuncture of psychic, narrative, cinematic, and capitalistic economies mentioned at the outset of the preceding chapter. An Eisler score, designed to unmask contradictions throughout *Mildred Pierce*, would surely just sound wrong to an audience thoroughly steeped in—and paying for—identification of the kind Adorno and Eisler rail against. "Progressive" music alone will not raise consciousness in the classical Hollywood framework of expectations.

Part II

Three
Analyses

CHAPTER VI

Vigo/Jaubert:
Zéro de conduite
and Problems
of Methodology

The Film

Zéro de conduite is the first of two collaborations by Jean Vigo and composer Maurice Jaubert. Among his thirty-eight film scores, Jaubert also composed for the Prévert brothers (*L'Affaire est dans le sac*), Clair (*Quatorze juillet, Le Dernier milliardaire*), and Carné (*Drôle de drame, Quai des brumes, Hôtel du nord, Le Jour se lève*). However, his partnership with Vigo strikes a particularly rare resonance, and according to P. E. Salles Gomes, *Zéro de conduite* established Jaubert as a film composer. Jaubert's critical concerns regarding narrative and expressive possibilities of film music, which he voiced during the thirties, may account for some of the distinctive qualities that postwar critics have seen in *Zéro de conduite*.[1] Here I propose first to examine his principles at work in the film, and second, to consider some methodological problems involved in the analysis of film music in general.

Zéro de conduite was arguably the most autobiographical film of the three that Vigo made before his untimely death in 1934. Its scenes loom out with the concreteness, as well as the distortion, of memories from childhood. Salles Gomes documents Vigo's modeling of the scenario on remembrances of his past. The film's curious discontinuity (due partly to severe time and budget restraints during shooting, but also an integral component of its "quasi-nihilistic" style)[2] contributes to its evocation of a nostalgia for what we've never experienced.

Thematically speaking, the school in the film acts as a social microcosm, a locus for a revolution of the imagination. What is "childlike" does battle with "adult" values; the schoolboys' seemingly natural collectivity takes action in the face of the staff's comically rigid hierarchy. While the administrators form a calcified system, an illogical, indeed caricatured, application of meaningless values (meting out zeros for conduct and decreeing Sunday confinements), the children, through intuitive logic, and bolstered by the film's narrative point of view on their side, address the problem of how to live with such a system. The film sets up a dialectic of orders: neat disciplined lines imposed by the school—a static order—versus the boys' unruliness and collective spontaneity, which at least temporarily spawn an order stronger than the imposed one.

Vigo's film does not try to account for everything in "good narrative" fashion. (Why does Gas-Snout patrol the lavatories on Alumni Day?) The curious effect of the elliptical segmenting—Caussat and Colin walk alongside a fence and ceremoniously bow to each other, Caussat stays on Sunday with a bourgeois family whose putative father is lodged behind a newspaper and whose daughter hangs a goldfish bowl precariously from a wire traversing the salon—is not to distance or to puzzle, but rather to make one feel privileged to participate in them, as if in flashes of memory. In brief enigmatic scenes like these, Vigo's reputation as a surrealist is justified. The dreamlike quality arises from a tension between the real and the imagined, the present and the past, the communicable and the incommunicable.[3]

Zéro de conduite exemplifies how stylistic choices are also moral and aesthetic decisions. One notes evidence of Vigo's debt to earlier filmmakers of the imagination in subtle parallels to films of Méliès (Caussat's balloon disappearing act in the classroom), Cohl (Huguet's cartoon coming to life), and Clair (madcap chases in the streets), as well as Chaplin (Huguet imitates Chaplin; children watch him while his back is turned and flee when he faces them . . . *Easy Street*) and Linder. But *Zéro* goes beyond Clair or Méliès in straining at the bounds of narrative logic and visual classicism. In scenes of joyous freedom, such as the classroom under Huguet's non-rule, bodies literally hang from the rafters; pairs of legs dangle into the frame from above; other characters are only partially included in the composition. It is as if the narrator were saying "merde" to the (anal-retentive) regularity of the rectangular film screen. The viewer gets pleasure not only from witnessing the students' freedom of movement, but also from violations of the classical rules of visual order. (This particular scene moves from freedom to imprisonment, however, for as Dry-Fart takes over the class we fade out on an image of straight rows of desks and now-unnatural silence punctuated only by the proctor's repetition of the word "No". . .)

At issue is a set of values and the way the film portrays them. Liberty, anarchy, and repression find their expression in a plot and in a style. Those who draw a direct line of descent from the political anarchist Almereyda— Jean Vigo's father—to the story of *Zéro de conduite* most staunchly assert that *Zéro's* unruliness (on all levels) is its message. The film's final sequence, the Alumni Day disturbance, certainly fuels the perspective that the film is anarchistic. Into the courtyard, where authority is depicted more cartoonlike than ever (the Prefect sits at a small pavilion flanked by dummies), garbage suddenly plummets down, hurled by the four young revolutionaries on the roof. The ceremonies' participants scatter in all directions. Where will the boys' revolution lead them? Certainly the children will not assume control of the school the next day. But the surprise bombardment is a complete success within the context of the film, and that is what counts.

On the other hand, a film professing *stylistic* anarchy would appear much more unglued than *Zéro.* Instead, this story proceeds in a number of brief, tailored segments—episodes that all focus around the freedom-repression polarity, and which most often end with the repressive forces of authority gaining the upper hand. Only when the boys organize does the tide change: Tabard's "merde" to the principal sets in motion the series of scenes that lead to the students' Alumni Day "triumph." Exteriors and interiors take on positive and negative values respectively through their placement in the story, as do movement and stasis. The promenade sequence, alternating between shots of the group's joyous rambling and the principal's stifling office, between their noisy fun and his officious verbosity, demonstrates how Vigo's structuring and narrating principles coincide. The "unglued" realm of the imagination does take over completely in the film's final moments: while in the third-to-last shot the four boys crawl atop the school roof, the final image shows them climbing up toward the summit as if somehow they had not arrived there yet. Although the film ends on a spatially illogical note, the episodic patterning that builds up to this ending involving the notion of visual disorganization as one *pole in a stylistic system* has narratively and stylistically prepared it as the logical result. Music plays a central role in the process.

Method

Although writers on film music frequently allude to specific parts of scores, exhaustive analyses of an entire score and its narrative functioning have been rare. *Zéro's* brevity renders it a good object for close scrutiny: barely sixteen minutes of music are included in its forty-five minutes. In the course of this analysis, attention will be paid to rhythm, form, and representation in both film and music. *Zéro de conduite* consciously deploys music not only in terms of its emotive and rhythmic properties, but also exploits music as a *physical sound phenomenon*, and as a *recorded* soundtrack element.

The score exploits, explores, breaks conventions of the music-film relationship: Jaubert, who among early sound film composers was perhaps most conscious of the breadth of music's narrative possibilities in film, devoted careful attention to these issues in his articles and lectures during the thirties. To what extent did his critical writing agree with his film-music practice?

Here we must open a parenthesis: how is it possible to describe accurately the film-music practice? What is relevant to the description of a scene and its music—short of another screening/audition of the film itself? Can a standard methodology develop, and if so, how should it appear on paper? We are confronted with problems of notation, priorities, principles of pertinence. Writing about the ways in which film music, coinciding with dialogue and images, functions in the story film, means not merely copying down the composer's printed score: for the score by itself tells us at best about the instantaneous music-shot relationships, and virtually nothing about music's effects in the narration. The prevailing scarcity of close, accurate analyses of narrative film music results from this dilemma of notation.[4]

Along this line, Raymond Bellour pinpointed the exasperating nature of films in general as "unattainable texts": the filmic text is unattainable because it is an unquotable text.[5] In literature, "nothing is more immediate, simpler than to quote a word, a phrase, a few lines, a sentence, a page. Omit the quotation marks that signal it and the quotation is invisible" [p.20]. "The written text is the only one that can be quoted unimpededly and unreservedly"[p. 21].

Similarly, an independent musical work is quotable, says Bellour, since the score is codified into a standard written notation—although with the important difference that

> the musical text is divided, since the score is not the performance. But sound cannot be quoted. It cannot be described or evoked. In this the musical text is irreducible to the text, even if it is metaphorically, and in reality thanks to the plurality of its operations, just as textual as the literary text. [p. 22]

The sound film

> conjoins five matters of expression, as Christian Metz has shown: phonetic sound, written titles, musical sound, noises, the moving photographic image.

> The first two of these pose no apparent problems for quotation . . . [although dialogue] undergoes a certain reduction as soon as it is quoted: it loses intensities, timbres, pitches, everything that constitutes the profound solidity of the voice. The same is true of noises. . . . what might be called motivated noise, which can always be evoked more or less since it indicates the real, should always be distinguished from arbitrary noise, which can go so far as to serve as a score, then escaping all translatability since it is not even codified as the musical score is. . . . noise constitutes a greater obstacle to the textuality of the film the more it is one of the major instruments of its textual materiality. Musical sound obviously takes this divergence between text and text to the extreme: given the specifications implied by the phenomenon of combination which makes film music not a work in itself but an internal dimension of the work, we have here again the problems posed in this respect by musical works (code vs. performance). [pp. 23–24]

Bellour devotes greatest attention to the dilemma of quoting the moving photographic image (the fifth of Metz's "matters of expression"), which few would dispute is the definitive textual component of cinema. If one desired to quote the film's image-track as faithfully as one can quote literature, one would be obliged to show the film itself. Bellour concludes that the only solution can be found in the compromise of using stills: although

> The frozen frame and the still that reproduces it are simulacra. . . . Obviously the language of the analysis is responsible for the rest. It attempts to link together the multiplicity of textual operations between the simulacra of the frozen images like any other analysis. [p. 25]

And finally, since film analysis does not deal purely with separate textual images but must also contend with "that absolutely illusory thing known as its story,"

> Thus it constantly mimics, evokes, describes; in a kind of principled despair it can but frantically try to compete with the object it is attempting to understand. [p. 26]

I have quoted extensively from Bellour's essay to emphasize the problematic situation of even the relatively well-established field of close film analysis. Few such methodological considerations have even entered the picture in the field of film music, although the very disorganization of its critical literature has at times yielded curiously excellent results. If it is only since the seventies that the methodical use of stills became customary in film analysis, as early as 1938 Eisenstein described a sequence from *Alexander Nevsky* in stills juxtaposed to the musical score to demonstrate the exact audiovisual correspondence that he and Prokofiev supposedly

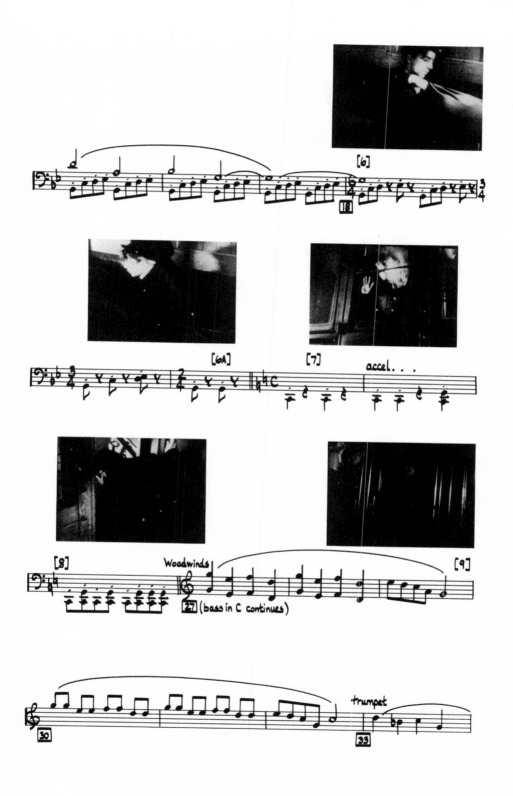

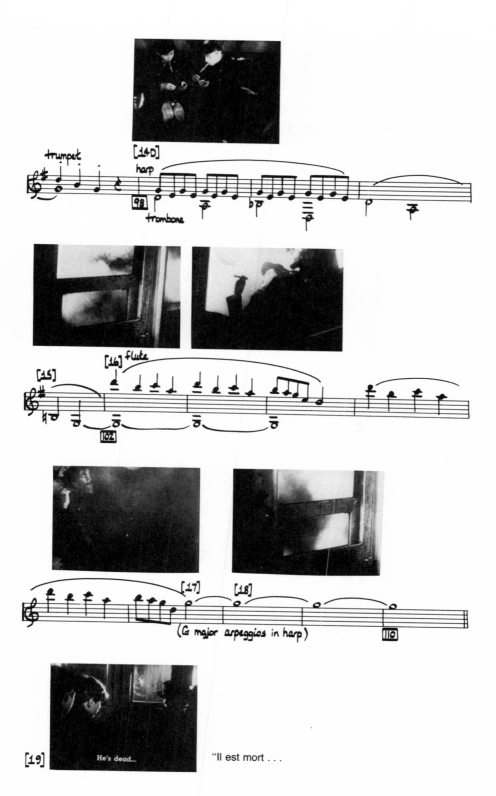

[Rhythms noted
from shots 21–38
are diegetic
sounds of trains.]

[20] trombone (G)

ff

. . . foutons le camp!"

[21]

[22]

[23]

[24]

Caussat:
"Violà Monsieur Pète-sec.
On ne rigolera encore pas
cette année."

[25]

Caussat & Bruel:
"Colin . . [?] Vieux Colin . .
. . [?] avec un mort!"   [26]

[27]

Caussat:
". .Eh! Fiche-nous la paix!"

[28]

Parrain:
"Dis-donc, Caussat,
finies les vacances."

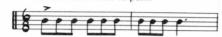

[29]

Parrain:
"Par ici, vous. Allons!"

[29 A]

(Jump cut)

[30]

Mme Tabart:
"Pardon, monsieur. René . .
René Tabart ne rentrera que
demain matin. Il a le
coeur gros ce soir."

Caussat:
"Un mort. . . .

[31]

. . . je te dis, un mort.
La preuve! . ."

[32] There's your co...

Colin:
"La preuve,
le v'là là-bas."

⪜ (train whistle)

[33] I'm Huguet...

Huguet: "Je suis le nouveau
surveillant . . .

[34]

[35]

. . . le surveillant
Huguet."

[36]

> train whistle, as
⪜ H. puts on his hat

[37]

[38]

Accel . . . .

𝆑   𝆏𝆏

achieved. In 1957 Roger Manvell and John Huntley used Eisenstein's basic format to cite segments of *Henry V, Louisiana Story, Julius Caesar,* and *Odd Man Out;*[6] regrettably, the authors did not follow up their transcriptions with any analysis. As for Eisenstein, his work has stood alone as a vigorous and thorough—if somewhat delirious—combination of transcription and analysis.[7]

The other approach, used by film composers, concentrates on transcribing the complete musical score itself: additional cues for images, actions, and lines of dialogue briefly evoke the music's position in the given scene. Needless to say, the composer and his/her notation system are weighted heavily toward the music at the expense of minimizing the visual importance of the moving compositions on the screen as well as the score's moment-by-moment relationship with the story.

Working with this mixed heritage of film music notation, I have set forth the inaugural sequence of *Zéro de conduite,* concentrating on the music's functioning with relation to the diegesis ("that absolutely illusory thing"). I have chosen to consider the sequence from the perspective of the musical rhythm that governs the soundtrack and often the images themselves. I have not deemed it essential to write out the entire score, but rather to indicate rhythm, principal melodies and harmonies, and instrumentation. The shot lengths are not described in absolute time (i.e., in seconds) but in terms of their co-incidence with the music. The "textual simulacrum" will then serve as a point of reference for analysis.

Structure

The musical organization of the "ragged" little sequence[8] closely follows its narrative organization. The story opens, we will recall, as the schoolboy Caussat and the adult Huguet wordlessly share a compartment on the moving train (shots 1–7, meas. 1–20). The train slows to a stop—first division—and schoolmate Bruel clambers on. The ride continues, joyously now, as Caussat and Bruel play tricks with fingers, trumpets, feathers, balls, balloons, and cigars. As the train screeches to a halt, the sleeping Huguet thuds to the floor, and the boys half-seriously mistake him for a corpse. Second train stop, second division. The boys join their colleagues on the station platform. Parrain (Dry-Fart), Colin, Tabard and his mother, and the decidedly undead schoolteacher Huguet are presented. Finally, after everyone has filed out of the station, a fade-out ends the sequence as a fade-in began it.

So the first of these three sections consists of an exposition: vacation finished, the train in motion. The music that accompanies this rather mournful collection of shots plays in G minor; it is dominated by a bassoon playing the principal four-note motif, and the low strings playing a "trainlike" rhythmic ostinato in the bass (see example, Part I). The music then decelerates with the train; as a matter of fact, there is no way for the viewer to know that the train is slowing down *except* for the musical decelerando on the soundtrack.

Part Two, the leg of the voyage with Bruel, begins in the major subdominant of the original G minor (C major); woodwinds play the theme in double-time (see example, Part II).

I have labeled melodic elements *a* and *b* to indicate how *b*, the train-rhythm accompaniment for Part One, actually incorporates itself into the melody for Part Two: not in its original form, but with one passing-tone added, and in melodic inversion (I have re-inverted it, and placed it in the bass clef, as "*" so that the musically untrained reader may compare it to *b* of Part One). It may be noted also that the exact intervals among the four melodic components of *a* have not been retained (except for the semitone between the second and third notes), but the shape of the melody is unmistakable.[9] Jaubert's economical choice and manipulation of motifs results in continuity in score and in filmed segment. One may consider Part Two the real development section of the sequence, in several capacities. It is the longest and most eventful of the three parts, and is distinct from its neighboring sections by virtue of its joyful mood. Narratively, it gives a first view of the marvels that seem to occur whenever the schoolboys are left to interact freely with one another. In addition it introduces visual thematic material that will crop up throughout the film giving it further formal cohesiveness. The scene presents visual motifs as playthings: the body, various balls, feathers, a trumpet, smoke.[10] Musically, this is a section of development and recapitulation: moving from C major and voyaging harmonically through a tonal menagerie (A^b, D^b, C, E, and G major), the four-note melody (*a*) is performed by a zoo of solo instruments, undergoes melodic variations, and comes to rest on an elephantine trombone rendition in G minor—which magically resolves to G major as the boys puff contentedly and the train pulls into the station.

At this juncture, the train's arrival, the third segment begins. Huguet slides to the compartment floor, and one of the boys whispers loudly, "He's dead!"—the first nonmusical sound in the film. The instrumental music ends with an onomatopoetic flourish and thump in G major to underscore Huguet's fall and the ride's end.—"Let's beat it!" Beginning with shot 21, the "natural" sounds of the train station are heard, and thus between shots 19 and 21, tonal music has given way to dialogue and sound effects, the soundtrack elements that will finish out the sequence exclusively.

This does not mean that the "music" is over. For music is *rhythm*, and the soundtrack continues just as rhythmically as before. First the ambient steam-locomotive sounds are heard in a 3/4 rhythm (cf. shot 21) and then, beginning with shot 22, they form another rhythmic pattern with a steady repetition of eighth notes. The most elegant evidence that this section is planned musically is to be found in shots 26 and 27. Caussat and Bruel shout in resonant stage whispers to their pal Colin that they have just shared their train ride with a dead man (their words are unfortunately indistinguishable to my ears, and the dialogue in *L'Avant-scène du cinéma* is inaccurate at this point,[11] but what is all the more discernible for my lack of comprehension is the *rhythm* of their speech:

A

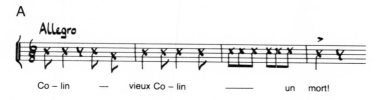

What follows, in perfectly continuous timing, is a battery of "natural" locomotive steam sounds as if in response to the rhythm of the boys' speech (example B: the several measures are reduced to their rhythmic and not their "realistic" or representational content).

B

[boys' voices]   [train sounds]

Furthermore, just as various solo orchestral instruments punctuate certain actions on the train ride, a "concrete" solo instrument now performs schoolteacher Huguet's "theme" on the platform. After Caussat says "The proof? There's your corpse," a nearby train whistle toots loudly on the soundtrack to punctuate Huguet's approach into the shot's foreground. The whistle happens to sound again exactly at the moment when Huguet, having presented himself to Dry-Fart, tips his hat. A ridiculous punctuation, the toot informs Huguet's character with a note of the fantastic and lighthearted, and from the outset it sets him apart from the other adults, redeeming him from the stifling musical silence that envelops his stuffier colleagues at the school.

The boys and their teachers walk off into the night to the offscreen accompaniment of a train accelerating and leaving the station, and the image fades to black. Again, this first fade-out in the film lends support to the idea that the film's beginning is organized into one continuous sequence from shots 1 through 38. The musical score's *tonality* changes after Part One (meas. 1–20)—from G minor to C major and related keys; its *instrumentation* changes after Part Two (meas. 21–110)—from orchestral instruments to organized noise. Thus the entire sequence unmistakably comprises a musical-poetic whole.[12] Jaubert had a pioneering concern with the porous nature of the wall separating music and natural sound, and with the unique possibilities that cinema offers for organizing sounds into music:

> Freed from all academic impedimenta (symphonic developments, orchestral "effects," etc.), music, thanks to the film, should reveal to us a new character. It has still to explore the whole territory which lies between its frontiers and those of natural sound. . . . Music must never forget that in the cinema its character of *sound phenomenon* outweighs its intellectual and even metaphysical aspects. . . .[13]

Instrumentation

The composer sarcastically reproaches his contemporaries for the conventions of instrumentation they perpetuated:

> Generally speaking, music is asked to provide commentary on the action. Is the scene tragic? A few accents on the horn or trombone will emphasize

the image's darkness. A sentimental scene? Give it a violin solo: that will, it is believed, render the hero's declaration of love more convincing.[14]

Zéro's score avoids the instrumental clichés that were so wholeheartedly adopted in Hollywood. Instead, each solo completes and gives unique definition to actions on the screen. In this perspective, Eisenstein spoke of Prokofiev's intuitive genius in scoring solos for *Alexander Nevsky*: "It seems to me that it's precisely from the tonality and timbre chosen for the image that the melodic and orchestral musical equivalent emerges."[15]

Equivalent—not illustration, commentary, or explanation. To understand this distinction in Jaubert's practice, turn to measures 45 to 48 in *Zéro*. The violin and oboe introduce a sprightly rhythmic three-note motif as one of the boys one-ups the other with a ball-and-spring toy. Perhaps an oboe alone would have done about as well here—but the violin brings in special qualities. The movement of the ball popping up from the spring mechanism is amplified by the bouncy, almost pizzicato notes from the resonant violin. Elsewhere, from measures 70 to 74 and 98 to 104, the trombone plays the four-note motif, corresponding to the images of Bruel's mammary-suggestive balloons, and the friends' sucking and smoking cigars. The trombone, full and blowy, comically reinforces these physical aspects of the images it accompanies. In every case throughout *Zéro*'s score the *physical* qualities of the solo instrument—register, timbre, articulation—correspond in some way to the physical and dynamic content of the images. (The train ride sequence also has "motivated solos," a different use of solo instruments: for example, the trumpet that plays on the soundtrack as Caussat plays his toy trumpet. Here, the music is clearly aping *representational* functions the way musical accompaniments did for silent films.)

Just as remarkable as Jaubert's efficiency with melodic motifs and solo instruments is the tonal variety he achieves with such a small ensemble. According to his biographer, François Porcile, the orchestra for *Zéro* consisted of only eleven instruments: four woodwinds, percussion, trumpet, trombone, harp, piano, violin, and violoncello, and additional singing in three scenes. The score is based on extreme orchestral economy and imaginative choice of solo instruments.

Rhythm

For Jaubert, the function of film music

is not to be *expressive* by adding its sentiments to those of the characters or of the director, but to be *decorative* by uniting its own rhythmical pattern with the visual pattern woven for us on the screen.

That is why I believe it to be essential for film music to evolve a style of its own. If it merely brings lazily to the screen its traditional interest in composition and expression, then instead of entering as a partner into the world of images, it will set up alongside a separate world of sound obeying its own laws. Even if this autonomous sound-structure reveals all the marks of genius, it will never have any point of contact with the visual world which it ought, nevertheless, to serve. It will live its life, sufficient unto itself.

Let film music, then, free itself from all these subjective elements; let it also, like the image, become realistic; let it,—using means strictly musical and not dramatic—support the plastic substance of the image with an *impersonal* texture of sound, accomplishing this through a command of that mysterious alchemy of relationships which belongs to the essence of the film composer's trade. Let it, finally, make physically perceptible to us the inner rhythm of the image, without struggling to provide a translation of its content, whether this be emotional, dramatic, or poetic.[16]

From this eloquent statement of film music's objective functions let us extract Jaubert's comments on rhythm. Music ought to "make physically perceptible . . . the inner rhythm of the image." Exactly what is meant by the inner rhythm of an image? Does Jaubert invite the reader onto Eisensteinian grounds again, suggesting an equivalence between spatial compositions and temporal ones? Is he referring to movements within a shot, or to the rhythms of editing itself? or to the "subjective tempo" of an image in its narrative context? Jaubert might agree with all three of these attempts to corner him—although, I suspect, he would not be wholly pleased. Let us examine some of these aspects of rhythm in *Zéro's* train sequence.

First, the bass ostinato: its rhythm *is* the train's rhythm, its variable pace reflecting, really denoting, the speed of the train. Music is functioning as noise (and in doing so invites us to perceive everyday sounds as permeated with musical rhythm). Here the rhythm acts as a representational element: since there is no diegetic sound at all until shot 19—we are in effect watching a "silent film"—the music takes over the iconic duties of the soundtrack in the meanwhile. Vigo evidently considered establishing shots prosaic, for there is none at the beginning of the scene (the only shot defining the space of the compartment is the fifth in the sequence). Merely the door-window, smoke outside, and the rhythmic bass on the soundtrack provide the narrative information.

Between measures 17 and 20 we (musically) hear the train slow down to a halt. After Bruel has climbed on, the rhythm picks up again (meas. 21 to 24) in the 'cello, indicating that the train is once more on the move. This rhythm is much faster than the original bass rhythm. Aside from its loosely representational role, the rhythmic bass has an emotive function; it serves to indicate a rise, a quickening, in spirit with the entry of Caussat's comrade. *Allegro* becomes equivalent to *allégresse*, pointing also to a politics of tempo (auditory) and motion (visual) that pervades *Zéro*. The schoolmasters, seemingly impervious to motion, are usually seen standing, ordering, sitting, sleeping. The boys are happiest running, playing, and in kinetic states with respect to the film frame as well; and sprightly music is very often present to insist on the rhythms of their movements.

Editing to music. If *Zéro*'s style capitalizes on the poetic interrelationships "found" between musical rhythm and natural rhythm, we might expect Vigo to edit shots according to the same rhythmic patterns as well. Indeed, he does: it is clear from the transcription of the sequence on the preceding pages that musical rhythm is a primary principle according to which the sequence is constructed. Following are examples of cuts to music.

1. The beginning of shot 2 coincides exactly with the beginning of the repetition of the four-note G minor motif in the bassoon.

2. The theme's recapitulatory statement, beginning in meas. 13, begins at the same time as shot 5. In the images as well as in the music, several disparate introductory materials have been presented, and the composition of shot 5 recapitulates them in a manner similar to the way the music recapitulates its own thematic material.

3. Shot 16, the low angle shot of the boys and their cigars, begins in precise conjunction with a final statement of the motif, this time in G major by the flute.

4. Other shots are cut so as to begin on a musical downbeat: examples are shot 4 (meas. 9), shot 6 (meas. 18), shot 10 (meas. 35), shot 11 (meas. 39), shot 15 (meas. 101), and shot 16 (meas. 102). Additionally, other shots that are edited to logical rhythmic beats within a measure, usually the third beat, are shots 1, 3, 8, 12, 13, 14, and 17.

Further, *movements within a shot* often are timed to match the rhythm on the soundtrack. Several of these image-music orchestrations occur during shots 12 and 14, the lengthy two-shots of the friends as they play "épater le copain" with their successive amusements. For instance, measure 45 inaugurates the three-note motif in A♭ major, as Bruel gets out his ball toy. Measure 58 seemingly motivates Bruel to play the notes on the trumpet that Caussat is blowing. With a transition in the score from C major into E major at the beginning of measure 64, Bruel takes a balloon out of his coat pocket.

Caussat feels Bruel's right balloon in time with measure 66, and the left balloon to the rhythm of measure 67, and so on.

In fact, it is in this extraordinary concern on Vigo's/Jaubert's part to match auditory with visual rhythm that we may find a partial explanation for two of the awkward jump cuts in the sequence. Notice the timing of the jump cut that occurs near the end of shot 12, when Caussat removes the mouthpiece from his toy trumpet before he plays it through his nose. Caussat's original playing lines up well with meas. 56ff, and the match continues acceptably through Bruel's playing (meas. 58, 59). In order that the close-up of the "nose-trumpet" should not end up out of synch with the music's rhythm, Vigo seems to have deemed it necessary to cut a few frames out of shot 12's final moments when Caussat removes the mouthpiece. If this was indeed the reason for that jump cut, we can see to what unorthodox lengths Vigo would go to preserve the audiovisual integrity of the rhythm behind this sequence.

The transcription and discussion of the music in this first sequence brings to light several important aspects of Vigo's and Jaubert's approach to film and film music. We have noted Jaubert's economy of composition and instrumentation achieving a remarkable variety of narrative effects. We have cited Jaubert's concern with music as physical sound, and consequently have seen that *Zéro*'s score assumes representational functions, and conversely that sound effects assume musical functions. We have uncovered some formal relationships between soundtrack and image-track: the musical demarcations and subdivisions of the diegetic action, correlations between musical phrases and actions on the screen, and so on. Above all, it becomes evident how important rhythm is in the poetic unfolding of the sequence—important enough to influence strongly the sequence's actual editing and important enough to necessitate discontinuity cutting. What should be quite clear at this point is the close interdependence of music and images. It may surprise the reader that Jaubert wrote in 1936 that "music must remain the servant of the image." But let us recall that there are dumb, slavish servants and there are indispensable, imaginative ones, like Molière's Dorine and Renoir's Marceau.

Filmed Riot, Musical Organization

An analysis of *Zéro*'s music would not be sufficient which neglected to consider the sequence of the dormitory revolt near the end of the story. Two additional film-music factors demand attention here: musical themes and electronic recording.

First, to understand the treatment of musical themes, let us list some of the recurrent melodic figures. Two principal motifs run through the train music (see p. 128): the ascending eighth-note figure in the bass, which we labeled *b* (subsequently transformed but retaining its intervallic integrity), and the slower, four-note figure, *a*, which moves a skip down, a step up, and another skip down. Another of the film's repeated melodies is the boys' song (*A*) over the beginning credits, diegetically sung later as their marching song during their outing in the village.

A

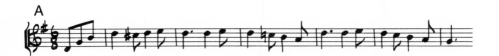

Solo snare drums also briefly intrude on two occasions: when Dry-Fart jumps out to awaken his sleepy students in the morning, and when Huguet herds them from the courtyard into the classroom. Aside from this the only music remaining (not repeated in the score) is the ensemble music accompanying the strollers' increasingly wild pursuit of a woman they spot on the street. For reasons which will become clear, we shall note here two closely related motifs from that music:

B

C

B accompanies the boys' chase after Huguet, and, soon after, the entire group is chasing the elusive gentlewoman; *C*, a demure version of the latter half of *B*, plays while Huguet and the boys first tip their hats respectfully to the fashionable lady.

The nondiegetic music on the soundtrack during the nocturnal revolt includes bits and pieces of all the motifs heard previously on the soundtrack. I shall not reproduce the score for the revolt—an unnecessarily laborious undertaking for both writer and reader—but shall merely note down some motifs from the music, and trace their origins.

As the boys begin their "revolution," running atop the beds, screaming, and generally disheveling everything within their enthusiastic reach, the music begins militantly in the piano's lower register (*D*).

The figure is reminiscent of other motifs heard in previous contexts: (1) the very opening of the score, the "train motif" in the 'cello, also consisting of eighth notes played staccato, also in a minor key. The motifs differ in instrumentation, and the melodic direction is inverted (as it was, for that matter, in Part Two of the train sequence). (2) the latter half of the boys' marching song contains the same descending melodic figure, only in triple rhythm (*E*).

(3) the lady on the street is introduced to a descending melody (*F*),

and as I have just pointed out, the cousin of this same figure is found in the chase music for the promenade sequence as well.

A comparison of all these motifs to the C minor motif launching the dormitory riot (see *G*) shows that while each motif has a distinct musical identity, each also bears a fundamental relationship of similarity to the C-minor figure.

Likewise, we can find a family tree for virtually every other motif in this crowded selection of riot music. *H* is another example.

Each of the motifs in the riot sequence serves as a *combinatoire* of anterior musical material. But only in a generalized sense do they convey thematic significations associated with the narrative. In other words, the C minor figure does not make the listener consciously recall the train ride, the village outing, and the pursued lady: we would better make these connections if the music associated with them consisted of one stable, consistent motif. Here it is more a question of musical resemblances too subtle and evanescent

to generate denotation the way, say, Ford's Indian drum motif does in *Stage-coach*. The motivic *combinatoire* behaves less specifically, more "poetically"; in evoking similar music it has the effect of summing up previous musical material: mirror-fragments from the boys' lives are picked up, transformed, and placed in an apparently chaotic piece that plays while they riot.

This is music whose tonality, harmony, rhythm, continuity in general, keep threatening to disintegrate completely—again, an apt mirror of the frenetic activity on the screen. Suddenly the music leaps to an E major chord and stops dead, as on the screen Gas-Snout opens the dormitory door, pokes his nose in, and hastily retreats. A "controlled breakdown," musically speak-

ing; followed by silence, and then the famous backwards music to the boys'
slow-motion procession among the pillowfeathers.

Electronic Recording

> . . . Let us recollect that [the new film music] will be *recorded*. Once re-
> corded, the music . . . will stand equally to benefit from all the various ma-
> nipulations which the sound-track is able to undergo. It is well known that
> the sound-track receives its impressions from the vibrations of light caused
> by the vibrating diaphragm of the microphone, itself set in motion by the
> sound-vibrations of the orchestra. Indeed, one can say that recording consists
> in the *photographing* of sound. The director, with this photograph at his
> command, is in a position to treat sounds just as he treats images: the technique
> of mixes and cuts is just the same. Indeed, the device of re-recording allows
> him to go further still in manipulating the sound-track. A certain sound or
> musical phrase, or several, can be first recorded separately and then trans-
> ferred together to a single strip of film.[17]

To produce the haunting music for the slow-motion sequence in the dormitory, Jaubert had to go through several steps involving the manipulation
of his photographed sounds. He used for the melody a phrase in the boys'
marching song

which a soprano's voice transforms into a slow, mellifluous anthem without
words. First he had to record the melody, then rerecord it backwards, and
transcribe the backward version for his musicians to execute it, an extremely
difficult task owing to its awkwardly unmusical character in that form. This
is its state in the finished soundtrack. The music thus underwent two electronic reversals, so that we may hear the melody make musical sense for-
wards. At the same time, we hear all the instrumental articulations
backwards—i.e., a note's resonance will be heard *before* its attack—producing the otherworldly effect that matches the visuals so well.

All that Vigo had requested for the scene was "une musique de dessins
animés," cartoon music.[18] Why, then, did Jaubert go through all these mu-
sico-electronic contortions for a score otherwise made as simply as possible?
The answer lies in the scene's importance in the film. Although the actual
revolution does not take place until the following day when the boys open

fire and pelt garbage on the Alumni Day ceremonies, the nighttime dormitory riot makes the stronger impression. The slow motion photography purifies the "jeunes diables," cinematically transforming them into angelic figures clothed in white and surrounded by white. The cross-shaped standards the boys bear are both a parody of religion (this partially explains why *Zéro* was censored for so many years)[19] and a celebration of its rituals. The marching-song theme renders this music the triumphant marching song of the imagination: its electronic treatment parallels in beauty the slow-motion reproduction of the images. (The real technical analogue to the slow-motion photography would of course be to play the music in slow motion too: but anyone who has ever heard a 45 rpm phonograph record at 33 rpm knows that this doesn't work).

From the riot scene's rejection of conventional modes of representation arises not chaos but a different order. And in fact, can we not say the same for the music? To record a piece backwards makes chaotic non-sense of it: but to return it to its normal state via a second transformation restores it to a new order, creatively different from the original. It seems that *Zéro de conduite* accomplishes this in formal, thematic, and ethical terms. A line from *Zéro's* original story outline reads: "If we must be prisoners, at least let us choose our prison, let's be happy and have fun there, so that we will want to stay there for the rest of our lives."[20]

CHAPTER VII

Music and Sound Space in Sous les toits de Paris

When sound invaded the movies like a controversial in-law, partisans of the "pure" cinema feared that its mundane reality would debase what had evolved as an artistically self-reliant medium. But the harsh, noisily domineering relative had come to stay, and most enterprising filmmakers added it to their arsenal of crowd-pleasing effects, "deafening the audience with a meaningless multitude of noises: striking matches, creaking hinges, gurgling bottles, chinking glasses."[1] Buster Keaton sang. Clara Bow nasally chattered. Renoir treated his public to the sound of a toilet flushing (a noise not to be heard this side of the Atlantic for another thirty years). In the midst of such contempt on one hand and intoxication on the other arose a brief period of extraordinarily vigorous experiment with sound. Between 1928 and 1933, Sternberg, Hawks, Lang, Ford, Dreyer, Lubitsch, Pabst, Mamoulian, Vigo, and many others explored the seemingly limitless possibilities of sound in fiction films, and established the lion's share of modern sound film language.

Between the few "pure" filmmakers, procrastinating in despair, and the newly invigorated sound directors, stands René Clair. His ambivalence in the face of the talking picture runs forcefully through his criticism of the twenties and thirties.[2] His hostility to sound arose from fears—and confirmation of them—first, that the enormous new production costs it entailed would heavily industrialize the business aspect of cinema, thereby jeopardizing directorial integrity; second, that the sound picture would succeed only in tying the camera down to its cumbersome recording equipment, necessitating both a static visual style and redundancy between sound and image; and third, that *talk* would threaten or even obliterate the primacy of the image.[3] Concerning the latter point, Clair had definite ideas before ever having worked with sound: "Imagine a film," he had said,

> in which the spoken text took the place of the written text of the intertitles, remained the servant of the image and made its appearance only as an 'auxiliary' means of expression; a brief, neutral text to which no efforts toward visual expression would be sacrificed. Only a little intelligence and good will would be needed for an agreement to be reached on this compromise.[4]

He made *Sous les toits de Paris* in a first attempt to deal with the "compromising" necessary to appease and integrate the loud newcomer to the cinematic family.

The film's plot does not have the classic proportion associated with Clair's silents, such as *Italian Straw Hat*, or his subsequent sound films, such as *Le Million* and *A nous la liberté*. Set in a movieland Parisian *quartier*, *Sous les toits* is about three men vying for the attentions of a pretty Rumanian named Pola who lives in the neighborhood. The first contender is Fred, a vaguely threatening thug with a street gang—a sympathetic character despite his occupation. The next chance goes to Albert, a street singer and the story's protagonist. An unexpected and undeserved prison sentence puts Albert out of the race, though, and his best friend, Louis, pairs up with Pola. Once freed from prison, Albert squares old accounts with Fred in a street fight, and then must ultimately accept Pola's happiness with his friend Louis. The film ends as Albert is singing once more in the streets of Paris.

Sous les toits de Paris arises from Clair's desire not to abandon the silently poetic ambience of his previous works, and not to wed soundtrack to image in prosaically redundant fashion. The first section of this chapter will investigate sound in relation to the images, to other elements of the soundtrack, and to the overall narration. The second section will review long-established criteria for discussing sound space, and suggest how a revision of critical vocabulary can be helpful in soundtrack analysis.

The Sound Hierarchy

Cinematic sound consists of spoken (or sung) words, music, and natural sound or sound effects. In this respect, the first things to strike the ear in *Sous les toits* are the predominance of music, the minimal role of speech, and an almost complete absence of natural sounds. These priorities on the soundtrack set *Sous les toits* off quite distinctly from other narrative films, which ordinarily favor dialogue and sound effects over music. One often hears no noise in *Sous les toits* to reinforce images of slamming doors, shattering glass, footsteps, and punches. Clair has stated, "It is unimportant to *hear* the sound of applause if you *see* hands clapping." Unimportant, we may remark, save for the (redundant) integrity of a "realistic" sound-image relation. Thus, where the film's visuals are not accompanied by the noises they would call for in real life, their unreality is accentuated.

A related phenomenon: to a large extent the soundtrack's three components are *mixed* in a nonrealistic way. Music often replaces natural sounds onomatopoetically; when, early in the film, Fred punches an underling, instead of the diegetic punching sound, we hear a piano thump a discordant pile of notes, mimicking the punch that would be potentially more upsetting. Music also tends to blot out entire conversations; for example, while Albert argues with a pickpocket friend in a doorway, we hear only energetic music and none of the argument. In fact, most of the film's dialogues are not dialogues at all on the soundtrack, but musical overlays, much in the style of American part-talkies of 1927–28.

If we note that Clair derives poetic effects from manipulating sound-image relationships, and from manipulating relationships among the three elements of the soundtrack, we note also that the film even edits together phrases of music itself in such a way as to produce nonrealistic effects. The most striking case of this comes early in the film. There is a sequence in which each person of the neighborhood, in the privacy of his or her own flat, is singing the theme song "Sous les toits de Paris"; the lives of all seem to intersect as they each sing a phrase or two of the song, which the film's editing connects with absolute musical continuity. How do we conceive of narrative time during these shots of characters singing their individual strains? We could understand the shots as not necessarily temporarily related—that the (invisible, omniscient) narrator has plucked the shots and tune fragments out of the evening air at different moments and has "edited in" his own musical flow. The second possibility is that this narrator is catching all the tune's phrases as they are magically sung in a real temporal continuum. In fact, the film produces this second effect.

Had the narrator simply assembled a group of silent shots of the neighborhood's residents, we may have interpreted time more openly, that is, we could have a sense of simultaneity of the shots, or loose narrative continuity. But since by nature tonal music is continuous in time with strict logical structures of rhythm, melody, and harmonic progression, it obliges us to read strict temporal contiguity into the shots that it accompanies. The narrator thus leads us to believe in an unbelievable event: people, unaware of one another—all of Paris, it would seem—are singing the same tune all exactly at the same time, in the same tempo, and in the same key. Clair's narrative voice, like that of many later musicals, does not hesitate to set up a tightly controlled realm, and takes for granted that no one will question its iron rule over cinematic time and space.

Once the film has established its auditory hierarchy—music first, speech second, natural sound third—it topples the whole structure in the dramatic street fight at night, when Albert defends his honor against Fred. The scene is all the more ominously exciting for its total lack of music: voices and natural sounds predominate. There is much indistinguishable noise, largely consisting of the shouts and mutterings of Fred's gang as they watch and encourage. In the context of a film of such clearly delineated visual and auditory contours, this scene virtually defines the very opposite of clarity. Nowhere else does the film allow stray voices; moreover, nowhere else does it accord such preeminence to one single noise—the train that (apparently) passes during the tensest moment of the struggle.

Why this reversal of the auditory hierarchy? Because of the scene's position of importance in the narrative. For once, the characteristically passive Albert is shifting into action, opting to fight it out with Fred. Although Albert has waited too long to win Pola, this transcendence of his natural passivity figures crucially in the film's overall dramatic structure.

So while the film may previously have set up various functional poetic tensions, this scene brings palpable dramatic tension to the fore. Serious threats and violence are not a comfortable element in the Clair universe. He portrays them here by placing as many obstacles as possible between the action and the viewer. In visual terms, this placement of obscuring factors is called masking. Here the spectator's view is hampered by every mask conceivable: darkness, fences, posts, obscuring camera angles, the backs of Fred's cronies as they watch, and finally the train's all-obliterating smoke. Most of the struggle between Albert and Fred is thus left to the imagination.

At the same time, what may be called auditory masking also works to obfuscate the fight. As soon as the gang's collective utterances begin to subvert the principal action on the soundtrack (dialogue between Fred and Albert, punches)—since these moments are too "serious" for music—the sound of an approaching train encroaches on the auditory field. Finally, the combination of the train's whistle in the auditory foreground and smoke in the visual foreground produces a virtually complete mask over the action at its point of greatest tension, the height of the fistfight. Note that the masking here *displaces* tension, it does not relieve it; it makes an audiovisual abstraction of the story events. Then, when the fight breaks up owing to the arrival of friend Louis on one hand and the police on the other, the usual auditory hierarchy resumes its status. Music plays as the police round up the enemy and lose track of Louis and Albert; music has brought relief, restored narrative order.

Though the film's masking tendency attains its strongest expression in this scene, its presence should not be ignored throughout the film, in both visual and auditory dimensions. Image-masking occurs as early as the fourth shot of the film. Umbrellas temporarily obscure two women on a sidewalk as well as Albert and Louis behind them—until the umbrellas collide and part to reveal everyone at once. In another scene, the angle at which the camera peeks into Pola's window hides Fred's identity behind a sloped ceiling. Some latticework in a cafe, and later an insignia on the door of a restaurant create similar effects. As for auditory masking, its most predominant form is in the "diegetic" musical overlays, which take up a large portion of the soundtrack as a whole. The masking tendency is a predominant stylistic feature in this first foray by Clair into cinematic sound space.

Auditory Space

I have mentioned the "auditory field" or auditory space because I wish to elucidate the differences between it and the visual field, and to reevaluate existing terminology for these subjects.

A resonant voice in this arena was Siegfried Kracauer. In the chapter on sound in his *Theory of Film*[5] he outlined three categories of distinctions relevant to the sound-image relationship. First, in the category of *synchronism* vs. *asynchronism*, he distinguishes between the visually identifiable source of a sound and the sound itself. A shot of a speaker, whose voice is heard simultaneously with his speech, demonstrates synchronism. A shot showing the listener while we hear the speaker on the soundtrack provides an example of asynchronism. Other examples of asynchronism involve further separation of image and soundtrack in time or space—an image in the present, for instance, coupled with a flashback or a commentator's voice on the soundtrack.

These terms lead to confusion as often as not. Does Clair's train/fight scene feature synchronous or asynchronous sound? In connection with what exactly would we speak of synchronism, the visually masked street fighters or the passing train offscreen? And what shall we do with moments elsewhere in the film when there is no sound, where people talk behind windows out of earshot? This definition seems to work solely in the context of the visual, saying little about sound space after all. How shall we name shots showing several sound sources? And even if we agree on some cases of synchronism and asynchronism, would not finer distinctions be helpful?

Kracauer presents the second pair of sound-image parameters as *parallelism* and *counterpoint*. If the word and image "carry different meanings," then they bear a contrapuntal relationship to each other. Imagine a speaker on the screen: "perhaps," says Kracauer, "a close-up of his face reveals him to be a hypocrite who does not really mean what he says."[6] If the synchronism-asynchronism pair already laid doubtful claims to precision, this second distinction really leads to arbitrary and subjective judgments. What if the character isn't sure of what he means to say? What if a sound or line of dialogue or music cue neither parallels nor contradicts the visuals? "Parallel" and "counterpoint" are terms that actually serve little use in looking at real movies. Rather, relations of complementarity, or mutual implication, are what usually result between soundtrack and image.

Kracauer's third category pertains more directly to auditory space itself. Sounds can be *actual*, that is, arising from an identifiable source within the narrative, or *commentative*, part of the soundtrack, not localizable in the story—such as verbal commentary or background music. I have been using the terms *diegetic* and *nondiegetic* in the same way.

Kracauer's attempts to objectify and classify sound-image relationships shed light on the issue, but writers on film have remained largely mystified as to the applicability of these distinctions, especially the first two of the three. More workable criteria would define both pertinent aspects of visual space and pertinent aspects of auditory space, and then examine how these specific "spaces" combine to form the perceived or inferred audiovisual space.

Let us for a moment reiterate definitions of onscreen and offscreen visual space. *Onscreen* refers to space perceived within the rectangular bounds of the image. *Offscreen* refers to inferred space, space that the diegesis gives us to believe exists, but which is not perceived because it lies outside the rectangular bounds of the image.

The pertinent factors for this definition of the visual field are that (a) offscreen space, by its very nature, is linked to and implied by the diegesis,[7] and (b) onscreen space is directly perceived, whereas offscreen space is not perceived but inferred.

We find, then, that the corresponding basic factor for characterizing auditory space is not whether sounds are on- or offscreen but whether or not they are directly perceptible on the soundtrack. Thus, *"on-track sound"* is sound that is heard (diegetically or nondiegetically) on the soundtrack, and "*off-track sound*" is sound that the diegesis gives us to believe exists, which we infer, but do not hear on the soundtrack.

Masking figures in this definition as follows: an element subject to visual masking is presumably still onscreen, contained in the rectangular image, though not perceived. Likewise, a masked element in auditory space is still presumably on-track, though buried by other sounds and thus not perceived. Masking, then, is a special case of onscreen image and on-track sound, by diegetic inference.

The Kracauer notion of synchronism covers more than one combination of audiovisual elements. Most obviously, asynchronism occurs with offscreen sound. But it also occurs with off-track sound when the sound source is visible, and in cases of auditory and/or visual masking.

Let us now briefly consider some of these elements of cinematic space and the audiovisual combinations relevant in *Sous les toits de Paris.*

The film refers frequently to offscreen visual space. The classical cinema deploys offscreen space very frequently in the device of the eyeline match; Clair in particular uses offscreen space as a locus for humor. For instance, a minor character is humming the romance-filled theme song at one point; a delayed downward movement of the camera eventually reveals what was below the screen—his feet soaking in a tub of water.

Sous les toits makes emphatic use of off-track auditory space. On several occasions the camera shows people talking animatedly behind cafe windows. Recalling Clair's curious statement about the redundancy of the sound of applause heard in conjunction with an image of hands clapping, note that in putting dialogues behind glass on the screen, he is diegetically justifying his suppression of dialogue. Similarly, as mentioned above, many conversations are never heard, because they are supplanted by music, sometimes diegetic and sometimes nondiegetic.

Most instances of off-track auditory space reveal an arbitrary narrator. One scene in the dance hall begins with diegetic accordion tunes on the soundtrack (there are glimpses of a musician playing the tunes for the dancing clientele). Louis and Albert leave the premises to settle a squabble they had begun there. As they emerge outside on the street, the music continues to play from within, its volume having hardly diminished at all. We hear nothing of the pair's shouting at each other as the music presumably drowns out their voices. According to the logic of realism, the sound mix is incorrect outside the dance hall. Either the music has suddenly turned diegetic or the microphone curiously remains in the dance hall as the camera turns outside. In many such moments *Sous les toits* becomes a silent film (relying on silent and part-talkie conventions and expectations) with weakly diegetic, or even aggressively antidiegetic music acting as the movie house's piano. In the context of Clair's "poetic" or antirealistic treatment of the acoustic landscape, the discussions behind those glass windows take on a self-consciousness of presentation that borders on what might simply be termed adiegetic. The fluctuations in the new sound cinema's terms of spatial verisimilitude, combined with the liberty which the musical genre took with these terms from the beginning, and with Clair's own playfully imperious directorial stamp, render suspect the integrity and credibility of the diegesis.

A great deal of what one judges as diegetic or nondiegetic in sound depends on whether the rule of *auditory depth of field* is observed. This is as essential to cinematic realism as perspective is to the photographic image. Only when the soundtrack abuses auditory depth of field to a considerable extent is the spectator's sense of spatial integrity actually disturbed. Such a disturbance takes place during Louis and Albert's argument outside the dance hall when their shouting continues to be "drowned out" by the accordion inside, which ought to be at minimum volume.

A screening of any thirties Clair film, followed by a screening of any thirties Renoir film, clearly demonstrates Clair's *planar* conception of filmic space in contrast to the depth, fluidity, and continuity of Renoir's. *Sous les toits* uses two planes of acoustic space, foreground and background. Even these two dimensions are violated so often that we come to doubt the diegetic existence of *any* continuous acoustic space situating the action. The single great exception is the crane shot at the beginning that descends from the Parisian rooftops to Albert and the others singing, and this shot's reversal at film's end, when the camera rises from the street and its chorus of residents to the rooftops again. The singular care with which Clair remains faithful to auditory depth of field in this pair of crane shots suggests their structural and thematic significance. This exception, these shots celebrating spatial continuity, calls attention to the norm—planar space—much as the sequence of the street fight perturbs the soundtrack's hierarchy and emphasizes that hierarchy in its very transgression.

Offscreen sound is a variable of cinematic space found frequently in *Sous les toits*, just as one would expect in a film by one who wrote so unequivocally about the necessity for asynchronism in sound pictures. It is with curious consistency, though, that even where Clair allows offscreen sound to give information, he has almost always already transmitted it visually through context—thereby undermining the communicative value of the soundtrack. An example among many of this treatment of offscreen sound: when Albert hears a knock at his door and the authoritative offscreen command to "open

Sous les toits de Paris. Depth in audiovisual space as camera and microphone move in toward sheet-music peddler Albert (Albert Préjean). This production-still shows the edge of Lazare Meerson's set at right. *Courtesy of Orbitron and the Cinémathèque Française.*

up in the name of the law," he complies the first time in the film, when it's not the police at all, and ignores the command the second time, when it *is* the police. The image can be trusted, but words by themselves cannot.[8]

A brief comparison between *Sous les toits de Paris* and other early sound films' use of offscreen sound might be illuminating here. Tod Browning's *Dracula* (1931), for one, provides a direct contrast. Rather than being an untrustworthy masking force, sound emerges as a trusted indicator, a supplier of clues and answers. Van Helsing and his friends collectively wonder who might be the feared killer in their midst; the maid offscreen, as if by coincidence, announces Count Dracula, who then enters the scene. In a scene where Dracula meets heroine Mina at a concert, auditory depth-of-field encourages an implicit acceptance that a concert is going on although at no point are musicians or stage ever shown on the screen. In Mamoulian's *Dr. Jekyll and Mr. Hyde* (1932), Hyde's strangling of his girlfriend offscreen underneath a statue of nude lovers is marvelously enhanced through the use of offscreen sound. Similar trust in the soundtrack's informing qualities is evident in Hawks's *Scarface* (1932) (offscreen automobiles, gunshots, whis-

Sous les toits de Paris. Sound "contradicts" image in this street-singing scene, where police and criminals alike are threatening to disrupt the pleasant tune sung by passersby and a worried Albert. *Courtesy of Orbitron and Cinémathèque Française.*

tling) and in Lang's *M* (1931) (automobile sounds as Elsie Beckmann starts to cross a supposedly busy street, Lorre's self-incriminating offscreen whistling of the Grieg leitmotif).

The most memorable occurrences of offscreen sound in *Sous les toits* are in the long crane shots at the beginning and end of the film, which we have already noted. In the first descending shot, the singing is very faint while the camera explores the rooftops, and the music gradually strengthens until the camera reaches the middle of the crowd with the musical source now onscreen (the opposite progression operates in the latter shot). It is tempting to call these shots audiovisually "redundant"—the transgression Clair wished at all costs to avoid. But in the first shot, since we have not yet seen the source of the music, we have no reason to believe that the music is diegetic. In the film's final, ascending shot, closure requires redundancy. In one continuous movement through cinematic space, Albert once more is shown assuming leadership of that music which pervades the narrative world, from street level to the "heavenly" reaches of the rooftops and chimneys.

A major poetizing force of the film, sound *de-realizes* image. During the final restaurant scene, where Albert sees he has lost Pola to Louis, a record player is cranking out the William Tell Overture. Albert and Louis briefly engage in a physical struggle with each other. The record, as mystically as the carousel in Ophuls's *La Ronde*, gets stuck concurrently with this snag in the plot. When Albert has resolved his differences with Pola and Louis, he puts the tone arm on the record again—the same side of the same record—which now plays "Sous les toits de Paris." A small detail, but one that tells us a great deal about Clair's manipulation of his narrative universe.

CHAPTER VIII

Anempathy: Hangover Square

Films about music and musicians—melodramas like *Intermezzo* (1939), *Humoresque* (1947), *Letter from an Unknown Woman* (1948), *Rhapsody* (1954), as well as countless lives-of-composers and -songsters films, starting with *The Jazz Singer*—permit the Hollywood cinema to play out themes and variations on the human psyche. Music diegetized as the product of a character can serve double duty in a film score. First, it provides semiotically rich "keys" to delineate the character—all the more so owing to music's ideological status as gaining access to emotional "truth" (especially Romantic music). Thus, melodrama's predilection for classical musicians, men of "obvious" depth and passion—and incidentally, the ironic twist this convention takes in *Letter from an Unknown Woman*, whose female protagonist is "tricked" by a decadent womanizer's beautiful piano music into believing that he is a sensitive romantic hero. Second, the music's connection to the musical character also partakes in the usual illustrative functions of the film score, namely, providing emotional and rhythmic accompaniment to the picture.

Hangover Square (Twentieth-Century Fox, 1944), directed by John Brahm and scored by Bernard Herrmann, is particularly rich territory for investigating how Hollywood invests music with meaning. Set in turn-of-the-century London, it has as its protagonist a musician who virtually composes himself to death. Pop Freud met Dr. Jekyll and Mr. Hyde in more than a few films of the era, and *Hangover Square* shares with them the preoccupation with madness and doubling.[1] Music in the film provides access to the character's madness; since it is also functioning as the film score, music insistently links the character's subjectivity with the spectator's.

George Harvey Bone (Laird Cregar) is a well-mannered (read repressed) composer who has psychotic episodes triggered by music: during blackouts set off by "discordant sounds," he metamorphoses into a murderous, bug-eyed aggressor, a strangler and a pyromaniac. His schizophrenia is expressed via music—the discordant music that triggers his psychosis. The Scotland Yard psychologist, Dr. Middleton (George Sanders), stands in the middle of George's two personalities, tracking down the "Fulham Road murderer" on one hand and suspiciously observing George on the other.

George is engaged to Barbara, a classical pianist. Her father, Sir Henry, urges George to complete his piano concerto, for he would like to conduct it during a prestigious musical soirée. But George, increasingly anxious and overworked, is prone to "spells" during which he cannot account for his actions. Trying to relax one evening on Dr. Middleton's orders, he meets Netta, a singer. He writes her one song, then more, until they develop an association of sorts: he falls in love with her, she uses his songs to advance her career. The wind of sexuality that blows into his life only exacerbates his psychic turmoil: for every note of the piano concerto he's composing for Barbara and Sir Henry, he is compelled by the manipulative Netta to write a sentimental popular tune. Netta, figurative castrator, even steals a melody from his concerto ("It's such a little thing! your concerto would never miss it"), adds lyrics, and appropriates it for her act.

The narrative therefore defines the terms of George's conflicts not only via the opposition of women characters—the "good" Barbara and the scheming, sexual Netta—but musically as well. Symphonic concert music aligns with respectability, repression; in the other column goes lowbrow music, desire, sexuality. George is torn between two women (at differing moments he'll want to marry each, and try to strangle each) and two corresponding musical styles. Just about everyone else (except the psychiatrist), not only George, is a musician in this film, and music seems to be everywhere: snippets of George's own concerto turn up unaccountably on the street, at nightclubs, at public festivals, and nondiegetically on the soundtrack. The viewer starts to notice music from all sources—George's concerto, Netta's tunes, incidental diegetic music, and nondiegetic music—interpenetrating in the most disturbing manner. Concurrently with the progressive blending of musical types and levels of narration, the distinction between George and his murderous alter ego begins to break down.

Classicism

Hangover Square's score conforms to the classical paradigm, yet foregrounds music; that is, the film self-consciously uses music to structure the
narrative. The *kind* of music in the score is unconventional as well. Herrmann
wrote George's piano concerto (which actually contains all the motivic material of the entire score) not in Hollywood's usual nineteenth-century Romantic idiom but in a distinctly twentieth-century style straining toward
atonality and dissonance (characteristically, it begins on a tritone—tonal music's most ambiguous and tense interval).[2]

The danger of dwelling on the "classical Hollywood model" of film scoring
is that it might give the erroneous impression of uniformity and sameness
in studio era film music. The model must not prevent us from seeing the
enormous variety of musical discourses and figures it was able to encompass.
However unconventional or avant-garde a Hollywood musical score might
be, the film always motivates it in conventional ways. Thus there is little
that's progressive or subversive about jazz in the milieu of drug addiction
in *The Man With the Golden Arm*, the electronic sounds that waft over the
strange *Forbidden Planet*, or the electronically generated music complicit
with the alcoholic dementia of Ray Milland in *The Lost Weekend*. David
Bordwell in fact cites *Hangover Square's* score to argue for Hollywood's
capacity for "non-disruptive differentiation," as the film's discordant music
is narratively motivated by its connection to a deranged character.[3]

So while Herrmann's score might strain some formal and stylistic boundaries, at no point does it violate the basic principles of the Hollywood scoring
model. The film uses music for continuity, and for underscoring moods and
narrative events; all music is motivated by the narrative. True to Hollywood
form, the beginning and ending are accompanied by "appropriate" music;
the first notes of George's concerto set a tense and gripping mood to the
opening credits, and the obligatory orchestral swell closes the film. (In fact,
since the self-immolating George has just finished performing his concerto
on the solo piano, the tacked-on orchestral ending seems gratuitous: but the
rules about end-title music must be observed to the letter.)

In typical classical fashion, scenes of rapid action or dramatic tension are
paralleled by appropriately fast and tense music. Distinct idioms and moods
of music match characters and narrative moods. "Stinger" chords typify the
music's mission to provide dramatic underscoring. Even mickey-mousing is
present (for example, a thundering trombone and tympani flourish underlines the lighting of each torch to a bonfire), and other rhythmic devices

dramatically accentuate screen events. The music redundantly reinforces visual information; thus, as George falls into a trance, an eerie-sounding chord accompanies the distorted subjective shots showing his altered perceptions.

The score faithfully observes the rules of continuity: it provides scene transitions, sets up thematic parallels from scene to scene, and otherwise smooths over discontinuities of space and time. Distinctions between diegetic and nondiegetic music remain intact, although the freedom of passage enjoyed by musical themes (from diegetic to nondiegetic and vice versa) is certainly exploited in this story about a composer. We may question logically how the opening (diegetic) organ-grinder tune can occur nondiegetically later, and then find its way into George's concerto at the end. But this kind of diegetic/nondiegetic confusion, although it exerts pressure on verisimilitude, *characterizes* the Hollywood model rather than challenges it.

The score of *Hangover Square* remains faithful to the classical system of film music, at the same time that it foregrounds important aspects of film music itself. I will examine the seven opening shots to show how the film establishes patterns of repetition and variation of both musical and visual elements. Then I will explore the film's treatment of musical themes, and third, its narrative engagement of "anempathetic music."

The Opening: Shot Breakdown

Shot 1: Fade-in to CU of fire at end of barrel organ; iris-out and dolly-out to MS, organ-grinder turning the crank,[4] removing hat, and mopping brow. Crane up and out to general high shot of street full of revelers. Pan L to follow lamplighter crossing street, in front of a horse and cart. Tilt up to follow lighting lamp. Crane R and into window of room cluttered with antiques [ominous dissonant chord now overlaps with organ music]; over-the-[killer's]-shoulder of Ogilby in MCU, trying to defend himself; Ogilby throws three objects at camera. [Dissonant chord in steady crescendo, organ music fading.]

Shot 2 (cut from shot 1 on 3rd throw): forward dolly from killer's p.o.v: CU of Ogilby as he is stabbed. [On his cry, all music ceases.] Crane to follow killer's arm reaching for kerosene lamp; as lamp is thrown down onto Ogilby's body, tilt down to body and flames on stairs [and low orchestral rumbling trill on soundtrack].

Shot 3: Low-angle MCU (reverse shot) of George looking down. [Musical stinger: orchestra with high brasses]

Shot 4: High-angle shot of flames in stairway [Musical stinger: orchestra with low brasses]

Shot 5: Organ-grinder in street (*not* playing his music); daylight; policeman behind him; organ-grinder points R and cries, "Look! It's old Ogilby's place!" pan R to follow him running across street to the shop [tense, racing nondiegetic music begins at shop].[5] Crowd gathers with organ-grinder and policeman.

Shot 6: Crowds gather and shove for a look into the storefront; pan R to follow policeman ringing fire alarm [nondiegetic music continues].

Shot 7: Horse-drawn fire wagon careens down street, its bells ringing loudly [along with continuing music]; exits R as George walks L, away from fire in the opposite direction [wagon's alarm bell fades; orch. music closes quietly, on variant of film's opening tritone].

Fire. By means of a close-up that only subsequently will open out to a general view of the organ-grinder, shot 1 pointedly begins on fire. All the more curious since fire has no logical narrative motivation: what business do flames have issuing from the end of a barrel organ, particularly on a hot summer's night? Perhaps no realistic motivation, but its strongly marked appearance (as the first diegetic image) inaugurates a code, a series of repetitions and variations on fire.

In the very next shot, a fire of greater magnitude will consummate Ogilby's murder. Fire is spectacle (that's what catches the organ-grinder's eye, the immediate evidence of foul play). Like the fragile psyche, it can be harmless (scattered through the film: streetlamps, kerosene lamps, candles and fireplace in George's flat), unless it goes out of control. George's murderous episodes are linked with fire as a figure of his loss of control. In his third trance, he murders Netta and carries her body in a sack to the Guy Fawkes Day bonfire. The bonfire is a public ritual of cultural inversion: the holiday allows for destructiveness as a safe outlet of aggressive energy. Participants throw sacks of junk, symbolizing Guy Fawkes's body, onto a huge fire and watch them burn. Ironically, George the madman re-inverts the inversion; he uses the bonfire as a perfect front for disposing of a very real corpse.

In the final concert sequence George runs amok; his two "selves" having joined in an impossible union, he is compelled both to perform his piano concerto and to set the concert hall on fire, which will immolate him.

Turning in Threes. The film makes structural use of threes, often in connection with turning, or with circles. The organ-grinder turns the crank of his music machine, and this turning produces a circular, mechanical music in triple time (theme *B*). After an evening of drinking, George and Mickey explain to Netta the neighborhood's walking cure for a hangover: "three times 'round the Square, and a drink at the pub." Or later, George telephones from a restaurant for symphony tickets. As he hangs up, there's a curious and otherwise unmotivated dialogue with the attendant, who obliges George to turn the crank on the phone: "Ring off, Sir, ring off. Turn the handle like this, three times—that's called ringing off, Sir."

The circles grow in magnitude. George murders Netta and carries her body to the Guy Fawkes bonfire. As citizens shout instructions about stacking the dummies to be burned, a trio of musicians slips by, innocently playing the organ-grinder theme *B*. When the fire is lit, revelers dance around the fire in a large circle, chanting "Guy! Guy! Guy!" as on the soundtrack, the organ-grinder's theme plays.

Elaborate circular camera movements establish the scene of the final concert sequence. There are tripartite structures, as well: when the police arrive, George plays the piano and watches with increasing agitation as his music "coincidentally" punctuates their arrival at three separate doors. A strikingly Eisensteinian series of three subjective shots—each showing George putting the cord around Barbara's neck, attempting to strangle her—show his remembering his attack on his fiancée. (The musical passage he's playing happens to be none other than the organ-grinder's theme.)

Transgression vs. the Law. Shots 1 and 5 set up the opposition between night and day, rational and irrational, desire and law. In the very atmospheric Shot 1 are music, indices of heat (sweating, fire, removing the hat), drunken dancing, singing, the brandishing of bottles. From a reverse angle, shot 5 returns to apparent daylight, *lack* of music, a policeman standing behind the street organ. It's the same place, but now suddenly occupied by the Law, not boozers—all the more dramatically and sharply delineating between the nightmare at Ogilby's and "normalcy" outdoors. The schizophrenic mise-en-scène points up the paradigm upon which the narration will subsequently elaborate: in the form of oppositions, for example, between Eddie Carstairs, the sleazy musical impresario (on the side of Netta), and Sir Henry, the classical musician and the very embodiment of George's superego (on Barbara's side).

Guy Fawkes Day commemorates the 1605 "Gunpowder Plot" to blow up Parliament and King James I in protest against his suppression of Catholicism. George's madness, also based on incendiary terrorism, thus finds an apt historical/political setting. His ultimate attack on law and culture (locking up Dr. Middleton, igniting a concert hall full of patricians) is, like the 1605 plot, unsuccessful—although, of course, it's the transgression in both cases that brings us back to such stories again and again.

"Moods." As Dr. Middleton says, "The mind is a delicate mechanism: if

a man upsets the balance between work and play, it may cause him to do strange things, even dangerous things." Dr. Middleton may serve as the voice of reason here, but he also ambiguously embodies the same duality as George. More than once he flirts gallantly with Barbara under George's nose. He advises George to "find some new emotional outlet," and George duly meets Netta, who contributes to his downfall. The doctor has literally written the book on methods of murder, including the East Indian devices known as "thuggee-cords," which George in his trances adopts to kill Barbara and Netta. The mise-en-scène emphasizes the George-Middleton doubling in numerous ways—a doubling heightened by a physical resemblance between the two men.

"All my life I've had blank little moods, but just for a minute or two," explains George. The film opens as his "moods" are becoming deeper and longer from tension and overwork. Medical literature since the 1930s documents a rare disorder called musicogenic epilepsy, in which epileptic seizures are brought on by hearing specific types of music or even specific melodies.[6] (The film even accurately depicts the "aura" or onset period of the seizures—George's distorted vision and characteristic clutching the back of his head—accompanied on the soundtrack by an eerie, shimmering chord. Where the horror film takes license is in giving George not a *grand mal* attack, but rather, purposeful mobility and a predilection for murder.)

The film opens, as it will close, in mid-"mood." Not until the second scene will it establish the protagonist's character and provide tentative explanations for the shocking opening. A departure from usual Jekyll-Hyde conventions, this *in medias res* beginning disorients the viewer, for lack of expository material: did this decent fellow really murder someone, or was it someone resembling him—perhaps Dr. Middleton?

During George's second trance, triggered by the sound of lead pipes falling into a ditch, he tries to strangle Barbara. The narrative is in place by now, and George's murder attempt has an explicable psychological motivation: Barbara is "in the way"; George wants Netta now. His third trance, brought on by classical stringed instruments falling cacophonously to the floor, structurally balances the second, for now he murders Netta, who has rejected him. The fourth and final psychotic episode occurs at the concert. No sudden "discordant noise" brings it on, but the ongoing dissonant music itself.

Musical Themes. Hangover Square begins in a social microcosm where the precarious balance between order and transgression is violently disrupted. The protagonist is introduced in mid-trance, as the monster, not the "distinguished composer" promised in the opening titles. Only a scene later is it clear that the monster is indeed the composer, who has "moods" set off by discordant sounds. Retrospectively, we might ask what brought on George's first psychotic episode in Fulham: the dissonant waltz of the street organ outside? This music (theme *B*) will be heard several times more. Slowed down, it plays on the soundtrack as George buys a newspaper for a report on the murder in Fulham Road. Already associated with that murder, it now serves as a vague, repressed connection between George reading about murder and his alter ego who committed it.

Theme *B* dominates at the Guy Fawkes bonfire scene, as socially institutionalized madness provides a backdrop for George's own. The musicians snake through the crowded frame. The fact that they are playing the out-of-tune organ-grinder's waltz makes no sense in terms of verisimilitude. But it makes all the more sense in firming up textual connections among George, madness, fire, desire, mayhem. Once the fire is lit and George watches Netta's body burn, the soundtrack lets out all the stops: the celebrants chant and dance, and the orchestra pounds an orgiastic variation of theme *B*.

Let us skip to the final occurrence of theme *B*, during the concerto performance. It appears in George's concerto; it's written in. But now the concerto *as the musical score* takes over the film's action, relentlessly, dictating camera movements, editing, and even plot events. So when theme *B* is announced in the course of George's concerto, it triggers in him a forbidden memory, the moment of trying to strangle Barbara. Now he plays the musical accompaniment to his own subjective images, bound to his piano, condemned to see the plot literally played out to the end.

Are we to assume that George heard the organ-grinder while doing away with Ogilby in Fulham Road, and would this explain theme *B* finding its way into his composition? In narrative cinema, music actively crosses narrational boundaries—between the objective and subjective, the diegetic and nondiegetic and metadiegetic—and *Hangover Square* foregrounds this liberty of the musical score to a hallucinatory degree.

Although fragments of his concerto-in-progress are heard through the film, the concerto is not performed in its entirety until the final concert sequence. It turns out to contain all the film's significant musical motifs,[7] including the waltz of the Fulham organ-grinder. One has the curious impression of hearing this as a musical *summa* at the end—this music which seemingly issues from George's mind.

I have defined a theme as any significant repeated music in a film. Herrmann's themes are distinctive in their general rejection of melody; he tended to work with fragments, harmonies, and instrumental colors rather than anything resembling a theme song.[8] In fact, the only singable melodies in *Hangover Square* are the ones George composes for Netta. As far as she is concerned, these tunes' value lies in advancing her nightclub career; but for him, they are "true," they prove to be deceptive lures. "All for you, I'd change my way of living . . . there's nothing I wouldn't do": George takes the lyrics seriously as he reiterates them to a cold and mocking Netta.

Anempathetic Music

> For some reason, 'needle drops'—scenes depicting
> someone playing a record—are prevalent in killing scenes. . . . [9]

A street organ plays while a murder is taking place. When the camera enters the scene of the struggle, the organ music continues to play (for a while). An ordinary sound (organ) accompanies an extraordinary, catastrophic event. Music is blind to the subsequent catastrophe; having been set in motion, it continues to play innocently, in its own sweet time, its own rhythm, its own universe. Ironically, it reminds us of what the situation *was*, pleasant or joyous, when no one could have anticipated the morbid turn of events. Music doesn't know, couldn't know; furthermore, in light of the bitter juxtaposition of music and scene, *music doesn't care.*

At the end, a concerto plays while a symphony hall is burning down. Fire, music, and murder again, condensed: this time, the musical agent and the victim are one and the same; George, in playing the piano, "grinds the organ" to his own death. He's the pyromaniac, organ-grinder, and victim all at once, and musical temporality wins out. *The music must finish,* no matter what; he has become enslaved to musical logic. (George's) music still plays oblivious to (George's) human catastrophe.

French musician and critic Michel Chion distinguishes three types of soundtrack music, the third of which is the heedless music of the organ-grinder: (1) "empathetic" music, the sort most frequently heard on soundtracks, which participates in the characters' emotions, vibrates in sympathy with their actions; (2) music of *didactic counterpoint*—nondiegetic music to signify a contrapuntal idea, demanding to be *read* and interpreted;[10] and (3) *anempathetic music*, music, in relation to the intense emotional situation on screen (death, crisis, madness), that shows

> an ostensible *indifference* by following its own dauntless and mechanical course. . . . [E]motion arises not from identifying through music with the character's feelings (which are normally treated as the most important thing in the world); on the contrary, emotion is born from seeing the individual's drama as it unfolds to the world's indifference. . . . We call this music anem-

pathetic (with the privative a-), since it doesn't care, and for this very reason takes on, in a *massive transference* often due to mere coincidence, the weight of a human destiny which it at once sums up and disdains.[11]

Anempathetic music is mechanical or robotlike in its failure to adjust to changes in the surroundings. In fact, in having a rhythmic and harmonic temporal logic of its own, music offers a counterpoint to what Henri Bergson identifies as alive and human—precisely, the capacity to perceive and accommodate to change in environment. For Bergson, laughter is a form of social punishment for the person who behaves like an automaton, mechanically, failing to respond spontaneously to changes around him. We laugh at the character who doesn't notice the banana peel in his path and slips on it. What distinguishes anempathetic music from the comic character is that music is not "punishable" in the same sense. First, it is *not* human; it is not expected to have awareness of its surroundings. Second, it doesn't slip and fall; it is capable (in some situations) of playing on independently, and, indeed, almost sadistically—it is capable of *rubbing it in*, this ironic audio-visual juxtaposition of the musically pleasant and the catastrophic occurrence.

No surprise, then, that this dichotomy—musical, regular, internal logic vs. human, dramatic representational logic, tied to the aleatory real—is often borne out all the more clearly in film with the use of, precisely, *mechanical* music: the record player, the hurdy-gurdy, the music box, the player piano once set in motion, even with its human agent eliminated by catastrophe, can still play on, agreeable and (seemingly) innocent. Hitchcock's *Strangers on a Train* is emblematic: at a fairground a woman is strangled to the music of a nearby merry-go-round, and at the end the same mechanical music becomes the maddening accompaniment to the life-and-death confrontation between hero and villain. As Jean Renoir's marquis Robert de la Chesnaye unveils his monumental music machine in *Rules of the Game* and sets it in motion, gamekeeper Schumacher murderously hunts down Marceau, his wife's poacher. In the thirties gangster film it was common to "poetically" murder the character who had started a tune playing on the record player or player piano.

What is the psychic explanation for the power of anempathetic music in film? For Chion, it is the subject's fear of the mother's indifference:

> Only the one being who forces us to *wait* for everything can represent absolute indifference. Her resistance or delay in responding, the absence of echoes to our cries, is what constitutes her as intolerably indifferent—that is, alive somewhere but not for us, and at the same time dead, since dead to us: or else, treating *us* like one dead, making of us a dead person.
> This indifference of music is thus not an anomaly, a perverted form of the

emotional mechanism, it is the basis from which all emotion arises. In a way, anempathetic music corresponds to a simple re-framing: instead of occupying the whole field with the individual character's emotion [as figure], it shows us the context [ground] of the world's indifference. Such re-framing does not diminish emotional intensity, but on the contrary, shifts it to a broader scale.[12]

At the end of *Hangover Square*, the score seems to take the story into its own hands. Diegetized as George Harvey Bone's first and last piano concerto, it goes beyond anempathy. The plot has conflated the agent and the victim of the action; each (the composer and the psychotic) has a different relationship to the music. But the music cares about neither one, and proceeds independently in its role as the film score too, motivating entrances, exits, actions, camera movements, cuts, flashbacks. Chion, for his part, focuses on music that motivates irony through juxtaposition. But this piano concerto motivates the events themselves: the causality of "musical illustration" is reversed when, for example, the three doors open, each revealing a Scotland Yard detective—as if these actions are obeying the dictates of three accents in the music.

In the way it acts on the spectator, music in film narrative performs roles it cannot have in theater, and certainly not in the novel or other narrative forms. The irony or the ambivalence of the music is that in terms of its use at a dramatic moment (the concerto/fire sequence in *Hangover Square*), it functions as spectacle, signifier of emotion. It involves the spectator more actively. Yet in its relation to the narrative events, it creates this sensation of indifference. Chion speaks of the infant's ambivalence toward the mother (i.e., she is both nurturer and threat). Somehow music also proves capable of both, providing emotion and indifference. But in cinema there is a split, between *spectator's place* and *place of the character* within the narrative. The ambivalent function of music is possible *because* it can easily move back and forth across the film's narrational boundaries.

Afterword

The latter part of this book's title, "Narrative Film Music," contains a deliberate ambiguity. It refers to *music as a narrational force* in films; also, it restricts the investigation to *music for narrative films*. Limiting the discussion to narrative cinema, and a rather traditional narrative cinema at that, has allowed me to avoid locking horns with films and genres that "complicate" the issues (e.g., film music's roles in textuality and spectatorship) as I have presented them.

But since I began work on this book, a phenomenon has emerged with ever greater insistence in popular movies. As any filmgoer notices who lingers to watch closing credits for music, the movies are using more and more recorded popular music. This tendency is due in large part to the meteoric rise and influence of the music video in its kaleidoscope of forms. The changing status of music in films is, in turn, producing an altered system of relationships between music and image.

But is the use of popular music in eighties films really different in kind from its use in the traditional Hollywood musical, where it is a matter of convention for the flow and space of the narrative to be disrupted by a musical number? A thirties Busby Berkeley number, playing out fantasies of bodies arranged in patterns of rhythm and space, is surely a forerunner of rock videos. Not so clearly demarcated from the "story," but still obviously belonging to the realm of fantasy, are numbers by Astaire and Rogers as they dance and sing their way into each other's hearts, or Gene Kelly and his buddies dancing with diegetic props such as taxi cabs and trash cans. But the pop-musical number in current dramatic films (the very distinction "musical vs. dramatic" seems to be wearing thin), set in a context of naturalistic acting, is most often performed on the soundtrack by musicians with no pretense of a relation to the diegesis. A hybrid is emerging, unlike diegetic music which is normally not listened to, and also not as focused as musical numbers issuing from the magic world of the musical.

Behind this phenomenon, of course, lies the motive of commercial profit through the consolidation of large financial interests: the music recording industry, the television and home video industries, and the film industry mutually advertise one another through music. But the changing position of music in films is also having an effect on the norms of narrative film viewing, on the way we watch and listen to a story film.

A recent TV program on the movies tellingly compared similar segments from two adventure dramas. The first clip showed the takeoff and flight of the vintage airplanes in *The Blue Max* (1966), for which composer Jerry Goldsmith had written "soaring" orchestral music of Wagnerian grandeur. In the second clip, the takeoff and flight of fighter jets in the 1986 *Top Gun* had for musical accompaniment a rock song with lyrics. Goldsmith commented that this music served little use but as a vulgar advertisement for the rock group, the music video, and the soundtrack album. Was he right to suggest that such music has little effect on spectators (and, if this is the case, did the soundtrack music play no role in making *Top Gun* the top grossing film of 1986)? Although the effect of the *Top Gun* music is certainly not "stirring" in the manner of the *Blue Max* score, it is nevertheless compelling in its high-tech, driving energy and sexual exuberance.

Have listening habits and responses changed in response to commercial interests? Has it become "normal" to listen to a rock song with lyrics at the same time we follow a story? A semiotic phenomenology of the evolving relations between music and image, and, overall, of changes in the "diegetic effect" or disposition of representation, needs to emerge. No less essential is an understanding of music's place in the changing relations among the recording industry, TV and video, and film. Music belongs to a number of systems, an economy of desire. What is being marketed, to whom, and how successfully? How does the market alter pleasure and demand?

Notes

Introduction

1. Certainly, today's media provide some examples. Some "serious" dramas, including those of Ingmar Bergman, convey a sense of philosophical depth and stark realism by virtue of a scoreless soundtrack. TV news broadcasts and some documentaries appear more real and immediate for lack of music. TV sitcoms may have no background music, but their laugh tracks assume emotive and interpretive functions of music. Other dramatic TV shows lacking music during scenes nevertheless play music—often the show's musical logo—every few minutes for commercial breaks.

2. Maurice Jaubert, "Music on the Screen," in Charles Davy, ed., *Footnotes to the Film* (New York: Oxford University Press, 1937), 111 and 115.

3. See Royal S. Brown, "Herrmann, Hitchcock, and the Music of the Irrational," in Gerald Mast & Marshall Cohen, eds., *Film Theory and Criticism*, 3rd ed. (New York: Oxford University Press, 1985), 641.

4. William Fleming, *Art and Ideas* (New York: Holt, Rinehart, and Winston, 1955), 33–34.

5. Didier Anzieu, "L'enveloppe sonore du soi," *Nouvelle revue de psychanalyse* 13 (Spring 1976), 175.

6. For an outline of principles of classical film narrative and continuity editing, see chapters 4 and 7 of David Bordwell and Kristin Thompson, *Film Art: An Introduction*, 2nd ed. (New York: Knopf, 1986).

Chapter I

1. Sir Arthur Bliss, for example, in *Grove's Dictionary of Music and Musicians*, wrote: "In the last resort film music should be judged solely as music—that is to say, by the ear alone, and the question of its value depends on whether it can stand up to this test."

2. Interview in *Cahiers du cinéma* No. 223 (August 1970): "I'm trying to make films that have no language, and when I sense that there is a cinematographic language I try to destroy it before it is born. I'm trying to eliminate all the obstacles between the spectator and what I'm showing of reality."

3. For a detailed study of the parallelism-counterpoint debate, see Douglas W. Gallez, "Theories of Film Music," *Cinema Journal* 9, 2 (Spring 1970), 40–47.

4. Siegfried Kracauer, *Theory of Film* (New York: Oxford University Press, 1965), 141.

5. Eisler and Adorno, *Composing for the Films* (New York: Oxford University Press, 1947), 70.

6.

7. "Pas de trou, surtout pas de trou, c'est un des cris de terreur des cinéastes. Et si trou il y a, bouchons-le. Avec de la musique." Henri Colpi, *Défense et illustration de la musique de film* (Lyon: Société d'édition, de recherches et documentation cinématographiques [SERDOC], 1963), 51.

8. Diegetic: having its source in the film's narrative "world"—as opposed to nondiegetic sound, for example, which is heard on the soundtrack but not presumably perceivable by characters in the narrative world. For a fuller discussion of these terms, see below, "Narrative/Diegesis," pp. 20–22.

9. Gérard Genette, "D'un récit baroque," in *Figures*, v. II (Paris: Seuil, 1969), 211. The primary narration designates the principal level of narration, as opposed to stories-within-the-story, which Genette terms metadiegetic narration, and as opposed to narrative instrusions from without (e.g. metalepsis, participatio) or extradiegetic elements.

10. Originally: "dans l'intelligibilité (comme dit M. Cohen-Séat)."

11. Etienne Souriau, ed., *L'Univers filmique* (Paris, 1953), 7. Translation mine. See also chap. 4 of Christian Metz, *Film Language* (New York: Oxford University Press, 1974), 97ff.

12. See my article on *Nights of Cabiria*: "Music as Salvation: Notes on Fellini and Rota," *Film Quarterly* 28, 2 (Winter 1974–75), 17–25.

13. See for example Mark Evans, *Soundtrack: The Music of the Movies* (New York: Hopkinson and Blake, 1975). Even Roger Manvell and John Huntley thoughtlessly perpetuate this distinction: see their 1957 *The Technique of Film Music* (rev. ed. New York: Hastings House, 1975), 45.

14. This example is taken from my article on *Nights of Cabiria*.

15. Christian Metz, "Outline of the Autonomous Segments in Jacques Rozier's Film *Adieu Philippine*," in *Film Language*, p. 150. Actually, the last few moments of the credit sequence may be seen as a new and different recording session—since, precisely, a new piece of music is heard on the soundtrack. Under no circumstances, however, can the film's beginning be correctly read as a discontinous "bracket syntagma."

16. Jack M. Stein, *Richard Wagner and the Synthesis of the Arts* (Detroit: Wayne State University Press, 1960), 75.

17. Stein, 94.

Chapter II

1. Barthes states that printed captions for photographs (whose polysemy could evoke "terror") serve as "ancrage": language, in the form of the caption, "guides . . . interpretation, constituting a kind of vice which holds the connoted meanings from proliferating." "Rhetoric of the Image," in *Image, Music, Text* (New York: Hill and Wang, 1977), 39.

2. It should go without saying that accepting black and white as normal or "diegetic" is itself purely a matter of convention, and that to account for the naturalization of black and white, we must turn to the history of signifying practices from line-engraving through painting and photography, and the uses to which they were put.

3. Manvell and Huntley, *The Technique of Film Music*, (rev. ed. New York: Hastings House, 1975), 16. In England, famous producers of melodrama were the

Bancrofts and Henry Irving; in the United States, Augustin Daly, Steele MacKaye, and David Belasco were among the best-known creators of the spectacles.

4. A. Nicholas Vardac, *From Stage to Screen: Theatrical Method from Garrick to Griffith* (Cambridge: Harvard University Press, 1949), 99.

5. James L. Smith, *Melodrama* (London: Methuen, 1973), 31.

6. "Music to Stage Plays," *Proceedings of the Musical Association*, 1910–11; cited in Manvell and Huntley, 16–18.

7. Peter Brooks, *The Melodramatic Imagination*. (Orig. 1976; repr. New York: Columbia University Press, 1985), 48.

8. Max Winkler reminisces: "We turned to crime. We began to dismember the great masters. We murdered the works of Beethoven, Mozart, Grieg, J. S. Bach, Verdi, Bizet, Tschaikowsky and Wagner—everything that wasn't protected by copyright from our pilfering."

9. For a history of collections of short musical pieces catalogued according to mood, plot event, etc., and for more on the economics and aesthetics of silent film scoring, see Manvell and Huntley, chapter 1, and Charles Hofmann, *Sounds for Silents* (New York: Drama Book Specialists, 1970).

10. Indeed, in the early cinema many audiovisual combinations flourished. The *benshi* in Japan accompanied films with spoken commentary and dialogue and attained the status of stars who eclipsed the movie actors themselves. In the United States and Europe, live spoken commentary and/or sound-effects machines also gained a considerable measure of popularity.

11. Kurt London, *Film Music* (Orig. London, 1936) (Repr. New York: Arno, 1970), 27–28.

12. Manvell and Huntley, *The Technique of Film Music*, 28.

13. Sabaneev, *Music for the Films: A Handbook for Composers and Conductors*, trans. S. W. Pring (London: Pitman & Sons, 1935), 18.

14. London, 35–36.

15. London, 34.

16. London, 35. See also Jeffrey Embler, "The Structure of Film Music" (orig. 1953), repr. James Limbacher, ed., *Film Music: From Violins to Video* (Metuchen, N.J.: Scarecrow, 1974), 61–66.

17. Jean Mitry, *Esthétique et psychologie du cinéma* (Paris: Klincksieck, 1965), vol. II, 118–19.

18. Noel Burch, *Theory of Film Practice* (New York: Praeger, 1973), note, p. 100. London remarks that musical rhythm gives "auditory accentuation and profundity" to the overall filmic rhythm.

19. Manvell and Huntley, 20–21. See also Kurt London: "The pictures thereby gained in vividness in the mind's eye of the onlooker; their inferior and unnatural colours took on a semblance of reality. The characters depicted in them assumed real dimensions and stepped out of their tableaux. The musical accompaniment had created an atmosphere of individuality." London, 26.

20. Eisler and Adorno, *Composing for the Films* (New York: Oxford University Press, 1947), 75.

21. Hence the cinema spectator's essentially fetishistic structure of belief. Freud defines the fetish as the object chosen to signify the missing phallus; at the same time, it is what permits the disavowal of that lack.

22. Eisler and Adorno's analysis comes closest to the Freudian model of fetishism. See especially chapter 5 of *Composing for the Films*. The links between magic, ritual, fetishism, and belief are rich territory for further investigation in film music.

23. Christian Metz has written on this subject in his essay "Aural Objects," *Yale French Studies* 60 (1980), 24–32.

24. Eisler and Adorno, 21.

25. Eisler and Adorno, 59.

26. Alan Williams, "Is Sound Recording Like a Language?" *Yale French Studies* 60 (1980), 51–66.

27. Manvell and Huntley, 35.

28. Nancy Wood, *Text and Spectator in the Period of the Transition to Sound*, Ph.D. Thesis, University of Kent: Canterbury, 1983, p. 110.

29. For example, one area of renegotiation that Robert Sklar notes was the social and physical behavior of audiences. The sense of community, including conversation, which often characterized silent-era audiences, greatly diminished: "people who talked aloud were peremptorily hushed by others in the audience who didn't want to miss any spoken dialogue. The talking audience for silent pictures became a silent audience for talking pictures." Sklar, *Movie-Made America: A Cultural History of American Movies* (New York: Random House, 1976), 153.

30. Ed Branigan, "Color and Cinema: Problems in the Writing of History," *Film Reader* 4 (1979), 24.

31. Comolli, "Machines of the Visible," in T. DeLauretis and S. Heath, eds., *The Cinematic Apparatus* (London: Macmillan, 1980), 121–142. (Slight translation changes mine.)

32. Heath, "The Cinematic Apparatus: Technology as Historical and Cultural Form," in DeLauretis and Heath, *The Cinematic Apparatus*, 1–13. Buscombe, "Sound and Color," *Jump Cut* 17 (April 1978), 23–25. Thompson, "Implications of the Cel Animation Technique," *The Cinematic Apparatus*, 106–120. David Bordwell and Janet Staiger discuss principles governing technological change with respect to mode of production in chapter 19 of Bordwell, Staiger, and Kristin Thompson, *The Classical Hollywood Cinema* (New York: Columbia University Press, 1985).

33. One needs hardly to emphasize the difficulty of gauging contemporary audience reaction to films by extrapolating from such texts as industry publicity, trade press, reviews, and box office statistics.

34. Film reviewers, too, marveled at the fidelity of sounds and their spectacularly lifelike effect.

35. The reader may think of the similar "taming" or naturalization of the jump cut since its self-conscious introduction in the sixties.

36. Harry Geduld disagrees that the musical score reflects a silent-film mentality. His analysis of the placement of musical selections vis-à-vis characters and actions "demonstrates that *The Jazz Singer* is scored like a modern picture. Music is used to create moods and psychological effects, to build an inner drama parallel to the outer action, to suggest and emphasize dramatic conflicts, and to create and develop character." Geduld, *The Birth of the Talkies* (Bloomington: Indiana University Press, 1975), 190.

37. David Cook, *A History of Narrative Film* (New York: Norton, 1981), 240.

38. See Noel Burch's article "Narrative/Diegesis—Thresholds, Limits," *Screen* 23, 2 (July–Aug. 1982), 16–33. Here he continues to elaborate on his model of the cinema's Institutional Mode of Representation.

39. Welford Beaton, quoted in Alexander Walker, *The Shattered Silents: How the Talkies Came To Stay* (New York: William Morrow, 1979), 105.

40. Two examples. Tremendously popular at first, musicals were produced less and less, until by 1931 and 1932 interest in them had waned so much that almost none were produced. Second, an improved two-strip Technicolor process boomed in popularity with its release in 1929; Crosland's *On With the Show* (1929) was the first all-color sound musical, and more all-color musicals were released in 1930. By 1932, use of color had "faded."

41. The historical iconography that has built up around the figure of Gilbert attributes his failure in the talkies to his "uncinematic" voice; Walker argues to the contrary.

42. *Variety*, October 9, 1929; quoted in Walker, 167.

43. A March 1929 review in *Photoplay* for the film *My Man*, for example, calls it a "three-quarters talkie." Evidence suggests that the part-talkie was an aesthetically unstable regime. A *New York Times* review of *The Lion and the Mouse* (1928): "It is . . a mistake to have silent sequences and then to hear a character who has been silent suddenly boom forth into speech." Quoted in Geduld, 201.

44. Tony Thomas quotes Max Steiner saying that until 1932 music "had not been used very much for underscoring—the producers would ask 'Where's the music coming from?' unless they saw an orchestra or a radio or phonograph." Tony Thomas, *Music for the Movies* (S. Brunswick & New York: A. S. Barnes, 1973), 113.

45. *Photoplay*, November 1929.

46. See Stephen Handzo, "A Narrative Glossary of Film Sound Technology," in Elisabeth Weis and John Belton, eds., *Film Sound: Theory and Practice* (New York: Columbia University Press, 1985), esp. 385–91.

47. Some Laurel and Hardy shorts as early as 1930 have some background music, but the state of technology prevented good-quality dialogue-music mixing until 1932.

48. Mamoulian gets credit for devising the first double-channel recording for a scene in *Applause* (1929). The capability for four-track sound emerged in 1932.

Chapter III

1. Michel Marie, "Comment parler la bouche pleine?" (How can you talk with your mouth full?) *Communications* 38 (1983), 56.

2. *Variety*, October 31, 1929. Quoted in Alexander Walker, *The Shattered Silents: How the Talkies Came to Stay* (New York: William Morrow, 1979), 171.

3. See, for example, the argument of T. W. Adorno's 1938 essay, "On the Fetish Character in Music and the Regression of Listening," in Andrew Arato and Elke Gebhart, eds., *The Essential Frankfurt School Reader* (New York: Urizen, 1978), 270–299. See also chapter 5 of this book, on "Eisler/Adorno's critique."

4. Richmond Cardinell, *Music In Industry: Principles of Programming*. New York: American Society of Composers, Authors and Publishers [ASCAP], 1944. See also Wheeler Beckett, *Music In War Plants* (Washington, D.C: War Production Board, August 1943).

5. Cardinell (see n. 4) comments on music's effect of relieving nervous tension: "This has been noted in several plants by a reduction of strife between employees. A Red Cross Blood Doning Center installed a musical program and stopped all post-transfusion fainting."

6. "Played in public places or supermarkets, its purpose is to put to sleep . . . put what to sleep? *Painfulness*: it's a response to pain. When peasants sing while planting rice, they're counteracting pain." Roger G. Tallon, interviewed, "La Musique utilitaire," *Musique en jeu* 24 (Sept. 1976), 72.

7. See Dominique Avron, "Notes pour introduire une métapsychologie de la musique," *Musique en jeu* 9 (November 1972), 102–110.

8. Tallon, see n. 6. His formulation comes dangerously close, of course, to suggesting that musical listening is somehow a wholly unmediated phenomenon, as if music is more natural than other discursive registers.

9. This helps explain why the noise of the projector needed to be drowned out by live music in the days of the silent film.

10. Elmer Rice, *A Voyage to Purilia* (New York: Cosmopolitan Book Corp., 1930), 32.

11. Tony Thomas, *Music for the Movies* (S. Brunswick and New York: A. S. Barnes, 1973), 17.

12. Claude Lévi-Strauss, "Boléro de Maurice Ravel," *L'Homme* 11, 2 (April–June 1971), 5–14. (p.5.) Leonard B. Meyer also invokes myth, in specifying the difficulty

of pinning down any particular connotations of a piece of music: ". . . the flexibility of connotation is a virtue. For it enables music to express what might be called the disembodied essence of myth, the essence of experiences which are central to and vital in human experience." Meyer, *Emotion and Meaning in Music* (Chicago: University of Chicago Press, 1956), 265.

13. See I. H. Coriat, "Some Aspects of a Psychoanalytic Interpretation of Music," *Psychoanalytic Review* 32 (1945), 408–418. For an excellent digest of the psychoanalytic literature on music to 1965, see Pinchas Noy, "The Psychodynamic Meaning of Music," in five parts in the *Journal of Music Therapy*: 3, 4 (Dec. 1966), 126–134; 4, 1 (March 1967), 7–23; 4, 2 (June 1967), 45–51; 4, 3 (Sept. 1967), 81–94; 4, 4 (Dec. 1967), 117ff.

14. See, for example, John Booth Davies, *The Psychology of Music* (London: Hutchinson, 1978).

15. F. Teller, "Musikgenuss und Phantasie," *Imago* 5 (1917), 8–15.

16. Guy Rosolato, "La Voix: Entre corps et langage," *Revue française de psychanalyse* 38, 1 (Jan. 1974), 75–94; Didier Anzieu, "L'enveloppe sonore du soi," *Nouvelle revue de psychanalyse* 13, (Spring 1976), 161–179.

17. Mary Ann Doane, "The Voice in the Cinema: The Articulation of Body and Space," *Yale French Studies* 60 (1980), 44.

18. Doane, 45.

19. Francis Hofstein, "Drogue et musique," *Musique en jeu* 9 (November 1972), 111–115.

20. Avron, "Notes pour une métapsychologie," 104. See also H. Racker, "Contribution to Psychoanalysis of Music," *Am. Imago* 8 (1951), 129–163, linking music with the primary infant-mother relationship.

21. André Michel, echoing ego psychologists such as Heinz Kohut, suggested in a 1951 study that music's primary appeal is that of "whistling in the dark" for fear of silence. It provides a reassuring language of rhythm and sound. Or perhaps the child fears "being abandoned by his auditory world, at first indistinguishable from the mother" (p. 30): *Psychanalyse de la musique* (Paris: Presses Universitaires de France, 1951).

22. See Jean-Louis Baudry, "The Apparatus," *Camera Obscura* 1 (December 1976), 104–126; and Constance Penley, "The Avant-Garde and Its Imaginary," *Camera Obscura* 2 (Fall 1977), 3–33.

23. Penley, 15.

24. This is actually Christian Metz's description of daydreaming in *The Imaginary Signifier* (Bloomington: Indiana University Press, 1982), 106.

25. Philip Rosen, "Adorno and Film Music: Theoretical Notes on *Composing for the Films*," *Yale French Studies* 60 (1980), 174.

26. Quoted in Manvell and Huntley, *The Technique of Film Music* (rev. ed. New York: Hastings House, 1975), 244.

27. Eisler and Adorno, 71.

28. Mary Ann Doane, "Ideology and the Practice of Sound Editing and Mixing," *The Cinematic Apparatus*, ed. T. DeLauretis and S. Heath (London: MacMillan, 1980), 48–49.

29. Metz, *The Imaginary Signifier*, 40.

Chapter IV

1. Christian Metz, "Story/Discourse (A Note on Two Kinds of Voyeurism)," in *The Imaginary Signifier* (Bloomington: Indiana University Press, 1982), 93.

2. André Bazin, *What Is Cinema?* trans. Hugh Gray, vol. 1 (Berkeley: University of California Press, 1967), 30.

3. Metz, "Story/Discourse," 91 and 94.

4. Charles F. Altman, "The Technology of the Voice," Part II, *Iris* 4, 1 (1986), 110.

5. Tom Levin, "The Acoustic Dimension," *Screen* 25 (May–June 1984), 63: "By locating the source of sounds *within* the image or the diegesis, sound is once again subordinated to the visual. At the same time, by focusing attention on the image, the effect of the acoustic 'enigma' is to shift an analytic gaze *away* from the activity of the sound technology which can subsequently function with even less risk of exposure."

6. Milton Lustig, *Music Editing for Motion Pictures* (New York: Hastings House, 1980), 75.

7. Leonid Sabaneev, *Music for the Films: A Handbook for Composers and Conductors*, trans. S. W. Pring (London: Pitman, 1935), 22.

8. Sabaneev, 44–45.

9. Sabaneev, 19.

10. Quoted in Tony Thomas, *Music for the Movies* (S. Brunswick and New York: A. S. Barnes, 1973), 30.

11. W. A. Mueller, "A Device for Automatically Controlling Balance Between Recorded Sounds," *Journal of the Society of Motion Picture Engineers* 25, 1 (July 1935), 79–86.

12. Response to W. A. Mueller, "A Device . . . ," p. 85. This model of film and perception, stemming from William James's writing on psychology, was elaborated upon in 1916 by Hugo Munsterberg, and by others, including Pudovkin, with respect to the image track.

13. Quoted in Tony Thomas, *Music for the Movies*, 34–35.

14. Sabaneev, 21.

15. Another reason for the prevalence of this idiom: the majority of the first wave of Hollywood film composers were thoroughly steeped in it, either because of national origin or by musical training.

16. Quoted in Manvell and Huntley, *The Technique of Film Music* (New York: Focal Press, 1957), 255. Emphasis mine.

17. See Kathryn Kalinak, "The Fallen Woman and the Virtuous Wife: Musical Stereotypes in *The Informer, Gone With the Wind*, and *Laura*," *Film Reader* 5 (1982), 76–82.

18. Sabaneev, 30.

19. Pam Cook, "Duplicity in *Mildred Pierce*," in E. Ann Kaplan, ed., *Women in Film Noir* (London: BFI, 1978), 79.

20. Quoted in Tony Thomas, *Music for the Movies*, 72.

21. Tiomkin, quoted in Thomas.

22. Quoted in Irwin Bazelon, *Knowing the Score: Notes on Film Music* (New York: Van Nostrand Reinhold, 1975), 112.

23. According to Rozsa, Selznick's studio executives summoned him saying "they had a psychological picture and that they wanted something unusual." Rozsa also used the theremin for Billy Wilder's *The Lost Weekend* "to denote·[sic] Ray Milland's craving for alcohol." Roy Prendergast, *A Neglected Art* (New York: New York University Press, 1977), 69–70.

24. Alex North was actually one of the first film composers to use the jazz sound, in *A Streetcar Named Desire*—not until 1951. Elmer Bernstein accounts for his own choice of the jazz idiom four years later, for *The Man With the Golden Arm*, in these terms: "The script had a Chicago slum street, heroin, hysteria, longing, frustration, despair and finally death. . . . There is something very American and contemporary about all the characters and their problems. I wanted an element that could speak readily of hysteria and despair, an element that would localize these emotions to our country, to a large city if possible. Ergo,—jazz." Quoted in Prendergast, 109.

25. Eisler and Adorno's Brechtian project for film music is put forth in *Composing*

for the Films (New York: Oxford University Press, 1947). Eisler did score a number of Hollywood films, of which the most well-documented is Fritz Lang's *Hangmen Also Die*. But their sermon on stripping film music bare of its tired connotations and its redundant function of illustration fell, as far as the public was concerned, on deaf ears.

26. Quoted in Kurt London, *Film Music*, 160–161.

27. Eisler and Adorno, *Composing for the Films*, 13 and 17.

28. Eisler and Adorno, 15.

29. Mark Evans, *Soundtrack: The Music of the Movies* (New York: Hopkinson and Blake, 1975), 226.

30. Tony Thomas, *Music for the Movies*, p. 17.

31. For Eisler, the Hollywood director "knows the danger of nonaction, of absence of suspense, and therefore prescribes music." Eisler, 12.

32. Bazelon, *Knowing the Score*, 22. Maurice Jaubert writes in 1937 about the Steiner score for *The Lost Patrol*: "He inflicts upon us—without giving us a moment's rest—a score whose constant presence threatens to destroy the images' own reality with its gratuitousness." Quoted in Henri Colpi, *Défense et illustration de la musique dans le film* (Lyon: SERDOC, 1960).

33. Evans, 32–33.

34. Colpi, 44–45.

35. Thus, the musical theme contributes strongly to the film's opening duplicity, which poses Mildred—this character played by Crawford—as the murderer. Joyce Nelson's interesting analysis of "false suture" emphasizes the omission of the reverse shot that would have shown the murderer. Her thesis, in *"Mildred Pierce* Reconsidered" (*Film Reader* #2, 1977, 65–70), is taken further by Pam Cook in "Duplicity in *Mildred Pierce,*" in E. Ann Kaplan, ed., *Women in Film Noir* (BFI, 1978), 68–82.

36. Quoted in Tony Thomas, *Film Score: The View from the Podium* (New York: A. S. Barnes, 1979), 81.

37. Peter Brooks, *The Melodramatic Imagination: Balzac, Henry James, Melodrama, and the Mode of Excess* (New Haven: Yale University Press, 1976).

Chapter V

1. Kathryn Kalinak gives a good rendering, for example, of positions for and against film music that underscores/parallels/supports the narrative events, in the first chapter of her dissertation, *Music as Narrative Structure in Hollywood Film* (University of Illinois, 1982).

2. The reader seeking a more thorough treatment of the theoretical milieu of the Frankfurt School and its formative influence on *Composing for the Films* should consult: Philip Rosen, "Adorno and Film Music: Theoretical Notes on *Composing for the Films,*" *Yale French Studies* 60 (1980), 157–182; Max Horkheimer and T. W. Adorno, *Dialectic of Enlightenment* (orig. 1944) (New York: Seabury, 1972), especially "The Culture Industry: Enlightenment and Mass Deception," 120–167; T. W. Adorno, "On the Fetish-Character in Music and the Regression of Listening" (orig. 1938), in Arato, Andrew and Elke Gebhardt, eds., *The Essential Frankfurt School Reader* (New York: Urizen, 1978), 270–299; and Arato and Gebhardt's essay "Introduction: Esthetic Theory and Cultural Criticism," in *The Essential Frankfurt School Reader*, 185–224.

3. The book appeared first in English (New York: Oxford University Press, 1947), signed only by Eisler. Eisler warmly acknowledges Adorno in his preface: "The theories and formulations presented here evolved from co-operation with him on general aesthetic and sociological matters as well as purely musical issues." Some sources assert that Adorno withdrew his own name as co-author in the wish to avoid

being associated, in the brewing climate of American anticommunism, with the Eisler name. The House Un-American Activities Committee's persecution of Eisler's brother Gerhart soon resulted in a hearing for Hanns Eisler himself; he would be forced to leave the United States in 1948. Subsequent editions of *Composing for the Films* in German and French attribute authorship to both Adorno and Eisler.

4. Manfred Grabs, Introduction, in Manfred Grabs, ed., *Hanns Eisler: A Rebel in Music* (Berlin: Seven Seas Publishing, 1979), 10.

5. Albrecht Betz, *Musique et politique: Hanns Eisler.* Trans. Hans Hildebrand (Paris: Le Sycomore, 1982) (orig. München 1976), 103. There is an English translation: *Hanns Eisler Political Musician.* Trans. Bill Hopkins (London and New York: Cambridge University Press, 1982).

6. 1939: *The 400 Million* (Ivens), *Pete Roleum and His Cousins, Soil*; 1940: *White Floods, Rain* (Ivens); 1941: *The Forgotten Village*; 1943: *Hangmen Also Die* (Lang); 1944: *None But the Lonely Heart* (Odets); 1945: *Jealousy* (Machaty), *The Spanish Main* (Borzage); 1946: *Deadline at Dawn* (Clurman), *A Scandal in Paris* or *Thieves' Holiday* (Sirk); 1947: *The Woman on the Beach* (Renoir); 1948: *So Well Remembered* (Dmytryk).

7. He composed fourteen possible musical accompaniments for a sequence in Joris Ivens's 1929 film *Rain* (this work became a concert piece in its own right), and musical alternatives for short segments from other documentaries and newsreels as well as from two fiction films, Herbert Kline's *Forgotten Village* and John Ford's *The Grapes of Wrath.*

8. Arato and Gebhardt, "Introduction," 191.

9. Horkheimer and Adorno, *Dialectic of Enlightenment*, 127.

10. Eisler and Adorno, 58.

11. In *Introduction to the Sociology of Music* as well, Adorno compares music for opening credits to a barker's spiel: "Look here, everyone! What you will see is as grand, as radiant, as colorful as I am! Be grateful, clap your hands and buy. . . ." T. W. Adorno, *Introduction to the Sociology of Music* (New York: Seabury, 1976), 46.

12. See Adorno, "On the Fetish-Character in Music" (see note 1).

13. Adorno, *Introduction to the Sociology of Music*, 31.

14. Adorno, *Introduction to the Sociology of Music*, 46.

Chapter VI

1. A compendium of critical reactions to Vigo's works can be found in P. E. Salles Gomes, *Jean Vigo* (Berkeley: University of California Press, 1971), particularly 220–238.

2. ". . . the spirit of this film, its fierceness and gaiety, the total absence of well-constructed 'constructive' diagnosis and prescription, the enormous liberating force of its quasi-nihilism, its humor, directness, kindliness, criminality, and guile, form for me as satisfying a revolutionary expression as I know." James Agee, *Agee on Film: Reviews and Comments* (Beacon, 1958), 263.

3. For his part, John M. Smith calls the film Expressionist; cf. his *Jean Vigo* (London: Praeger, 1972).

4. There are a few exceptions, such as Fred Steiner's analysis of *Psycho's* score: "Herrmann's Black-and-White Music for Hitchcock's *Psycho*," in two parts in *Filmmusic Notebook*, I (Autumn and Winter, 1974–75). But even this work, by virtue of the author's choice of what is pertinent to his description, largely ignores many of the score's narrative functions. Steiner illustrates his discussion with the relevant musical selections (in standard musical notation, including cue marks), pairing these in his text with skeletal descriptions of the scenes they accompany. Thus the music-image relationships and the music-action relationships are reduced to a verbal plane. Though he declares a concern for achieving a just balance in his analysis, aware as

he is of the "difficulty of trying . . . to strike a balance between information of musical interest and that of cinematic interest" (part 1, p. 29), Steiner chose to concentrate more heavily on the musical codes than on the film-musical codes. For other recent approaches, see the work of Royal Brown, Kathryn Kalinak, and myself.

5. Raymond Bellour, "The Unattainable Text," *Screen* 16, 3 (Autumn 1975), 20.

6. *The Technique of Film Music*, (rev. ed. New York: Hastings House, 1975), 96–107, 120–125, 130–131, 140–149.

7. His "delirium" stems from his idea that we perceive the melodic and dynamic contours of music analogously to the actual visual dynamics of shot composition. His analysis of the music-image relations in the "Battle on the Ice" sequence in Alexander Nevsky rests on the further assumption that we read a filmed image from left to right as linearly as the music's progression on the soundtrack. See his famous article, "Form and Content: Practice," in *Film Sense*, trans. and ed. Jay Leyda (New York: Harcourt Brace & World, 1947), 156–216.

8. Fully three "jump cuts" (shots 6, 12, and 29) appear within 38 shots, apparently a consequence of Vigo's lack of money and shooting time for the film. However, the jump cuts prove to have a more systematic basis; see below, under "Editing to Music."

9. This is normal in any tonal composition that undergoes modulation and variation.

10. For example, consider Vigo's treatment of the visual motif of cigar smoke. Smoke and steam come to connote movement, life, (scatological) immersion in one's atmosphere. The film has as its first shot the train compartment's door with steam billowing outside it. This same shot is repeated twice more (shots 15 and 18), accumulating resonance with each occurrence: if at first the shot simply indicates the interior of a moving train, it also comes to rhyme with the schoolboys' smoke-filled interior, etc., and the two-shot of Caussat and Huguet (shot 5) also includes the smoke. Huguet appears on the station platform breathing steam, recalling both the train steam out the window and the boys' cigar smoking, further reinforcing the aspect of smoke as a visual rhyme.

11. *L'Avant-scène du cinéma* (No. 21, 12/15/62) prints the original screenplay, so the line it gives here is "Haricot fils! haricot fils! on a voyagé avec un mort!" (Kid Beans, Kid Beans, we've been on the train with a dead man!)—not helpful, but interesting in that it suggests that the line was changed in order to form the rhythmic whole.

12. Therefore I take issue with Manvell and Huntley's narrow view of the music in *Zéro*. They mention the film briefly in their *Technique of Film Music* (p. 107); on shots 19 to 22: "As the train jerks to a standstill, a sleeping youth [sic] falls to the floor of the compartment. 'Il est mort!' shouts one of the boys; he has fallen with a heavy, musical thud. The natural sounds of the station flood in on the track, the boys get out of the train. The game is ended; the fantasy world becomes a real station platform. The sequence ends as abruptly as it began. The music is finished."

13. From "Music on the Screen" (p. 112), in *Footnotes to the Film*, ed. Charles Davy. This is a translation of what was originally a lecture Jaubert gave in London on December 10, 1936, entitled "La Musique dans le film," and which was subsequently printed in *Cinéma* (Cours et conférences de l'IDHEC), 1, 1944. It was also reprinted in *Ecran français* no. 522 (June 26, 1946).

14. Jaubert, "La Musique dans le film."

15. S. M. Eisenstein, *Réflexions d'un cinéaste* (Moscow: Editions du progrès, 1958), 178.

16. *Footnotes to the Film*, 111–112.

17. *Footnotes to the Film*, 113.

18. Quoted by François Porcile, in *Maurice Jaubert: Musicien populaire ou maudit?* (Paris: Editeurs Français Réunis, 1971), 205.

19. The French Board of Censors banned *Zéro de conduite* soon after its release in April 1933, giving no explanation for their action. Whether they were pressured to do so by the Catholic authorities, or whether they took offense at scatological references and a brief shot of a penis, or whether they deemed it subversive—a threat to public order—is a matter of speculation. Its public rerelease did not occur until twelve years later, after the Liberation. It opened at the Panthéon in Paris, in November 1945, on the same bill with Malraux's *Espoir*. For an account of the film's exhibition history, see Salles Gomes's study.

20. Salles Gomes, 98.

Chapter VII

1. Ralph Stephenson and J. R. Debrix, *The Cinema as Art* (London: Penguin, 1965), 180.

2. See his *Cinema Yesterday and Today*, trans. Stanley Appelbaum, ed. R. C. Dale (New York: Dover, 1972). The Soviets also, of course, took an intermediate position; see particularly the famous manifesto on sound drawn up in 1928 by Eisenstein, Alexandrov, and Pudovkin.

3. This fear was grounded in the rise of Pagnol's and Guitry's "canned theater" filmmaking in his own country, as well as countless talkies made in Europe and the United States whose staginess had the effects feared by Clair, Eisenstein, critics at *Close Up*, and many others who prized the aesthetic freedom from literalness that the techniques of silent cinema had found.

4. Clair, *Cinema Yesterday and Today*, 145.

5. Siegfried Kracauer, "Dialogue and sound," Chapter 7 of *Theory of Film*, (New York: Oxford University Press, 1960).

6. Kracauer, 113.

7. Although offscreen space is necessarily diegetic, onscreen space may either be diegetic or nondiegetic. An example of nondiegetic onscreen space is the insert.

8. The fact that the very first lines in the film are spoken in a sort of Parisian pig latin, answered by a line in Rumanian, successfully unnerves any audience. From the outset, we are wary of dialogue.

Chapter VIII

1. In Patrick Hamilton's novel *Hangover Square*, from which the scenario was adapted, the protagonist is not a composer at all; neither does the novel contain the systematic doubling of characters found in the film.

2. Let's label this motif *A*:

Graham Bruce traces the tritone through *Hangover Square* in *Bernard Herrmann: Film Music and Narrative* (Ann Arbor: UMI, 1985), 88–90.

3. David Bordwell, Janet Staiger, and Kristin Thompson, *The Classical Hollywood*

Cinema: Film Style and Mode of Production to 1960 (New York: Columbia University Press, 1985), 70.

4. Organ-grinder theme, *B*:

5. Call this music *C*:

6. See, for example, the fascinating case histories in D. D. Daly and M. J. Barry, "Musicogenic Epilepsy: Report of Three Cases," *Psychosomatic Medicine* 19, 5 (1957), 399–408.

7. With the exceptions of "Have You Seen Joe," the vaudeville song Netta performs when George first sees her, and "So Close to Paradise" and "All for You," songs that George writes for her.

8. For much more on Herrmann's film composing strategies, the reader is referred to Graham Bruce's study (see n. 2).

9. Irene Kahn Atkins, *Source Music in Motion Pictures* (E. Brunswick, N. J.: Fairleigh Dickinson University Press, 1983), 122, footnote 6.

10. For example, in *Padre Padrone*, "when the Blue Danube waltz resonates with the arid and hostile landscape shots of the poor Italian countryside, there is no affective response but the statement of an idea: the classical/bourgeois culture which the hero is going to try to acquire." Michel Chion, *Le Son au cinéma* (Paris: Cahiers du cinéma/Editions de l'étoile, 1985), 124.

11. Chion, 123.

12. Chion, 125.

Selected and
Annotated Bibliography
on Film Music

I. Critical Works

Applebaum, Louis, "Hugo Friedhofer's Score to *The Best Years of Our Lives*," *Film Music Notes* 9, 5 (1947). Description and analysis.

Atkins, Irene Kahn, *Source Music in Motion Pictures*. E. Brunswick, N.J.: Fairleigh Dickinson University Press, 1983. History, dramatic functions of diegetic music. Useful bibliography.

Bartush, Jay, "*Citizen Kane*: The Music," *Film Reader* 1 (1975), 50–54. Analysis of the score, as part of issue devoted to "Semiotics and *Citizen Kane*."

Batchelor, Jennifer, "From *Aïda* to *Zauberflöte*—the Opera Film," *Screen* 25, 3 (May–June 1984), 26–38. Traces history of the opera film and suggests why it has flourished in the seventies and eighties: it renders a potentially elitist medium (opera) more popular and profitable. Uses of the genre by e.g. Bergman, Godard, Saura.

Baudrier, Yves, "Musique et cinéma," *Cahiers de l'IDHEC*, 1930. Emphasizes opposition between cinema's realist tendency and music's lyric tendency. Music must bring out the image's "temporal interior reality."

Bazelon, Irwin, *Knowing the Score: Notes on Film Music*. New York: Van Nostrand Reinhold, 1975. Sections on composer's art and method, functions of film music; useful statements and interviews by composers. Unevenly reliable.

Behlmer, Rudy, "Erich Wolfgang Korngold," *Films In Review* 18, 2 (Feb. 1967), 86–100. Overview of Korngold's career.

Berg, Charles Merrell, "Cinema Sings the Blues," *Cinema Journal* 17, 2 (Spring 1978), 1–12. Overview of jazz in the movies, from silent-film ragtime accompaniment, through cartoon, experimental, and musical shorts, and the wave of jazz in fifties and sixties feature films.

———, *An Investigation of the Motives for and the Realization of Music to Accompany the American Silent Film, 1896–1927*. New York: Arno, 1976. With bibliography.

Bernstein, Elmer, "A Conversation with David Raksin," *Filmmusic Notebook*; Part I: 2, 2 (1976), 14–21; Part II: 2, 3 (1976), 9–18. Raksin's career, and general film criticism. See also six other "conversations" with composers (Amfitheatrof, George Roy Hill, Goldsmith, Addison, J. Green, L. Shuken, R. R. Bennett), in issues from 1975 to 1977.

Bianco e nero 11 (May–June 1950), 5–6: Special issue on "La Musica nel film," ed. Luigi Chiarini.

Blanchard, Gérard, *Images de la musique de cinéma*. Paris: Edilig, 1984. Drawing on Frances Yates, Bachelard, Pierre Schaeffer, and others, Blanchard discusses how cinema music functions like an "art of memory." Sections on connotations of musical instruments and styles. Many references for film music recordings.

Bourgeois, Jacques, "Musique dramatique et cinéma," *La Revue du cinéma* 2, 10 (Feb. 1948), 25–34. Film music is reinventing principles Wagner established in *Opera and Drama* for dramatic music. Waxman's score for *Objective Burma* (1944). Historical overview concludes that Prokofiev is the only "great" composer to write great film music; the cartoon presents challenge for film music art.

Brown, Royal S., "Herrmann, Hitchcock, and the Music of the Irrational," *Cinema Journal* 21, 2 (1982), 14–49. Rev. and repr. in Mast and Cohen, eds., *Film Theory and Criticism*, 3rd ed. (New York: Oxford University Press, 1985), 618–649. Evolution of Herrmann-Hitchcock collaboration from *The Trouble with Harry* through *Psycho*. Analysis of Herrmann's harmonic and melodic strategies; Hitchcock aligns source music with rationality, and soundtrack cues to evoke the irrational.

———, "Music and *Vivre sa vie*," *Quarterly Review of Film Studies* 5, 3 (Summer 1980), 319–333. Legrand's music of barely 70 seconds is used structurally by Godard as "12 cadence-less measures which, like the film itself, form a kind of closed loop capable of indefinite repetition."

Bruce, Graham Donald, *Bernard Herrmann: Film Music and Film Narrative*. Ann Arbor: UMI, 1985. Examines BH's contributions in context of the "classical" Hollywood style and alternatives of Eisler, Brecht. Analyses of *Kane*, *Obsession*, *Taxi Driver*, *Vertigo*, *Psycho*, others.

Caps, John, "John Williams: Scoring the Film Whole," *Filmmusic Notebook* 2, 3 (1976), 19–25. Several other articles in Vol. 2 of *Filmmusic Notebook* on Rozsa, Goldsmith, Barry.

Chavez, Carlos, *Toward a New Music: Music and Electricity*. Trans. Herbert Weinstock. New York: Norton, 1937. Esp. chapter 5, "The Sound Film" (89–121). Technology of sound-on-film, music recording for films; sound libraries allow for great creative film music synthesis, so far discouraged by commercial interests.

Chion, Michel, *Le Son au cinéma*. Paris: Cahiers du cinéma/Editions de l'Etoile, 1985. Part II: Music in the Cinema (in 4 chapters). Insightful essays. Aesthetic specificity of film music; debt to older stage and musical forms for mickey-mousing, for tendency to pastiche; any formal specificity of film music lies in its discontinuity and fragmentation. Music as "humanized" displacement of mechanical rhythm of projector. Music's "indifference" to human time of narrative. Functions in relation to narrative time and space. Filming music.

Cinéma 64. Special issue on film music: no. 89 (1964). Cf. entry for *Ecran 75*.

Colpi, Henri, *Défense et illustration de la musique de film*. Lyon: Société d'Etudes, de Recherches et de Documentation Cinématographiques (SERDOC), 1963. Anecdotal and encyclopedic "appreciation" of film music, with sections on history, technology and economics, theory, the musical film. Sketches of Eisenstein, Jaubert, Grémillon, British documentary school, *Hiroshima mon amour*.

Comuzio, Ermanno, *Colonna sonora: Dialoghi, musiche, rumori, dietro lo schermo*. Milano: Edizioni il Formichiere, 1980. Part I: Technical description of the soundtrack; music in silent film and into the sound era; aesthetics of film music; composing, mixing, editing. Part II: Theoretical problems in film mu-

sic, e.g., music-image relations, leitmotivs, synchronism vs. asynchronism,
nontraditional musical styles, music in film genres, film musicals. Part III:
Overview of film composers in all film-producing countries.

Cook, Page, "The Sound Track," regular column on film music in *Films in Review*,
beginning in 14, 9 (1963).

De la Motte-Haber, Helga, and Hans Emons, *Filmmusik: Eine systematische Bes-
chreibung.* München: Carl Hanser Verlag, 1980. Five aesthetic models (Kracauer, Zofia Lissa, Eisenstein, Benjamin-Adorno-Eisler, Arnheim) examined;
follows with sections on theory, aesthetics, and practice.

Ecran 75 (15 September 1975). Special issue on film music, "Cinéma et musique
1960–1975." Updates *Cinéma 64* no. 89.

Ehrenstein, David, and Bill Reed, *Rock on Film.* New York: Delilah Books, 1982.
Lively history of rock music in commercial American films. Thorough listing
of films containing or featuring rock music: arranged by title, giving date,
genre, credits, summary including artists and songs.

Eisenstein, Sergei M., "Form and Content: Practice," in *The Film Sense* (New York:
Harvest, 1942), 157–216. On the score for *Alexander Nevsky.*

Eisler, Hanns [and Theodor Adorno], *Composing for the Films.* New York: Oxford
University Press, 1947. Neo-Marxist critique of Hollywood's film music industry and textual practice. Aesthetics; outline for progressive practice; report
on Eisler's film-composing experiments.

Evans, Mark, *Soundtrack: The Music of the Movies.* New York: Hopkinson and Blake,
1975. Anecdotal work for popular consumption, disorganized and inaccurate.
Historical samplings, sketches of most important Hollywood composers, some
Europeans.

Fano, Michel, "Film, partition sonore," *Musique en jeu* 21 (Nov. 1975), 10–13. Fano,
regular collaborator with Robbe-Grillet, advocates replacing concept "film
music" with "sound score," to emphasize soundtrack's ensemble of signifying
material.

Faulkner, Robert, *Hollywood Studio Musicians: Their Work and Careers in the
Recording Industry.* Chicago: Aldine Atherton, 1971. Sociologist's overview
of the film music industry: Hollywood musicians, their relations to composers
and music directors.

Film and TV Music. 1,1 (October 1941). Various titles: began as *Film Music Notes*,
1941–51; *Film Music*, 1951–56; *Film and TV Music*, 1956–58. Publication of
the National Film Music Council.

Filmmakers Newsletter 4 (April 1971). Special issue on film music.

Filmmusic Notebook. Elmer Bernstein's Film Music Collection (Calabasas, Calif.)
Vol 1 (1974–). Quarterly publication of the Elmer Bernstein Society.

Frith, Simon, "Mood Music: An Inquiry Into Narrative Film Music," *Screen* 25, 3
(May–June 1984), 78–87. Remarks on the coding of film/musical pleasure,
esp. regarding use of popular music in commercial films. The "realism" offered
by music (emotional reality and reality of time and place) differs from image's
"realism."

Gallez, Douglas W., "The Prokofiev-Eisenstein Collaboration: *Nevsky* and *Ivan* Re-
visited," *Cinema Journal* 17, 2 (Spring 1978), 13–35. Well-documented analysis of Eisenstein/Prokofiev's collaboration on *Alexander Nevsky* and especially
Ivan the Terrible.

———, "Satie's *Entr'acte*: A Model of Film Music," *Cinema Journal* 16, 1 (Fall 1976),
36–50. Satie's self-effacing music is written in repetitious short segments, in

accordance with his idea of *musique d'ameublement.* "Offers a model solution
to problems in sound film: . . . continuity, background for dialogue, and pro-
pulsion of action."
————, "Theories of Film Music," *Cinema Journal* 9, 2 (Spring 1970), 40–47.
Overview of key works in the literature.
Geduld, Harry, "Film Music: A Survey," *Quarterly Review of Film Studies* 1, 2 (May
1976), 183–204. Survey of books on music for silent and sound cinema (musical
theater, film musicals), records of film music.
Germain, Jean, "La Musique et le film," in Etienne Souriau, ed., *L'univers filmique*
(Paris: Flammarion, 1953), 137–155.
Gorbman, Claudia, "Music As Mirror: *Cleo from 5 to 7*," *Wide Angle* 4, 4 (1981),
38–49. Structural analysis of musical score's role in construction of narrative
time and point of view.
————, "Music As Salvation: Notes On Fellini and Rota," *Film Quarterly* 28, 2
(Winter 1974/75), 17–25. Music and narration in *Nights of Cabiria.*

Hacquard, Georges, *La Musique et le cinéma.* Paris: Presses Universitaires de France,
1959.
Hagen, Earl, *Scoring for Films.* New York: E. D. J. Music, Criterion Music Corp.,
1971. Mechanics and vocabulary of film composing. Timing, equipment, click
tracks (detailed explanation and charts), etc. The composer's responsibilities
(legal and other) from pre- to post-production. Symposium of composers'
views. Principles for scoring with dialogue, source music (diegetic), "closed"
(under dialogue) and "open" scoring (nondiegetic).
Haun, Harry, and George Raborn, "Max Steiner," *Films in Review* 12 (June/July
1961), 338–351. Overview of Steiner's career. Filmography to 1961.
Herrmann, Bernard, "Bernard Herrmann, Composer" (1973), in E. W. Cameron,
ed. *Sound and the Cinema: The Coming of Sound to American Film* (Pleas-
antville, N.Y.: Redgrave, 1980), 117–135. Working with directors; business
incentives of film music. Music affecting film time, unifying montage, expressing subjective states. *Kane, Fahrenheit 451, Psycho.*
Hofmann, Charles, *Sounds for Silents.* New York: Drama Book Specialists (DBS),
1970. Foreword by Lillian Gish. Veteran pianist's account of history and practices of musical accompaniment for silent films. Documents reproduced incl.
photos, cue sheets, sample scores, sheet music, quotes from composers, reviewers, trade press.
Huntley, John, *British Film Music.* Orig. London, 1947. Repr. New York: Arno,
1972. Though written in "film music appreciation" tone, an erudite work.
Sections on history (major composers and scores), the British documentary
and other non-feature genres, music recording, and "forum" on British film
music incl. K. London, B. Britten, P. Rotha, A. Bliss, M. Matheson,
M. Rozsa, R. Vaughan Williams, others. Indexes, bibliography.
————, "The Sound Track." Regular column in *Sight and Sound*, vols. 19–24 (1950–
55).

Irving, Ernest, with Hans Keller and Wilfred Mellers, "Film Music," in *Grove's
Dictionary of Music and Musicians*, Eric Blom, 5th ed., New York: St. Martin's
Press, 1954. With bibliography. Composer Irving's section details technical
procedures of composing and recording; denigrates film music as opposed to
concert music.

Jaubert, Maurice, "Music on the Screen," in Davy, Charles, ed., *Footnotes to the
Film* (New York: Oxford University Press, 1937), 101–115. Music's new roles
in sound film. J. rejects music for annotation or synchronism. Music brings

poetic element to the realism of sound film. Should have "impersonal" texture as sound element, take advantage of recording medium.

Johnson, William, "Face the Music," *Film Quarterly* 22, 4 (Summer 1969), 3–19. The physiological effects of music on the film spectator, through rhythm, dynamics, and pitch. Musical and cinematic form. Concert music in film. The early sound film score's "inherent weaknesses." Uses of ambient (diegetic) music. The theme tune. Many examples.

Kalinak, Kathryn, "The Fallen Woman and the Virtuous Wife: Musical Stereotypes in *The Informer, Gone With the Wind,* and *Laura,*" *Film Reader* 5 (1982), 76–82. Musical connotation as it figures in the Hollywood screen representation of woman.

———, *Music as Narrative Structure in Hollywood Film.* Ph.D. Diss., Illinois, 1982. Following a historical and aesthetic overview of film music, concentrates on the "classical" period to 1945. Analyses of *Captain Blood* (Korngold), *The Informer* (Steiner), *The Magnificent Ambersons* (Herrmann), and *Laura* (Raksin).

Keller, Hans, *The Need for Competent Film Music Criticism.* London: BFI, 1947.

Kracauer, Siegfried, *Theory of Film: The Redemption of Physical Reality.* New York: Oxford University Press, 1960. Chapters 7 and 8, "Dialogue and Sound" and "Music."

Lacombe, Alain, *Hollywood Rhapsody: L'Age d'or de la musique de film à Hollywood.* Paris: Jobert, 1983. Part 1: historical/anecdotal overview of film music economics, genres, composers, and critics in Hollywood's classical period. Part 2: biographical sketches of 25 composers; filmographies and discographies (incomplete).

Lacombe, Alain, and Claude Rocle, "Les Paramètres d'un silence indésirable," *Musique en jeu* 33 (Nov. 1978), 41–58. Early relations between music and cinema, until the talkies. Popular and "art" cinema; their respective economic and aesthetic determinations of musical accompaniment.

Lambert, Constant, "Mechanical Music and the Cinema," in *Music Ho! A Study of Music in Decline.* New York: Scribner, 1934.

Larson, Randall D., *Musique Fantastique: A Survey of Music in the Fantastic Cinema.* Metuchen, N.J.: Scarecrow, 1985. Genre study of music for science fiction, fantasy, and horror films. Includes filmography (by composer) and discography (by film title).

Levy, Louis, *Music for the Movies.* London: Sampson Low, 1948. Anecdotal first-hand account of work in musicals and scoring for dramatic films.

Limbacher, James, ed. *Film Music: From Violins to Video.* Metuchen, N.J.: Scarecrow, 1974. First section includes many short articles on film music, written by musicians and other Hollywood personnel. Main section is (sometimes inaccurate) index of films and composers.

Lissa, Zofia, *Aesthetik der Filmmusik.* Berlin: Henscheverlag, 1965.

London, Kurt, *Film Music: A Summary of the Characteristic Features of Its History, Aesthetics, Techniques, and Its Possible Developments.* Orig. London, 1936. Repr. New York: Arno Press, 1970. Historical survey of nature and uses of film music from silents to early sound era. Problems and methods of music in the sound film.

Manvell, Roger, and John Huntley, *The Technique of Film Music.* (London, 1957) Rev. ed. (Richard Arnell and Peter Day), New York: Hastings House, 1975. History and aesthetics of film music; sections on the music director and sound recordist, and composers' views. Films treated in depth: *Henry V, Louisiana*

Story, Julius Caesar, Odd Man Out, The Best Years of Our Lives, and, in 1975 ed., *The Devils, 2001, Second Best,* and *Zabriskie Point.*

Meeker, David, *Jazz in the Movies.* London: BFI, 1972. Repr. New York: Da Capo, 1981.

Mellers, Wilfred H., "The Musical Problem," final section of entry "Film Music" in *Grove's Dictionary of Music and Musicians,* 5th ed. New York: St. Martin's Press, 1954. Aesthetic problems of film music. Satie's reconciliation of montage with musical continuity in *Entr'acte.* Eisler as film composer. Copland's (*Of Mice and Men*), Thomson's (*Louisiana Story*), and French and Russian scoring examined. Film opera and cartoon.

Milano, Paolo, "Music in the Film: Notes for a Morphology," *Journal of Aesthetics and Art Criticism* 1, 1 (Spring 1941), 89–94. Maps out categories according to greater or lesser subordination of music to visuals.

Mitry, Jean, *Esthétique et psychologie du cinéma.* 2 vols. Paris: Editions Universitaires, 1963–66. Sections on film music.

Modern Music. Regular film music reviews variously titled "On the Film Front," "Films and Theatre," "On the Hollywood Front," 1936–1946. Authors incl. Lawrence Morton, Charles Koechlin, George Antheil, William Alwyn, Paul Bowles.

Morton, Lawrence, "Film Music of the Quarter." Column in *Hollywood Quarterly,* vols. 3–6 (1947–51). Thoughtful reviews of notable scores incl. *The Third Man, Sunset Boulevard, Broken Arrow, Forever Amber.* Also topics of current interest such as filmed opera, Hollywood orchestrating.

————, "The Music of *Objective: Burma,*" *Hollywood Quarterly* 1, 4 (July 1946), 378–395. Analysis of Waxman's 1944 score and its descriptive, narrative, psychological functions through deployment of themes.

Moving Picture World. Column "Music for the Picture," irreg. from Nov. 1910 to March 1919. For motion picture musicians, with information, practical advice, and musical examples.

"Music in Films: A Symposium of Composers," *Films: A Quarterly of Discussion and Analysis* 1, 4 (Winter 1940), 5–20. Results of internationally circulated questionnaire, incl. Blitzstein, Bowles, Britten, Copland, Eisler, Rathaus, Shostakovitch, Thomson.

Nelson, Robert U., "Film Music: Color or Line?" *Hollywood Quarterly* 2, 1 (Oct. 1946), 57–65. Color (for descriptive effect) vs. line (music's own discourse): film music is obviously "coloristic in its intention and effect." Examples. Advocates new emphasis on line.

Porcile, François, *Présence de la musique à l'écran.* Paris: Editions du Cerf, 1969. Aesthetics and criticism of film music. Bio-filmographies of many composers.

Prendergast, Roy M., *A Neglected Art: A Critical Study of Music in Films.* New York: NYU Press, 1977. Sections on film music history, aesthetics, and techniques of scoring, editing, mixing, dubbing. Interviews with contemporary film composers.

Pro Musica Sana. Publication of the Miklos Rozsa Society. 1970–78(?). Articles range from reviews of recordings of film music and interviews with composers to in-depth analyses of film scores.

Rapee, Erno, *Encyclopedia of Music for Pictures.* (New York, 1924) Repr. New York: Arno, 1970. Suggestions for musical accompaniment for films.

Reisz, Karel, and Gavin Millar, *The Technique of Film Editing.* Rev. ed. New York: Hastings House, 1968. History, practice, and principles of editing. Includes sound and music.

La Revue musicale. Special issue, "Le Film sonore: l'écran et la musique en 1935," 15, 151, December 1934. Articles by Hoérée, Honegger, Koechlin, Ibert, Sarnette, others, on aesthetic principles for music in sound film.

Rosar, William H., "Music for the Monsters," *Library of Congress Quarterly*, Fall 1983. Genre study of music for Universal's thirties horror films.

Rosen, Philip, "Adorno and Film Music: Theoretical Notes on *Composing for the Films*," *Yale French Studies* 60 (1980), 157–182. Adorno's theory of art and of the degradation of musical listening under capitalism; development of his thought in Adorno/Eisler's *Composing for the Films.*

Ross, T. J., *Film and the Liberal Arts.* New York: Holt, Rinehart and Winston, 1969. "Film and Music," 217–247, has essays by G. Antheil, O. Levant, D. Tiomkin, and Page Cook.

Rubsamen, Walter, *Descriptive Music for Stage and Screen.* Los Angeles: UCLA, 1949. Monograph on expressive/evocative music, drawing from nineteenth-century composers as well as film and radio composers.

———, "Music in the American Dramatic Film," *Juilliard Review* 4, 2 (Spring 1957), 20–28. Digest of emotive and connotative functions of music (diegetic and nondiegetic) in American feature films.

Sabaneev, Leonid, *Music for the Films: A Handbook for Composers and Conductors.* Trans. S. W. Pring. London: Sir Isaac Pitman & Sons, 1935. Early thirties state-of-the-art manual for film composers, explains conditions of recording (incl. orchestration), mixing, and editing, and advises on best composing methods. Section on sound-film aesthetics.

"Shooting the Music," *Photoplay*, March 1918, p. 41. Description by Joseph O'Sullivan, Mutual's music director, of process of preparing cue sheets to be distributed to movie theaters.

Steiner, Fred, "Herrmann's 'Black and White' Music for Hitchcock's *Psycho*," *Filmmusic Notebook* 1, 1 (Fall 1974), 28–36; 1, 2 (Winter 1974–75), 26–46. In-depth analysis of Herrmann's landmark score.

Steiner, Max, "Scoring the Film," in Nancy Naumburg, ed., *We Make the Movies* (New York: Norton, 1937), 216–238. Reminiscences about early film scoring in the studio system; observations on aesthetics.

Sternfeld, Frederick W., "Copland as a Film Composer," *Musical Quarterly* 37 (April 1951), 161–175. Musicological evaluation of Copland's film work, especially in *Of Mice and Men* and *The Heiress.*

———, "Film Music," in *Harvard Dictionary of Music*, 2nd ed. Ed. Willi Apel. Cambridge, Mass.: Harvard University Press, 1969.

———, "Gail Kubik's Score for 'C-Man'," *Hollywood Quarterly* 4, 4 (Summer 1950), 360–369. Analysis of Kubik's efficiently orchestrated score for low-budget film.

———, "Music and the Feature Films," *Musical Quarterly* 33, 4 (October 1947), 517–532. A musical score can serve twofold purpose of accompanying the film and introducing the public to modern music. Musicological analysis of Friedhofer's score for *The Best Years of Our Lives.*

———, "The Strange Music of Martha Ivers," *Hollywood Quarterly* 2, 3 (April 1947), 242–251. Description and analysis of Rozsa's "craftsmanship" for Milestone's 1946 film.

Stravinsky, Igor, "La Musique de film?—du papier peint!" *Ecran franqis* no. 125, (November 1947), 3. Films need music in the same way the composer's studio might need wallpaper. Music as decorative, as bearing conventional meaning, does not interest Stravinsky.

Sutak, Ken, "The Return of *A Streetcar Named Desire*," (in 4 parts) *Pro Musica Sana* 3, nos. 1 (Spring 74) and 4 (Winter 74–75); 4, nos. 2 and 3 (1975–76). Detailed analysis of Alex North's influential score.

Thiel, Wolfgang, *Filmmusik in Geschichte und Gegenwart*. Berlin: Henschelverlag Kunst und Gesellschaft, 1981.

Thomas, Tony, comp. and ed., *Film Score: The View from the Podium*. S. Brunswick and New York: A. S. Barnes, 1979. Twenty film composers' statements about their work. Includes film music discography 1970–78 by Page Cook, and select bibliography by Win Sharples.

————, *Music for the Movies*. S. Brunswick and New York: A. S. Barnes, 1973. Anecdotal, well-researched history-by-composer of Hollywood film music. Discography and filmography of twenty-four composers.

Winkler, Max, *A Penny From Heaven*. New York: Appleton-Century-Crofts, 1951. Autobiographical account of early days of film music.

Winter, Marion Hannah, "The Functions of Music in Sound Films," *Musical Quarterly* 27, 2 (April 1941), 146–164. Trends in film music composing, especially in the international avant-garde, to 1940.

II. Manuals and Technical Works

Beynon, George, *Musical Presentation of Motion Pictures*. New York: G. Schirmer, 1921. Survey of music for motion pictures, 1903–21. Principles of compiling and conducting film scores.

Dolan, Robert Emmett, *Music in Modern Media*. New York: G. Schirmer, 1967. Manual for preparing, composing, and recording music for tape and disc, film, television, and electronic music. Chapters 4–12 on film.

Kellogg, Edward W., "The ABC of Photographic Sound Recording," *Journal of the Society of Motion Picture Engineers* 44, 3 (March 1945). Basic essay on history and technique of optical recording.

————, "History of Sound Motion Pictures," *Journal of the Society of Motion Picture and Television Engineers* 64 (June, July, August 1955). Technical survey of development of motion picture sound.

Lang, Edith, and George West, *Musical Accompaniment of Motion Pictures*. (1920), repr. Arno, 1970. Manual for pianists and organists for silent pictures. 64 pp.

Lustig, Martin, *Music Editing for Motion Pictures*. (New York: Hastings House, 1980). Guide to procedures and technology, from the spotting session, timing on the movieola, click-tracks, to playback recording and editing. Includes illustrative sample timing sheets, charts, appendices.

Mancini, Henry, *Sounds and Scores: A Practical Guide to Professional Orchestration*. Northridge Music, 1967 (1962). Guide for the professional.

Nisbett, Alec, *The Technique of the Sound Studio*. New York: Hastings House, 1962.

Reisz, Karel, and Gavin Millar, *The Technique of Film Editing*. Rev. ed., New York: Hastings House, 1968. (see main entry)

Roberts, Kenneth H., and Win Sharples, Jr., *A Primer for Film-making: A Complete Guide to 16mm and 35mm Film Production*. Indianapolis: Bobbs-Merrill, 1971. See esp. chs. 5, 11, and 12: scoring, music editing, etc.

Sabaneev, Leonid, *Music for the Films: A Handbook for Composers and Conductors*. (see main entry)

Skiles, Marlin, *Music Scoring for TV and Motion Pictures*. Blue Ridge Summit, Pa:

Tab Books, 1976. Clear, complete manual for film and TV composers. Three sequences analyzed from cue sheet to finished score. Legal and financial issues. Interviews with six composers (Q. Jones, H. Friedhofer, D. Grusin, J. Green, A. North, L. Morton.)

Skinner, Frank, *Underscore*. New York: Criterion Music Corp., 1960. Manual for film and TV composers. Step-by-step, cue-by-cue explanation of the author's choices in scoring an entire film ("The Irishman"). Advice on instrumentation and arranging in various styles.

III. Bibliography and Reference

ASCAP—30 Years of Motion Picture Music. New York: American Society of Composers, Authors and Publishers, 1967. Writer and other credits listed chronologically, according to song titles.

Atkins, Irene Kahn, *Source Music in Motion Pictures*. (see main entry.) Has 50+ page annotated bibliography on sound and music in film.

"Composers on Film Music: A Bibliography," *Films: A Quarterly of Discussion and Analysis* 1, 4 (Winter 1940), 21–24. International (mostly in English) bibliography of thirty-seven composers' articles on film music.

Ehrenstein, David, and Bill Reed, *Rock on Film*. New York: Delilah Books, 1982. Has 171-page listing of films by title that supplies release date, credits, data on music, and short film description.

Elsas, Diana, ed. *Factfile: Film Music*. Washington: American Film Institute, 1977. Annotated bibliography. Data on film music organizations, schools with film music courses, sources for soundtrack discs and for background music, films on film music, oral history sources on film music, periodicals which cover film music.

Gorbman, Claudia, "Annotated Bibliography on Sound in Film (Excluding Music)," in Elisabeth Weis and John Belton, eds., *Film Sound: Theory and Practice* (New York: Columbia University Press, 1985), 427–445. For soundtrack theory, aesthetics, and practice, complements present bibliography.

Kinkle, Roger D., *Complete Encyclopedia of Popular Music and Jazz 1900–1950*. New Rochelle: Arlington House, 1974. Four vols. Biographical data on singers, composers, bandleaders, musicians; musical credits on 1,230 movie musicals; information on 28,000 popular songs; discographies.

Lacombe, Alain, *Des Compositeurs pour l'image (cinéma et télévision)*. Paris: Musique et promotion, 1982. Published for SACEM—the French ASCAP. Part 1: essay on the situation of film composing in France, 1930 to the present. Short bios on major French film composers of the past. Part 2: Exhaustive filmographies of living French film and TV composers, alphabetically arranged by composer.

Limbacher, James, *Film Music: From Violins to Video*. Metuchen, N.J.: Scarecrow, 1974. Large reference section: alphabetical listing of film titles and dates, year-by-year listing of film titles indicating composers; composers' filmographies, discography. Not highly reliable, prone to omission.

———, *Keeping Score: Film Music 1972–79*. Metuchen, N.J.: Scarecrow, 1981. Updates Limbacher's earlier *Film Music*. Added articles by composers and others in the film music business.

186 Selected and Annotated Bibliography on Film Music

Marks, Martin, "Film Music: The Material, Literature and Present State of Research," *Notes* (The Quarterly Journal of the Music Library Association) 36, 2 (December 1979), 282–325. Well-researched overview of literature, materials in the field, and directions for research.

McCarty, Clifford, *Film Composers in America: A Checklist of Their Work.* (1953) Repr. and re-ed. New York: Da Capo, 1972. Foreword by Lawrence Morton. Listing of composers, arrangers, orchestrators, musical directors. Complete composer filmographies through 1953.

———, "The Score of the Scores," Filmography of 24 major Hollywood composers, in Tony Thomas, *Music for the Movies* (S. Brunswick and New York: A. S. Barnes, 1973), 236–264.

Rapee, Erno, *Motion Picture Moods for Pianists and Organists.* (1928) Repr. New York: Arno, 1970. Some 200 compositions arranged for easy reference according to mood, setting, or story event.

Sharples, Win, Jr., "A Selected and Annotated Bibliography of Books and Articles on Music in the Cinema," *Cinema Journal* 17, 2 (Spring 1978), 36–67. Valuable, accurate, eclectic bibliographies of books, articles, periodicals, and organizations of film music.

Index

Disney, Walt, 2
Doane, Mary Ann, 62n, 67
Don Juan, 45–46, 55
Dracula, 148
Dr. Jekyll and Mr. Hyde, 148
Dr Mabuse der Spieler, 38

Easy-listening music, 5, 56–59
Eisenstein, Sergei, 15, 49, 117, 127, 127n
Eisler, Hanns, 89
    and T.W. Adorno, 15, 39, 40, 41, 58, 64,
    67, 68, 81, 86, 87; critique of Hollywood
    scoring practices, 99–109
Ennis, Bert, 35
Epic feeling, music and, 81–82. *See also* Spec-
    tacle
Evans, Mark, 93

Fantasia, 2
Fat City, 20
Fazil, 44
Fellini, Federico, 19, 24
Forbidden Planet, 153
Force of Evil, 7
Ford, John, 16, 27, 81, 137, 140
Forty Guns, 20
Fuller, Samuel, 20
Functional music. *See* Easy-listening music
Fury, 32

Geduld, Harry, 46n
Genette, Gérard, 20, 21, 22
Gilbert, John, 49, 54
Gilda, 19
Godard, Jean-Luc, 14, 19, 75, 78
Gold, Ernest, 77
Goldsmith, Jerry, 163
Gone With the Wind, 93
The Great Lie, 93
Grémillon, Jean, 22
Griffith, D.W., 21, 35, 49

Handzo, Stephen, 51n
Hangover Square, 151–161
Hawks, Howard, 140, 148
Heath, Stephen, 44
Herrmann, Bernard, 4, 7, 67, 151–161 *passim*
Herzog, Werner, 18
His Glorious Night, 49
Hit the Deck, 44–45
Hitchcock, Alfred, 23–24, 26, 160
Humoresque, 151
Huntley, John. *See* Manvell, Roger
Huston, John, 20
Hypnosis and music, 5–6, 55, 61, 64

Identification, film music's role in, 58–59, 65–
    69, 109; critique of, 106, 108, 109. *See also*
    Bonding

Illustration: music for, 87–88; critique of, 107;
    Mickey-mousing, 88, 153; stinger, 88–89,
    153
Impression of reality, 43–44, 45–49
In This Our Life, 93
"Inaudibility" of film music, 69, 73, 76–79
The Informer, 88
Instrumentation. *See* Orchestration
Interference, 48
Intermezzo, 151
Invisibility of film music apparatus, 71–76
Irving, Henry, 34

Jaubert, Maurice, 3, 18, 89, 113–139 *passim*
Jaws, 58
Jazz, 83, 85, 86, 86n, 153
The Jazz Singer, 46–47, 48, 151
Jezebel, 71, 93
Jolson, Al, 46–47
Jones, Quincy, 83
Le Jour se lève, 71
Jules et Jim, 16–19, 85

Kalinak, Kathryn, 80n, 99n
Kellogg, Edward, 77–78
King Kong, 51, 74–75, 77, 79–81, 87, 88, 90
Kracauer, Siegfried, 15, 144–145, 146

Lang, Fritz, 20, 32, 38, 109, 140, 149
Legrand, Michel, 14
Leitmotif. *See* Themes
The Letter, 93
Letter from an Unknown Woman, 75–76, 151
Levin, Tom, 75n
Lévi-Strauss, Claude, 60
London, Kurt, 37–38, 39, 40n
The Lost Weekend, 153
The Love Parade, 50–51
Lubitsch, Ernst, 50

M, 149
Ma Nuit chez Maud, 13
The Maltese Falcon, 71
Mamoulian, Ruben, 51, 52n, 140, 148
The Man Who Knew Too Much (1934), 23
The Man With the Golden Arm, 153
Manvell, Roger, and John Huntley, 33, 37,
    38, 42, 127, 130n
Marie, Michel, 54
Melodrama, 7, 33–35, 36, 151
Metadiegetic music: definition, 22–23; in
    Blackmail, 26. *See also* Point of view
Metropolis, 20
Metz, Christian, 26, 39, 40n, 64, 66n, 68–69,
    70, 72, 116–117
Meyer, Leonard B., 60n
Michel, André, 63n
Mickey-mousing. *See* Illustration

CLAUDIA GORBMAN is Associate Professor of Comparative Literature at Indiana University, where she teaches courses in film and literature. Her articles have appeared in *Yale French Studies*, *Wide Angle*, *Film Quarterly*, and *Jump Cut*.

EDITOR: Nancy Ann Miller
BOOK DESIGNER: Sharon Sklar
JACKET DESIGNER: Sharon Sklar
PRODUCTION COORDINATOR: Harriet Curry
TYPEFACE: Caledonia
COMPOSITOR: J. Jarrett Engineering
PRINTER: Thomson-Shore, Inc.